READINGS ON EQUAL EDUCATION

(formerly *Educating the Disadvantaged*)

MARGUERITE ROSS BARNETT is Professor of Political Science and Vice Chancellor for Academic Affairs of the City University of New York.

CHARLES C. HARRINGTON is Professor of Anthropology and Education, and Director of the Institute for Urban and Minority Education at Teachers College, Columbia University.

READINGS ON EQUAL EDUCATION

Volume 8

RACE, SEX, AND NATIONAL ORIGIN
Public Attitudes of Desegregation

Edited by

MARGUERITE ROSS BARNETT   *CHARLES C. HARRINGTON*

AMS PRESS, INC.
NEW YORK

Copyright © 1985 by AMS Press, Inc.
All rights reserved.

Library of Congress Catalogue Number: 77-83137
International Standard Book Number: 0-404-10108-9

International Standard Series Number: 0270-1448

Published by

AMS Press, Inc.
56 East 13th Street
New York, N. Y. 10003
U.S.A.

MANUFACTURED IN THE UNITED STATES OF AMERICA

TABLE OF CONTENTS

I. RACE DESEGREGATION

II. GENDER DESEGREGATION

III. NATIONAL ORIGIN DESEGREGATION

PREFACE

The 1980 presidential elections were a watershed for those concerned with equal education, and after these results were known it became apparent to us that the issue to dominate the remainder of 1980 and 1981 and beyond would be the stance taken by the new administration in regard to our government's commitment to desegregation. Would the new administration continue the policies of the past or would it radically alter course? What middle grounds might it pursue? With these concerns as background, plans were made for a series of lectures in the spring of 1981.

This lecture series was envisaged as an opportunity for some of our leading experts on school desegregation to review the issues upon which future policy should be built. The goal was not so much to directly influence the policies of the new administration—very few of the participants would have felt they could. The goal was rather to provide an honest and succinct overview of where the current policies had gotten us with an eye toward providing an adequate conceptual base for further federal policy in desegregation. The lectures were sponsored by the Institute for Urban and Minority Education and the Program in Politics and Education (of the Department of Philosophy and the Social Sciences) of Teachers College, Columbia University. The financial support of the Institute toward the lecture series upon which this book is based is gratefully acknowledged.

We therefore decided to change the usual format for this series and focus the volume on one topic. We include papers commissioned in 1981 for this volume and three other works published in 1980 which participants found useful (Kirp, Bornstein, and Liebowitz). Our purpose is not to judge the current administration but rather to provide the opportunity for a background, or rather a foundation, upon which new policies can be built.

viii   *Readings on Equal Education*

ACKNOWLEDGMENTS

Grateful acknowledgment is made to those participants in the lectures series upon whose work this book was originally conceived. We also wish to acknowledge the authors and/or copyright holders listed below who have granted permission to include articles related to the main themes of the book.

BORNSTEIN, RITA. "Title IX Compliance and Sex Equity: Definitions, Distinctions, Costs, and Benefits," originally published as Number 73 in the ERIC/CUE Urban Diversity Series by the ERIC Clearinghouse on Urban Education.

HARRINGTON, CHARLES C. "Bilingual Education in the United States: A View from 1980," also published as Number 68 in the ERIC/CUE Urban Diversity Series, by the ERIC Clearinghouse on Urban Education. Copyright © by the author.

FREEMAN, JO. "Women and Public Policy: An Overview," originally appeared in *Women, Power & Policy*, edited by Ellen Bonepath and published by Pergamon Press in 1982, and is included here with some revisions by the author. Copyright © 1982 by the author.

KIRP, DAVID L. "The Bounded Politics of School Desegregation Litigation," *Harvard Education Review*, Vol. 51, No. 3. Copyright © 1981 by President and Fellows of Harvard College.

LEIBOWITZ, ARNOLD H. "The Bilingual Education Act: A Legislative Analysis," reprinted with permission of the National Clearinghouse for Bilingual Education, Rosslyn, Virginia.

INTRODUCTION:
PERSPECTIVES ON DESEGREGATION
IN PUBLIC EDUCATION

Marguerite Ross Barnett
Charles C. Harrington

School desegregation is, for most citizens, a racial issue. *Brown v. Board of Education*, the school violence and riots of the sixties, and the undoing of the "separate but equal" principle as the basis for a legally segregated educational system are synonymous with attempts by blacks to secure for themselves a better education for their children. When these events culminated in the Civil Rights Act of 1964 it was widely noted at the time that the act was broader than educational concerns, as important as those might be. The act dealt with broader issues of enfranchisement in the voting booth, in public facilities, and employment. Less noticed was the fact that the act prohibited discrimination not only on the basis of race (and color), but gender (sex), religion, and national origin as well. [We will not mention the prohibition against religious discrimination again: it was an idea whose time had already come by 1964, but gender and national origin prohibitions each lead to separate controversies discussed below.]

The implications of federal law regarding gender and national origin discrimination took some time to reach local school districts which were understandably preoccupied with issues of race discrimination. However, as amendments to the act and various other laws reviewed below subsequently made clearer, discrimination on the basis of gender and national origin could necessitate what the government came to call desegregation as much as prior discrimination on the basis of race.

Since the earliest years of the 1970s these three issues—race, gender, and national origin—have been overt concerns of efforts of the federal government to redress prior discriminatory practices by local schools. Our book, therefore, reflects the fact that people of all three categories have not only been victims of discrimination, but also that legal efforts to redress that discrimination through desegregation efforts have been increasingly concurrent. To say that these efforts have gone on at the same time, however, does not mean that they represent the same effort. There are obvious differences in what constitutes discrimination by race, gender, and national origin when it does occur. All public school districts have both boys and girls, not all have blacks and whites, not all have Puerto Rican or Mexican students. Racism, sexism, and ethnic prejudice do not, therefore, affect individual school districts equally. Nor are they interchangeable when they do occur. Each has its own history, and their own function in the contemporary society, as the articles below attempt to illuminate. Just as they are not the same, or even aspects of the same, phenomena, so too are the solutions required for each different. For example, gender desegregation is more often concerned with school issues of curriculum and sports, while national origin desegregation can involve bilingual programming for many nationalities. Race desegregation (and to a lesser degree national origin) involves shifts among schools and inevitably raises questions about housing and, therefore, economic patterns of the larger society. In spite of this complexity, or indeed because of it, we felt a volume devoted to a comparative overview of desegregation efforts to date to be not only auspicious but essential.

RACE DESEGREGATION

We begin with articles discussing important issues in race desegregation since it is the antecedent of the other legal efforts as Crain's overview of the history of racial school desegregation since 1954 makes clear. Crain's article not only provides an introduction to such federal efforts but also reviews trends in school desegregation controversies such as busing, the much discussed 'white flight', the fight over solutions, e.g., magnet schools, and the relationship between school and neighborhood racial population. Crain's article concludes with an overview of the implication of desegregation efforts for black-run schools in general, and traditional Black colleges in particular, a theme that will re-emerge in Morris's article in this section.

Marguerite Ross Barnett's article explores three themes: 1) the relationship of school desegregation to the larger structures of racism in America (in which five elements are discussed: legal segregation as an overt marker of Black inferiority, the political disenfranchisement of blacks by law and custom, the economic segregation of blacks into secondary labor markets, the cultural marginalization of blacks, and the psychological stigmatization of blacks); 2) school desegregation as a type of institution challenging racial public policy (in which two issues are discussed: the locus of benefits received through change and the extent of the impact of 'change' on society); and 3) school desegregation in relationship to the overall dynamics of change from the 50s to the 80s. Barnett concludes:

> when all these things are seen together, it might plausibly be asserted that school desegregation can usefully be seen, not simply as a thing in itself, but as a manifestation, expression, reflection, of more fundamental ideological, political, economic and social conflicts in society. The goal then is to study school desegregation in such a way that it illuminates these underlying societal dynamics and conversely to utilize comparative knowledge about social change in order to enrich our understanding of specific school controversies.

Lorenzo Morris delineates the discrepancy between public fears about affirmative action (e.g., the Bakke case), and the actual demonstrated effects of the policies of the past decade. He provides an overview of black higher education in America, and the history of affirmative action in higher education. He concludes that "affirmative action has been treated as too demanding an imposition on institutional independence . . . because public responsibility for education has not been understood."

David Kirp puts school race desegregation into an additional context: the courts at various levels and their decisions since 1954, and the interface between other political institutions and the courts. He argues that the decision-making process in contemporary race desegregation cases is "both a political and a constitutional event."

GENDER DESEGREGATION

The 1978 regulations for the Civil Rights Act of 1964 define gender desegregation as the "assignment of students to public schools and within those schools without regard to their sex, including providing students with a full opportunity for participation in all educational programs regardless of their sex." Unlike race desegregation which is limited in the same regulations to the "disestablishment of segregation in *de jure* segregated schools" no *de jure* test applies to sex desegregation which is free to redress *de facto* segregation.

Jo Freeman begins with a brief overview of state and federal statute law, common law, and judicial interpretation that affect the position of women in American society. Commenting on the Civil Rights Act of 1964 she asserts that the inclusion of a prohibition against sex discrimination in employment in the act was one of the most "profound redistributive decisions of our century" and remarkable for the haphazardness with which it was made by Congress. She argues that it was, in fact, Congress's insensitivity to the consequences of such an inclusion rather that its sensitivity which "permitted sex discrimination to be prohibited so easily." Indeed the Equal Employment Opportunity Commission (EEOC) were slow in enforcement of the gender prohibition almost as if they found it difficult to believe that Congress could have meant what it said. However, in the ensuing years, a successful lobbying effort by women's groups, what Freeman calls incrementalism, and political self–interest—culled from the perception that half the voters are women—led to further congressional efforts culminating in the Ninety-Second Congress, responsible for the 1972 Equal Employment Opportunity Act, the ERA, and Title IX of the Educational Amendments, just to name the three major pieces of legislation affecting the status of women. Freeman brings her history up to date with a discussion of the efforts surrounding ERA and offers some thoughts on future trends.

Sacks's article offers the general reader an overview of the terminology about and explanations for the general issue of gender development in American society. The piece is included for the reader who may be unfamiliar with these basic issues.

Millsap and Wolfe pick up Freeman's discussion at the point of the 1972 activity and devote their article to the Women's Educational Equity Act of 1974. They discuss what led to WEEA, its implementation, issues surrounding its reauthorization in 1977-78, and the implementation of the 1978 Act to date. They conclude their article with a view of what future trends might be for WEEA.

Annette K. Baxter focuses on the issue of higher education for women. She reviews the history of our efforts in this regard, and the historical context in which current federal efforts are carried out. Her article parallels Lorenzo Morris's piece earlier in this volume, and reaches a similar picture in which little appears to have changed despite the trends identified by the authors. She comments: "We ought to bear in mind that discrimination against women anywhere is not easily eradicated. It goes against the grain of the culture. But discrimination in higher education is even harder to eradicate because the presence of women threatens to prove that human values can coexist with the disinterested pursuit of knowledge."

Rita Bornstein focuses our attention on attempts to improve compliance with Title IX with an eye toward problems, costs, and benefits of various implementation efforts. She usefully distinguishes between long term and short term benefits, and concludes with a prescription for strategies for change which she describes as the most efficient and least alienating way of fulfilling school districts' civil rights responsibilities.

As with the discussion of race, discussions which focus only on federal law and policy which ignore larger socio-historical-political realities can lead to a false sense of action. As Admiral Rickover said in testimony to Congress last year about unrelated issues, administrations are better at talking—law-making—than doing—enforcing the law. There is also the question of how rapidly enforcement can reasonably be expected to take given the entrenched behaviors at which the laws are themselves addressed. At any event, there is little justification in the articles reviewed for smugness.

NATIONAL ORIGIN DESEGREGATION

Congress in 1964 might also have been surprised to learn that what it had prohibited required actions promulgated over the last two decades. The federal definition of national origin desegregation introduces us into the realm of language more than ethnicity. National origin desegregation is defined in the Federal Register (Volume 43, no. 144, 6/26/78) as "providing whatever special services are necessary to insure that a student whose dominant language is not English is not limited in his or her participation in educational activities by a lack of proficiency in English." Charles Harrington reviews the history of federal involvement with national origin desegregation through a review of federal efforts in encouraging bilingual education and other programs for non-English dominant students. Reviewing the socio-political context in which such efforts are embedded, he identifies five larger issues in which controversy about national origin desegregation has become embedded: loss of local school and political autonomy, the conflict between legislative prerogatives on the one hand and the executive's use of regulations on the other, inconsistency over years of federal efforts, reliance on local as opposed to federal funds for implementation of federally mandated programming, and the limitations of compensatory models embedded in relevant law. He then reviews the practical problems facing those who would implement bilingual programming, and the appalling reality of our failures to fund research adequately, let alone to make provisions to evaluate adequately programming that has already been implemented. The piece ends with suggestions as to what exemplary bilingual programming ought to try to achieve and how. Harrington concludes "that bilingual programs to date have been able to demonstrate any success whatsoever is testament to the need for such programs, and the urgent need for critical research that would allow us to construct programs to achieve "equal educational opportunity for America's linguistic minorities." Some proponents of national origin desegregation have gone so far as to call for a constitutional amendment that would provide constitutional guarantees for the rights of non-English dominant students. However, the experience of ERA would suggest that such a route is unlikely. They are right that the courts have, to be sure, rested their opinions regarding national origin desegregation on statute rather than constitutional issues, but this is a reflection of the courts' mood of the 70s (see Kirp's article in our last volume) rather than their specific attitudes toward bilingual education. Courts were increasingly reluctant to decide such cases on constitutional grounds. In the end the best argument for national origin desegregation is the dismal statistics in regard to educational and economic achievement for the majority of such populations coupled with the extraordinary success some individuals can have.

Arias's article discusses a complicated issue: the interaction of attempts to desegregate by race and by national origin. Directing our attention toward important, but not well-researched or understood, situations of triadic desegregation contexts, Arias (creatively utilizing and extending the analysis in a prior study done by Willis Hawley), discusses six "myths" that surround school desegregation. They are:

1. Desegregation, generally, does not enhance the academic achievement of minorities, and indeed, may impede the cognitive development of minorities and of whites in many cases.
2. Desegregation increases interracial conflicts in schools, communities and in the society of large.
3. Desegregation is harmful to the development of the self-concept and racial and ethnic identity of minorities.
4. Busing children beyond the nearest school is harmful to their performance in school, destructive of a sense of community cohesion, and very expensive.
5. Desegregation does not enhance the post-high school opportunities and socioeconomic status of minorities.
6. Desegregation leads to white flight, which reduces the social class and racial heterogeneity of communities, thus eliminating the long-run opportunities for racial desegregation.

Reviewing each "myth" in turn, she contrasts black with Hispanic minority students and concludes by stressing the need for better designed more thoughtful research. She concludes:

> The goal for integrated bilingual education for Hispanics appears to be a significant step toward minimizing the differential minority status to which they have been socialized for generations. It is hoped that with the study of a new cohort of Hispanic students who are followed throughout their schooling experiences in integrated settings the dimensions of student ethnic interaction as well as student achievement for Hispanics will be greater understood and fostered.

Arias's argument rewarding the need for improved research studies is well taken. Not only is there a need for better understanding of the triadic situation but also for more in-depth, better designed research on dyadic desegregation.

Arnold Leibowitz provides a useful review of the federal legislation which is the foundation for many bilingual education efforts in the United States today. First, he sets forth the political background that led to the passage of the Bilingual Education Act of 1968 including a concern for the experiences of the Hispanic population in the southwest, the American Indian, and the European immigrant. The history of restriction and tolerance of non-English speakers is therefore set forth. The second section is an examination of the existing bilingual education legislation set forth analytically, but with some attention to the evolution from 1968 to 1974 and then 1978. Breadth of coverage, purposes, program design, the allocation process, the application process for program grants, and program administration are discussed. The concluding section addresses the questions raised by Congress and recent reports which suggest future directions and issues for bilingual education. Given the complexities of the legislative processes in this area, such a review was thought to be essential by other participants in the series.

Taken together the articles in this volume provide a rare opportunity to compare and contrast perspectives on three complex implementation issues: race desegregation, gender desegregation, and national origin desegregation. Despite the amount of attention given to desegregation in popular and academic publications, it is still an often misunderstood and improperly conceptualized public policy. Needed are better empirical data and a clearer focus on structures of inequality in American society. As Barnett states:

> While a theory of racial school desegregation involving Blacks might inform analysts interested in gender or national origin research, it would not be a substitute for developing a structural analysis of those forms of inequality as the basis for understanding gender and national origin desegregation processes. Each structure of inequality requires the integrity of autonomous analysis. Comparison, then, entails understanding the similarities and differences among race, gender, and national origin structures of inequality rather than creation of mindless analogies that equate all forms of discrimination with each other.

I.
RACE DESEGREGATION

SCHOOL DESEGREGATION:
FROM SIMPLICITY TO COMPLEXITY

Robert L. Crain

For one hundred and fifty years, blacks have asked for the right to be educated in the same schools that whites attend. During most of that time the issue was a moral one. In 1954, when the Supreme Court ordered the abolition of separate schools, the issue was still a simple one, with clear moral positions. But in the last decade, school desegregation has been swamped by complex ideological and scientific arguments. Today, it is hard to find anyone who will give unqualified support to the idea of separate schools and equally difficult to find anyone whose endorsement of desegregation is unequivocal. It is the thesis of this essay that school desegregation was never really a simple issue; but before desegregation became a well-established national policy, these complexities were not allowed into public debate. Even today, the legacy of school desegregation as a simple moral issue throws a stifling blanket over efforts to understand an issue of great complexity and enormous public policy importance.

A HISTORY OF SCHOOL DESEGREGATION SINCE 1954

What has happened since Brown can be best understood if the 28 years from 1954 to 1982 are divided into four intervals of seven years each.

1954 to 1960: Southern Massive Resistance

It seems safe to say that when the Brown decision was handed down no one thought that it had any implications north of the Mason-Dixon line. It also seems safe to say that no one in the South knew exactly what was going to happen there.[1]

1

A few of the northernmost southern cities—Baltimore, Louisville,[2] St. Louis—abolished formal segregation and allowed large numbers of black students to transfer to white schools near their homes. Farther south, school officials took a wait-and-see attitude. Gradually two strategies evolved. In Arkansas, Governor Orville Faubus attempted to confront the federal government; Little Rock Central High School became a virtual military outpost when U.S. Army paratroopers occupied the high school so that desegregation could proceed.[3] Other states followed Arkansas's lead, creating a not-quite-impenetrable maze of state laws to prevent desegregation. Some communities went further; after desegregation was ordered, public schools were closed in several Virginia communities and a white school boycott ran for the better part of a year in New Orleans.[4] A few school districts which were predominantly black before desegregation became all-black as whites fled to newly established "segregation academies." A second strategy evolved elsewhere in the South. In North Carolina, state officials guessed that voluntary desegregation, allowing a token number of blacks to transfer to white schools, would delay legal action, minimize violence and maintain segregated schools in all but name. The three largest cities in North Carolina called a joint press conference to announce their decision to desegregate schools. In fact, only a handful of black students entered white schools during the first year, and for years thereafter North Carolina reaped the benefits of its show of good faith by escaping the sort of harsh desegregation orders that fell on other states that had committed themselves to massive resistance. By the end of the decade it was clear that massive resistance was a failure as a policy. Miami desegregated in 1959; Houston and New Orleans in 1960. By 1964, there were desegregated school systems in every Southern state.[5]

1960–1968: Southern Tokenism and Northern Pickets

In the South, desegregated school systems did not necessarily mean desegregated schools for very many blacks. Under so-called freedom of choice plans, a small number of black students moved to formerly white schools and black schools remained largely black. During the early sixties the federal government became more aggressive, as the Department of Justice, HEW, and even the Department of Defense cooperated in pressuring Southern school districts.[6] By the middle 1960s nearly every Southern school district was technically desegregated, but most blacks remained in segregated schools.

It is probably not coincidental that litigation over schools was accompanied by the growth of nonviolent civil rights demonstrations. The creation of the bus boycott in Montgomery, Alabama, in 1957 and the invention of the sit-in in 1960 led to a full-blown assault on segregated public accommodations in the South. In the North, civil rights activists began expressing concern over desegregated schools. Marches, sit-ins, and other non-violent tactics were borrowed from the

South and resulted in the voluntary desegregation of a few small communities and some desegregation in larger cities such as New York City, Baltimore, and St. Louis.[7] However, Northern schools became steadily more segregated as black student enrollment increased.

1968–1975: The South Desegregates While the North Watches

The passage of the Civil Rights Act in 1964 created the machinery to enforce desegregation in the South. By 1968, federal officials in HEW began insisting on genuine desegregation plans: no more freedom of choice. In the next four years, thousands of Southern school districts negotiated with Washington to develop acceptable desegregation plans.[8] Those that did not were faced with threats of suits from the Department of Justice and a loss of federal funds from HEW. The plans generally called for racial balance—setting approximately equal white-black mixes in every school. By the fall of 1972 there were only three all-black schools in the state of Virginia, although there were a number of others which were unacceptable because they had only a small number of white students. Richmond city schools, for example, were totally desegregated with every school but one being more than fifty percent black and only two schools over ninety percent black.[9] During this period there was very little desegregation in the North, but a number of suits had been filed and were moving through the court system.

1975–1982: School Desegregation Comes to the North

In many Northern cities formally segregated schools had never existed and the issue was one of de facto segregation—assignment to neighborhood schools which were segregated because of housing segregation patterns. The Supreme Court was faced with a dilemma, for if it exempted these schools from desegregation, it would permit much more segregation in Northern schools than it had allowed in the South. At the same time, it was difficult to rationalize ordering desegregation when there was no evidence of governmental action creating segregation in schools. For years the Supreme Court simply refused to hear Northern cases. Finally, in the *Keyes* decision of 1973[10] it found a compromise position that would permit widespread desegregation in Northern schools. It ruled that if evidence of intentional segregative action was found which had affected a significant portion of the school district, the presumption could be made that intentional segregation in this portion of the school district had created additional segregation in other areas (creating an all-black school in one area would cause the creation of all-white segregated schools in other areas). While this was not the same thing as requiring the automatic desegregation of any racially imbalanced school, in practice it worked out that way; a well-prepared suit would stand a very good chance of achieving total desegregation in any Northern city. School desegregation in the North raised a new problem, however. There were many northern central cities whose school populations were predominantly black and which were surrounded by a white noose of suburbs. This was less true in the South, where there had been more annexation, more metropolitan governments had been created, and many county-wide school systems existed. (For example, every school system in the state of Florida is a county system.) Central city school administrators in Detroit sued to force the merger of the Detroit City Schools with the surrounding suburbs, but the Supreme Court refused to order a metropolitan plan and created a set of legal guidelines which made metropolitan solutions difficult, although not impossible.[11] Metropolitan plans were ordered in only two large communities: Jefferson County (Louisville), Kentucky and Newcastle County (Wilmington), Delaware. With a metropolitan solution foreclosed in many communities, the question of what to do with predominantly black central cities went unresolved. In Detroit, a city-only plan was drawn which created fifty-fifty black-white schools and left many black students "warehoused" in all-black schools. In many other cities, desegregation suits were thrown out or perhaps not filed, leaving predominantly black cities, such as Newark, unchanged. Cleveland was the only large predominantly black city in the North ordered to desegregate all its schools. Like Richmond, all of its schools were predominantly black after desegregation.

As federal court orders evolved into requiring more busing, local and state government support for desegregation declined. The number of communities voluntarily desegregating dropped and some state governments became more cautious in ordering local communities to desegregate. Los Angeles was ordered to desegregate under state rather than federal law, but a referendum produced a constitutional amendment which forced the court to reverse its position there. Local communities began to find alternatives to mandatory reassignments of white students; magnet schools and other devices for encouraging voluntary white transfer were developed in the 1970s. Cities such as Milwaukee and San Diego, which might have had mandatory busing orders, were instead allowed to desegregate with voluntary reassignment to magnet schools. In other cases, voluntary plans were used to escape the constraints imposed by the *Milliken* (Detroit) decision on metropolitan plans. Milwaukee, Indianapolis, St. Louis, Houston and other cities are experimenting with the voluntary reassignment of black students from central city schools to suburbs.[12]

The Status of Desegregation Today

The most obvious point to make about the status of desegregation in the beginning of the eighties is this: there are very few predominantly black schools in predominantly white school districts in the United States. The easy cases—small predominantly white cities in the South or Midwest—have almost all been desegregated. Advocates of school desegregation have begun to shift their attention to three kinds of more difficult situations: (1) the desegregation of predominantly black school districts through merger with other districts. Sometimes this means the merger of a central city with its suburbs. In other cases, such as East Palo Alto, California, or Braddock, Pennsylvania, it means the merger of a small predominantly black suburb with nearby white suburbs. (2) The desegregation of new ghettos developing in the suburbs. As blacks have moved out from the central city, school segregation has followed. Prince George's County, Maryland, outside of Washington D.C., and Baltimore County are examples of a pattern which has occurred in many metropolitan areas. (3) The resegregation of aging desegregation plans. In many cases, desegregation plans which were effective ten years ago have become out-of-date. Neighborhood change has resulted in resegregating schools which were once desegregated.

There is a fourth issue of desegregation, although not one which is likely to be pursued by litigation: this is the return of white families to predominantly black central cities. Reintroducing whites to segregated black schools is a new urban planning art form. The most common answer is the creation of magnet schools— schools with a specified racial quota serving volunteers from a large area.

The late 1970s also saw an increase in the intensity of the debate about the merits of desegregation. White flight became front page news. Earlier tentative proposals about community control as an alternative to desegregation evolved into demands for black schools of excellence. The disproportionate suspension of black students from newly desegregated schools became an issue. Polls found white parents willing to accept desegregation, but vehemently opposed to bussing. Many black intellectuals rose to defend black colleges which seemed threatened with extinction due to federal desegregation orders.

THE DEBATE OVER DESEGREGATION: THE NEW COMPLEXITIES

The evolution of the debate about desegregation from simple moral issues to complex cost-benefit argumentation partly reflects the progress that has been made. Conservatives can no longer simply insist on segregated schools. They must now argue that one form of desegregation—mandatory busing—is unacceptable; and when they do most whites (and many blacks) agree. Blacks are no longer faced with the need to close ranks behind the NAACP's effort to desegregate Southern schools, and they no longer feel compelled to accept a plan which clearly favors whites. So complexities that were ignored are now being brought into the open.

Desegregation is no longer a white vs. black issue. A person who has the position of school administrator, political or civic leader, or member of the intelligentsia has a stake in the desegregation conflict which may have more effect on his attitude about desegregation than will his skin color.

One cannot understand this debate without a clear sense of who the various stakeholders are, for each approaches the issue with a unique mixture of self-interest, ideological predisposition, and a particular perception of real costs and real benefits from alternative policies. A particular combination of self-interest and ideology may cause one person to stress one aspect of desegregation which another person might consider of little import. Which means that whichever aspect one focuses upon depends upon one's location in the social system. For the civil rights attorneys, a school desegregation case is primarily a matter of establishing the guilt of the defendant school district. Lawyers, of course, are not insensitive to the educational needs of children, but because this must be secondary to the legal issues, it is easy to accuse them of wanting to punish this generation's children for the sins of the politicians their grandparents voted for. For the great mass of white and black parents, the legal issues are irrelevant—the question is whether children will receive a better or worse education or be subject to physical danger. School administrators see the issue in a very different way; for them, the issues of corporate guilt and quality of education must be secondary to their need to maintain the school district as a viable institution. For them, desegregation is mainly a matter of trying to minimize the controversy which threatens to wreck the school system. Because desegregation always poses the threat of controversy, one rarely finds a school administrators, white or black, who are advocates of desegregating their own schools. (By the same token, few administrators will advocate massive resistance to desegregation, or advocate dismantling a desegregation plan once it is in place.) For central city political leaders, the priority is maintaining a tax base and getting reelected; which generally means they are concerned with "white flight" (if they are white) or the loss of black voters to the suburbs (if they are black). Finally, the books and magazine articles about desegregation are written by black and white intellectuals who see desegregation mainly as an idea, since ideas are the currency of their trade. Intellectuals are likely to relate school desegregation to themes about inequality, one of the major motifs of twentieth-century discourse. They are also likely to be fascinated by the nature-nurture controversy in the study of intelligence and may well wind up writing about school desegregation in terms of its implications for the "gap" between black and white IQ test scores. Ultimately, school desegregation may become fodder for a debate about ethnic cultural superiority or inferiority—it may be seen as a threat to the integrity of the white ethnic neighborhood, or as an attack upon black-run schools. Of course, no one lawyer, parent, school administrator, politician or intellectual would view school desegregation as simplistically as their respective views are portrayed here—but it is important to bear in mind that each group brings with it a particular bias which makes one aspect of the desegregation controversy more important than the others.

And one breed of intellectual, the newspaper reporter, must view desegregation as news, which means he must focus on conflict, controversy, violence, and that which is new, which means that intangible and "old" issues such as quality of education take a back seat to newer issues such as white flight, and are eclipsed by any incident of conflict.

Yet behind all these complexities is the urge to see all this in hard-edged moral terms—the white intellectual who opposes busing is a racist; the black intellectual who favors busing is a traitor to his people and so forth. Because intellectuals are often not directly involved in desegregation, and because their life revolves around the sweeping issues that dominate cocktail parties, desegregation becomes a symbolic issue. One side is racist, the other pure. Which also means it is a zero-sum issue; that which pleases whites or blacks must by definition harm the other group. Desegregation is not, fortunately, a zero-sum issue, there are some policies which benefit both whites and blacks. It is also not a symbolic issue— it involves each year the expenditure of millions of dollars, and affects the education of millions of children.

In the remainder of this paper we will look at some of the major issues in desegregation. We will see that there is plenty of room for people of integrity to disagree. There are not very many positions we can dismiss as simply immoral.

Desegregation and Quality Education

For black parents desegregation is a way of obtaining quality education; but for many white parents it is a threat to the quality education they believe their children are now receiving. It is important to bear in mind that very few parents are in a position to assess accurately the quality of their child's school. One may know if the principal is courteous or rude; one can see if the building has been recently painted; or one can hear rumors of widespread drug use. But whether the curriculum is effective or the teachers skilled is difficult even for an educational expert to determine. Parents assume instinctively that a school in a middle class suburb must be better than a low-income central city school. Educational research supports their instincts, but in a complicated manner. There is no evidence that the quality of curriculum, teaching or administration is superior in the suburbs—indeed, a good case could be made that it is inferior since those school have not benefited from infusions of Title I money and the development of special remedial programs. But the most important finding of the Coleman Report[13] is that the quality of education that a child experiences is less a function of the policies of the school and more influenced by the character of the other students in the classroom. Surrounded by middle-class students, the student will learn more. This leads our common sense to expect that black students, who on average come from poorer families and do less well on achievement tests, will benefit from being desegregated with higher income white students, and our common sense seems to be correct— a good deal of research has demonstrated that black achievement test scores go up after desegregation.[14] Our common sense also tells us that the presence of low-income students in the desegregated classroom will pull down the rest of the class, and here our common sense seems to be wrong; so far we have found no evidence that white students in desegregated schools suffer as a result of desegregation.[15] In nearly all desegregated classrooms the low-income minority students are in the minority. The teacher pacing his or her assignments to the mode of the class will be directing his or her teaching toward the middle class students, pulling the minority students along at that pace rather than slowing down. Teachers often complain about the extreme heterogeneity of the desegregated classroom. While it seems commonsensical that it is more difficult for the teacher to work with a classroom with a greater range of ability, the fact remains that the heterogeneous classroom is educationally more effective.[16] A wealth of research on homogeneous grouping of students indicates that it does not particularly benefit the more able students and is harmful to the others. There is also common sense attitude that education is a zero-sum game: if blacks benefit, white must have lost something. One is reminded of Stewart Chase's definition of common sense: it is that sense that tells us that the world is flat.

Desegregation and busing

Our common sense also tells us that schools in white neighborhoods should be superior to schools in black neighborhoods. The reason common sense fails here is that students do not go to school in a neighborhood—they are in a school that is physically isolated from the surrounding area. A predominantly white desegregated classroom is no different when located in a white neighborhood, a black neighborhood, or a cornfield. But fear of the black neighborhood is a root of the opposition to busing. Polls have found that most whites have learned to accept the desegregated classroom. A vast majority express no opposition to the notion of their child attending a school that is half white and half black.[17] At the same time, there is enormous white opposition to busing. To my admittedly biased view, most of the arguments against busing seem specious. There are great differences between the safety in high-income and low-income neighborhoods; but there is much less difference in the safety of schools in those neighborhoods. The NIE Safe Schools Study[18] puts it bluntly: In a low-income neighborhood the school is a haven of safety; in a high-income suburb, the school is the most dangerous part of the community. Neighborhoods differ; schools, if they have the same student body, do not differ very much. The other reason why busing is a red herring for white parents is that white children are bused very little. There is a mathematical rule of thumb; in a school desegregation plan, the number of years a student is bused is proportional to the percentage of his classmates who are of the opposite race. Thus, in a typically desegregated school where twenty percent of the students are minority, the average white student is bused twenty percent of the years he is in school—only two or three years.[19] The black students are bused eighty percent of the time—nine to ten years. Some research on Southern schools suggests that busing is more difficult for black students than for whites.[20] White students, even when bused into a black neighborhood, are usually the majority group in the school and always represent the dominant group in the society. They can expect to be well taken care of. Black students, arriving in a white neighborhood as the minority in the school and as members of a powerless and low-status group in the society, run the risk of being ignored. There are Southern desegregated high schools where not a single black participates in the school orchestra or the school play. Blacks complain about busing, but not as much as whites do, perhaps because it is obvious that as the petitioners for better schools they will be expected to make sacrifices. A black mother, testifying before a civil rights commission hearing in a community where blacks experienced most of the busing, commented, "Certainly it's difficult to get the children up to be on a cold street corner at 6:30 a.m. But I tell them that if they don't get out on that street corner now, they will be on that street corner the rest of their lives."[21]

"Second-generation" problems

Issues of discrimination against black students in desegregated schools are difficult to discuss because of the difficulties of doing good research on what is actually happening in classrooms. Of all the "second generation," post-desegregation problems, discriminatory disciplinary practices have attracted the most attention, since statistical records are available. There is widespread evidence that black students in secondary schools are suspended more often than whites. However, there is little evidence on the extent of unfairness of discipline—in many high schools black students are more disorderly and hence a greater suspension rate is not in and of itself an indication of discriminatory practice. The civil rights leaders have in some cases been able to use disproportionate suspension effectively to press for reforms in desegregated schools. Since it seems clear that suspensions, especially when used as a punishment for truancy, encourage students to drop out of school, successful efforts to reduce the use of suspension as a disciplinary device may reduce both white and black dropouts. There is also hard evidence of serious problems of internal segregation—blacks relegated to all-black classrooms within desegregated schools. Common sense, which leads us to expect discrimination against black students in desegregated classes, is probably right; but since not all teachers express racial prejudice in their classroom manner, and it is difficult to identify those who do, attacks on "second generation" problems in the school can often be ignored by school administrators.

Magnet schools, voluntary desegregation, white flight

The controversy surrounding James Coleman's writings on white flight is almost a textbook example of the difficulties social science has in dealing with public policy.[22] It was clear from the beginning that Coleman's writings were motivated by his own philosophical opposition to school desegregation. His main conclusion—that mandatory school desegregation is an unsuccessful public policy because it creates more segregation than it eliminates—is false. However, many of Coleman's critics painted themselves into a corner by claiming that school desegregation never caused white flight—a statement that is equally false. While it is understandable that advocates of desegregation take offense at the degree to which school administrators treat white flight as the only issue in desegregation policy, advocates of desegregation should be concerned that plans for desegregation minimize white flight, since unnecessary white flight means the unnecessary disruption of families, and an unnecessary risk of schools resegregating. Research has identified conditions that cause white flight.[23] White flight is increased by plans that reassign white students into predominantly minority schools and send them to minority neighborhoods. In most cities, any valid desegregation plan will require the reassignment of white students to schools in minority neighborhoods. Some of the white flight caused by this can be avoided if magnet schools are created and white volunteers are recruited to attend them. In smaller communities, where there is only a single ghetto school, it is often possible to convert the black school into a magnet and eliminate the need for mandatory reassignment, with black volunteers to white schools being complemented by white volunteers to the magnet. Magnet schools alone cannot desegregate large systems, however, and can be misused. In particular, magnet schools that cater to gifted whites seem especially prone to problems of racial inequity and tension.[24] The odds seem better with schools built on special interests, such as the performing arts or foreign languages.[5] Magnet schools can provide superior quality of education and assist the desegregation plan; the fact that they are transparently intended to appease whites is not a sufficient reason to oppose them.

The serious problems of white flight occur in predominantly black central cities where complete desegregation requires that whites be transported into minority neighborhoods and be in a minority in each school for over half of their school years. Under these conditions, white flight will usually be severe. There are honest differences among advocates of desegregation about predominantly black school districts. Some favor the total desegregation of all schools, as was done in Cleveland. Others believe the optimal racial composition should be fifty-fifty, even if it means leaving large segments of black students in segregated schools, as happened in Detroit after a metropolitan alternative was rejected by the courts. In most predominantly black northern communities total desegregation has not been ordered; Cleveland is the exception, Detroit the rule.

School desegregation and integrated neighborhoods

In focusing on the white flight caused by desegregation plans, little attention has been given to the white flight that results from segregated schools. Since families often move into a new neighborhood when their children reach school age, and since blacks are less likely to send children to Catholic schools, the public schools in a changing neighborhood are likely to become predominantly black while the neighborhood's adult population is still largely white. (This is true even though black families are no larger than white families today.) This means that a segregated neighborhood school policy tends to destabilize integrated neighborhoods. For this reason, the interracial community groups in integrated neighborhoods have long been the strongest advocates of school desegregation. The *Keyes* case was filed by the residents of the Park Hill community in Denver. They realized that with a neighborhood school policy their integrated neighborhood would become all black as each neighborhood school "tipped," pushed white families out. A school desegregation policy in effect places a quota on the number of black and white students in each school and guarantees to white families an integrated school regardless of where they live. This has the effect of discouraging white flight from integrated neighborhoods. We do not normally think of these actions as examples of integration, perhaps because the beneficiaries of this sort of integration are whites rather than blacks.

Metropolitan desegregation has encouraged whites to stay in the central city and return to the city, and also has encouraged blacks to move to the suburban schools where they know that their child will not be the only minority student and where they can avoid further busing.[26]

Non-black minorities in desegregation

Although most court cases, and most writing, has dealt with black-white desegregation, Latinos, with ancestors from Cuba, Puerto Rico, Mexico, South America, or from the Spanish colonies which are now part of the United States, Native Americans, and Asians make up a large segment of the minority school enrollment. Their presence raises two fundamental issues. First, is school desegregation, developed by one minority group, of value as a remedy to others? School desegregation is significant for Afro-Americans partly because of their history in the United States. Other minorities have been discriminated against in different ways, and may need different kinds of remedies. For example, there is much less residential segregation of Latinos than of blacks, but in 1975 they were educationally more segregated, and their degree of segregation was increasing at a time when segregation of blacks was declining.[27] Some of the important benefits of desegregation may accrue to Latinos just as they do to blacks. For example, Latinos have higher achievement test scores in desegregated schools, just as blacks do.[28] In Los Angeles, Spanish-speaking Chicanos supported school desegregation much more than did English-speakers, who are presumably residentially less segregated.[29] For other ethnic minorities, the question is more ambiguous. Asian-Americans are much less segregated then blacks, and have opposed school desegregation in San Francisco and Los Angeles. Asian-Americans, like Latinos, are not a single group, and a remedy appropriate for Puerto Ricans or Filipino-Americans may be meaningless to Equadorian or Cambodian-Americans. The second issue is whether desegregation should involve the mixing of minorities with each other as well as with whites.[30] A good case can be made for tri-ethnic desegregation, but it would markedly increase the amount of busing in cities such as Los Angeles.

Three Non-Issues

There are three issues often debated by intellectuals that have no logical relationship to the desegregation of public schools. One is the issue of the relative intelligence of blacks and whites; a second is whether it is possible for black-run schools to be good; the last is the future of the traditional black college. In some of the early writing about desegregation, white intellectuals treated desegregation as a compensatory program designed to prove that with an improved environment black IQ scores would equal whites. Although desegregation does raise IQ scores, it has not eliminated the "gap" between blacks and whites. Some writers have leaped to the conclusion that desegregation is a failure because of this. The question of the relative intelligence of blacks and whites and its possible genetic base for the "gap" has fascintated both white and black intellectuals. It is almost as if the entire moral worth of a human race could be decided with a pencil and paper test. A careful examination of this debate convinces me that the entire intellectual exercise is pointless. The statistical concepts and analysis which appears in debates between environmentalists like Jencks and heriditarians like Jensen[31] are so complex that relatively few professional social scientists can understand them. Yet intellectuals seem preoccupied by the issue—this despite Jencks' convincing evidence that racial differences in intelligence explain only an infinitesimal fraction of black poverty[32] and despite the fact that evidence on inheritance of intelligence is virtually irrelevant to claims about the physiologically-based intellectual inferiority of Afro-Americans. The uselessness of the debate is demonstrated by the fact that there is not a similar debate about the superiority of Asian or Jewish test scores. One does not hear white intellectuals arguing for the reform of the schools because they do not eliminate the IQ gap between Gentiles and Jews, or whites and Asians.

The failure of desegregation to raise black test scores by one standard deviation immediately is not evidence of the inferiority of blacks. At the same time, the fact that desegregation does raise black test scores to a considerable degree (although less than a standard deviation) is not evidence that black-run institutions are incompetent. Yet a number of black intellectuals have opposed school desegregation because they favor creating excellent all-black schools. Again, the debate is pointless. Given present desegregation policy there will be large numbers of all-black schools for the foreseeable future in which to demonstrate the excellence of black-run institutions. The fact that test scores are higher in desegregated schools does not indicate that white teachers are superior to black or that white culture is superior to black culture. The point should not require stating, but it seems that it does. There is a good deal of simplistic ethnic one-upsmanship in talk about the "gap" and "black excellence."

The other issue that is irrelevant to the discussion of the desegregation of public schools is the future of the traditional black college in America. Here the fault lies not with the intellectuals but with the federal government, which has not bothered to make a careful distinction between the desegregation of public schools and the desegregation of higher education. There is an important difference, since post-secondary schooling is voluntary. The present policy which pressures white schools to admit blacks but also offers opportunities to blacks to attend black colleges provides choice during the post-high school years, when school attendance is voluntary. The elimination of traditionally black colleges would be very harmful, since it would simply discourage some blacks from attending college at all, which is not beneficial to them or to the society.[33] Thus, condemning a black college because it is segregated is not the same thing as the mandatory reassignment of whites to desegregate a black public school. However, the two issues seem to be constantly entangled, partly because the federal government has not attempted to define its goals for the desegregation of higher education as distinct from its goals for the desegregation of public schools.

CONCLUSIONS

Perhaps we should be cheered by the realization that a simple moral issue—the elimination of intentional segregation of schools—has grown over the last twenty years to become a complex issue debatable in a variety of ways from a number of points of view. School desegregation was never a simple issue. The fact that we once treated it as a simple issue is a reflection on the sterility of the political climate in the 1950s. School desegregation, like any other public policy, must be evaluated in a complete fashion—which means that the debate will necessarily be complex. Given that segregated schools are illegal, the hard question becomes how a desegregation policy should be fashioned—how much attention to magnet schools, how much concern for maintaining housing integration in mixed neighborhoods, how much concern for inquities of busing, how much concern for elimination of discriminatory suspension in desegregated schools, etc. These are value judgments on which disagreements are unavoidable, but there may be optimal strategies which will do the best job of balancing the conflicting interests of the parties involved. This is, after all, what public policy debate should be about.

NOTES

1. Richard Kluger's *Simple Justice: The History of Brown v. Board of Education and Black America's Struggle for Equality* (New York: Harper & Row, 1976) covers the first reaction of the South to the Brown decision.

2. See, for example, Omar Carmichael, *The Louisville Story* (New York: Simon & Schuster, 1957); D. Shoemaker, *With All Deliberate Speed* (New York: Harper & Row, 1957); Benjamin Muse, *Ten Years of Prelude* (New York: Viking, 1964).

3. W. Record and J. C. Record, *Little Rock, USA* (San Francisco: Chandler, 1960).

4. B. Muse, *Virginia's Massive Resistance* (Bloomington: Indiana University Press, 1961); R. L. Crain, M. Inger, G. A. McWorter, J. J. Vanecko, *The Politics of School Desegregation* (Chicago: Aldine, 1968).

5. Crain, *et al.*, *Politics of School Desegregation*, ch. 14, has a statistical summary of the compliance rate of Southern districts.

6. Charles S. Bullock and Harrell R. Rodgers, "Coercion to Compliance: Southern School Districts and School Desegregation Guidelines," *Journal of Politics*, Nov. 1976, 987–1011.

7. R. Crain, *et al.*, *Politics of School Desegregation*, Part I, describes several of these early desegregation controversies.

8. For an analysis of federal action, see Gary Orfield, *The Reconstruction of Southern Education: The Schools and the 1964 Civil Rights Act* (New York: John Wiley, 1969).

9. Racial data for schools in most school systems from the Office of Civil Rights is published for 1967, 1968 and in each even year thereafter under the general title, *Directory of Public Elementary and Secondary Schools in Selected Districts: Enrollment and Staff by Racial/Ethnic Group* (Washington, D.C.: United States Government Printing Office).

10. *Keyes v. School District No. 1, Denver, Colorado* 413 US 189 (1973).

11. *Milliken v. Bradley* 418 US 717 (1975).

12. The St. Louis case attracted considerable national attention in 1981 because of the Department of Justice proposal that the state give college tuition grants as an inducement to encourage inter-district transfers.

13. Coleman, James S., Campbell, Ernest Q., Hobson, C. J., McPartland, J. M., Mood, A. M., Weinfeld, F. D., and York, R. L., *Equality of Educational Opportunity* (Washington, D.C.: U.S. Government Printing Office, 1966).

14. See R. L. Crain and R. E. Mahard, "Desegregation and Black Achievement: A Review of the Research," *Law and Contemporary Problems*, 1978, 42 (Summer), 17–56, and R. L. Crain and R. E. Mahard, "Some Policy Implications of the

Desegregation-Minority Achievement Literature," in Willis Hawley (ed.), *Effective School Desegregation* (Beverley Hills: Sage, 1981); Donald F. Krol, "A Meta-Analysis of School Desegregation and Achievement," unpublished doctoral dissertation, Western Michigan University.

15. See, for example, Nancy H. St. John, *School Desegregation: Outcomes for Children* (New York: John Wiley, 1975).

16. See, for example, James E. Rosenbaum, "Social Effects of Educational Grouping" in David C. Berliner (ed.), *Review of Educational Research VIII* (Washington, D.C.: American Educational Research Association, 1980).

17. See Wade Smith, "Tolerance of School Desegregation 1954–77." *Social Forces* 59:4 June 1981.

18. National Institute of Education, *Report of the Safe Schools Study* (Washington, D.C.: U.S. Government Printing Office, 1978).

19. For a longer discussion of this, see Crain, Mahard and Narot, *Politics of School Desegregation.*

20. Ibid.

21. U.S. Commission on Civil Rights, Hearings, Jefferson County, Kentucky, June 14–16, 1976. Excerpted in *Fulfilling the Letter and Spirit of the Law: A Report of the U.S. Commission on Civil Rights* (Washington, D.C.: U.S. Government Printing Office, August 1976, p. 83).

22. James S. Coleman, S. D. Kelly, J. A. Moore, *Trends in School Segregation, 1968–1973* (Washington, D.C.: The Urban Institute, 1975).

23. Christine H. Rossell, "School Desegregation and Community Social Change," *Law and Contemporary Problems* 42 (Summer) 1978, 133–183.

24. Janet S. Schofield, *Black and White in School: Trust, Tension, or Tolerance* (New York: Praeger, 1982).

25. Donald R. Waldrip, "Program Development as a Strategy for Racial Balance." Paper presented at AERA annual meeting, April 21, 1976.

26. Diana M. Pearce, "Deciphering the Dynamics of Segregation: The Role of Schools in the Housing Choice Process," *The Urban Review*, (Summer) 13:2, 1981, 85–102.

27. *Trends in Hispanic School Segregation 1970-1974*, Vol. II, and *Trends in Black School Segregation 1970–1974*, Vol. I (Washington, D.C.: Center for National Policy Review, Catholic University, 1977).

28. Rita E. Mahard and R. L. Crain, "The Influence of High School Racial Composition on the Academic Achievement and College Attendance of Hispanics." Paper read at the American Sociological Association annual meeting, August 1980.

29. Personal communication, David Armor.

30. This issue is discussed in Thomas F. Pettigrew's "Report to the Honorable Paul Egly in Response to the Minute Order of Feb. 7, 1978," Case 822–845, Los Angeles Superior Court, 11/14/78, and in other reports by other experts in this case.

31. Christopher Jencks, "Heredity, Environment, and Public Policy Reconsidered," *American Sociological Review*, 45: 6 (Dec. 1980) 732–735; Arthur M. Jensen, "How Much Can We Boost IQ and Scholastic Achievement?" *Harvard Educational Review* 39 (Winter 1969) 1–123.

32. Christopher Jencks, M. Smith, H. Acland, M. J. Bane, D. Cohen, H. Gintis, G. Heyns, S. Michelson, *Inequality* (New York: Basic Books, 1972).

33. Work in progress by Gail Thomas, Jomills Braddock II, and James McPartland at the Center for Social Organization of Schools, The Johns Hopkins University.

TOWARDS A THEORY OF SCHOOL
DESEGREGATION: A REVISIONIST VIEW

Marguerite Ross Barnett

INTRODUCTION

Much of the literature on school desegregation focuses on descriptions of specific plans, remedies or implementation experiences in various communities; research and evaluation of the impact of desegregation on academic achievement and racial attitudes; advocacy or opposition to desegregation as public policy and discussion and analysis of the long-run implications of school desegregation for local educational systems.[1] This literature has been extremely valuable in providing detailed description of one of the most significant social changes in American history—namely, desegregation of American education. Too little attention, however, has been given to conceptualization of school desegregation as a theoretical issue that illuminates and interprets the dynamics of American social and political change, particularly the development and implementation of racial public policy. A theory of school desegregation would be useful in providing a more general framework for understanding many specific problems and seemingly contradictory implementation experiences; it would provide general concepts for interpreting other instances of racial public policy and it would add to our knowledge of the dynamics of politics and policy formulation during the period from 1954 through 1980.

In this brief essay it is not possible to provide a detailed theory of school desegregation. However, I would like to situate school desegregation in a broader conceptual framework by exploring three major themes: (1) the relationship of school desegregation as a form of racial public policy to the larger structure of racism; (2) school desegregation as a type of potentially institution-challenging racial public policy; and (3) the overarching public policy shift (encompassing school desegregation as well as other policies) from expanded notions of the public interest and governmental responsibility (dominant in the 1960s) to narrower views of the proper role of government typified by the Reagan administration vision of the 1980s. I shall conclude by outlining an interpretation of school desegregation in relationship to broader dynamics of American social change in the last thirty years and by suggesting the linkage among the various conceptual elements discussed and their relevance to a comprehensive theory of school desegregation.

SCHOOL DESEGREGATION AND THE STRUCTURE OF AMERICAN RACISM

Various models have been used to interpret the Afro-American social and political experience. These models can be grouped into four major types: those that view Afro-Americans as "just another ethnic group" and therefore use a theoretical framework derived from and modeled on the experience of white ethnic groups in order to analyze the experience of Afro-Americans;[2] institutional racism models which argue that racism is embedded in American political and social institutions and therefore use this model to explain the continuation of discriminatory practices in various specific organizations;[3] cultural and/or class conflict models in which class and cultural factors are seen as the "real" barriers against Blacks[4] and caste models portraying Blacks as a separate caste in the U.S.[5] An extensive critical literature exists on all of these approaches. All have been criticized as insufficient, unsatisfactory, and only capable of partial explanation and, in some cases, as deliberate distortions.

Each approach fails to explain a crucial aspect of American race relations and/or ignores processes of social change for which it cannot account. The ethnic group model, for example, cannot account for the widely divergent experiences of white ethnic groups and Blacks; it must dismiss slavery and legal segregation of Blacks as inconsequential for subsequent history and as factors differentiating ethnic and Black experience, and elides past the nationwide, historically relevant hierarchy of whites over Blacks. Institutional racism, on the other hand, provides a framework which accounts for much of the history ignored by the "ethnicity theory," but becomes a static model because it has no way of accounting for institutional change and dynamic movement in the social and political systems. Beyond stating the obvious fact that racism exists in American life, the theory of institutional racism has little to offer the analyst who seeks to study racial policy change.

In their anxiety to acknowledge the obvious change that has taken place in the U.S. in the last thirty years, the third group of analysts have declared racism "dead." While wags may ask facetiously where did racism go, even the most serious proponents of the class/culture thesis have a difficult time explaining how the overtly racist attitudes manifested in both North and South less than thirty years ago could disappear so suddenly. What happened to the young rock throwers in the Gage Park demonstrations in Chicago? Where did the mobs of Selma, Birmingham, Little Rock go? Why is there such strong belief by Blacks that racism remains? But the major difficulty faced by the class/cultural analysts is the statistical and behavioral evidence of continuing racial prejudice.

Caste theoretists assert a caste-like system, similar in structure to the Indian caste system, exists in the U.S. In this scheme, Blacks and whites are the two castes organized hierarchically. Caste theory is tempting because the hierarchy and collectivism of caste are evident in American race relations. However, the essential components of the Indian caste system are not present in the American situation—caste in India is a system organizing all of Hindu society according to notions of religious purity and pollution. Castes in India are endogamous and were originally rooted in the Jajmani system which linked castes to specific occupations. Most important, caste, and the code for conduct which buttresses the system, is replicated in the ideological sphere by a religion in which varnashrama dharma (duty according to caste division or varna) is a main principle. Race in the U.S. differs fundamentally from Indian caste so that more confusion than enlightment results from linking the U.S. to India by analogy. Without a theoretical base, caste often degenerates into a form of academic name-calling without analytical significance.

How do we develop a theory that acknowledges the importance of history, particularly events as important as slavery and legal segregation; illuminates the continuing inability of major institutions to incorporate Blacks despite the legal changes that have occurred in the country; and also accounts for and provides an interpretation of institutional and system transformations where they have occurred? Elsewhere I have used structural analysis to describe the organization of American race relations and to interpret changes and transformations in that system.[6] In outline form the argument is that prior to 1954, the structure of racism in the American context in the twentieth century consisted of five elements: legal segregation; political disenfranchisement; economic exploitation; cultural marginalization, and psychological stigmatization.

Legal Segregation

Legal segregation is an overt marker symbolizing Black inferiority. Involving separation of Blacks and whites in every conceivable arena, legal segregation was a concrete and comprehensive manifestation of two principles fundamental to maintenance of Black subordination: (1) *enforced collectivism* in which all individual Blacks are treated according to rules derived for the group, making the phenotypical characteristic of skin color the essential factor in shaping all social interaction; and (2) publicly recognized *hierarchy* in which all whites are ranked above all Blacks. Legal segregation violated, in obvious and deliberate ways, two principles held to be central to American democratic life. One principle is *individualism,* manifested in public life by the right of individuals to participate in society without restraint based on their primordial characteristics. The second principle is *egalitarianism.* Notions of "personal guilt" and "individual liberty" are ideological and legal manifestations of western concepts of individualism and equality among individuals in public forums and secular arenas. Equality of opportunity, in its most minimal definition, entails freedom from prior restraints or participation in public life. Maintenance of hierarchy of one group over others entails enforced collectivism. Some degree of proximate equality of access to public life for individuals depends on either the elimination, or the equalization, of collective categories. Realization of even the illusion of individualism necessitates ending enforced collectivism and eliminating publicly sanctioned hierarchization of groups through use of social control.

Legal segregation, then, was extremely important as a public manifestation of white-Black hierarchy. It is important, however, to distinguish between legal segregation as the *marker,* sign, symbol of hierarchy, and hierarchy and collectivism as transcending system elements.

Political Disenfranchisement

Political disenfranchisement of Blacks by custom, violence, unequal enforcement of rules governing the franchise and implementation of regulations (such as the white primary, grandfather clause) specifically designed to disenfranchise Blacks meant that for most of American history, the majority of Blacks (that is, those living in the South) were excluded from the political community (those people who solve their political problems together) and therefore unable to work to change laws such as legal segregation. For those Blacks living in the South under legal segregation and political disenfranchisement, political life approximated more a closed, totalitarian regime than an open, democratic polity.

Economic Segregation

Economic separation of a disproportionately large number of Blacks into what economists term a secondary labor market characterized by low wages, high instability of employment, low or nonexistent benefit packages, seasonal work, poor working conditions and low levels of unionization constitutes the third element in the structure of racism. Economic separation and labor market inequality led to the oft-heard, painful comment that Blacks were (and are) the "last hired and first fired."

Legal segregation, political disenfranchisement, and economic separation have been obvious barriers facing Blacks. Legal segregation was public, enforced by judicial, legislative and executive branches of state governments and sanctioned in *Plessy v. Ferguson* by the Supreme Court of the United States. Similarly, political disenfranchisement was overt—articulated and defended publicly. Even economic separation was so deeply rooted and embedded in patterns deriving from slavery and sharecropping experiences that it has an obvious, overt character. Cultural marginalization and psychological stigmatization, the last two elements of the structure of racism, however, are more obscure, covert, subconscious and less obvious but nevertheless just as significant as legal segregation, political disenfranchisement and economic segregation as elements maintaining the structure of racism.

Cultural Marginalization

In the cultural marginalization of the Black community two forms of stigmatization took place. In popular culture, from the late nineteenth century throughout the era of segregation, Blacks were depicted as inferior—stupid, slow, criminal, bestial. These images, which appeared in advertising, entertainment, household items, and in every area of everyday life were disseminated throughout the nation. Even in areas in which no Blacks resided the message of Black inferiority was carried through the artifacts of everyday life.[7] Secondly, cultural stigmatization occurred through the relegation of Black aesthetic contributions to society to invisibility or irrelevance. Harold Cruse makes this point with power and perceptiveness:

For critics like Seldes, the Negroes were the anti-intellectual uninhibited, unsophisticated, intuitive children of jazz who functioned with aesthetic "emotions" rather than the disciplined "mind" of white jazzmen. For such critics, the real artists of Negro folk expression were the George Gershwins, the Paul Whitemans and the Cole Porters.[8]

. . . it typified the white cultural attitudes toward all forms and practices of Negro art. Compared to the Western intellectual standards of art and culture, the Negro does not measure up. Thus every Negro artist, writer, dramatist, poet, composer, musician, et al., comes under the guillotine of this cultural judgment. What this means is that the Negro is artistically, creatively, and culturally inferior; and therefore all the established social power wielded by the white cultural elite will be used to keep the Negro creative artist in his place. But the historical catch in all this is that the white Protestant Anglo-Saxon in America has nothing in his native American tradition that is aesthetically and culturally original, except that which derives from the Negro presence.[9]

Psychological Stigmatization

Psychological stigmatization is perhaps the most difficult concept to delineate precisely and briefly. In essence it means that skin color, in the American context, has become a culturally pervasive symbol—white skin color denoting superiority and Black skin color denoting inferiority. Internalization of this symbolic reference occurs early and is an intrinsic part of the psychic makeup of Americans. Joel Kovel states:

A really deep survey of white Americans would doubtlessly reveal a great mixture of racial patterns in everyone, but it might be predicted that the substantial majority continue to reserve their most intense feelings for the hallowed racial patterns of yore, that is, they hold to a mixture of dominative and aversive racist beliefs, according, one would expect, to their authoritarianism and the degree to which their superego has internalized aggression.[10]

and

. . . the best-adjusted, most productive, and most typical of Americans who respond aversively to Black people they have not personally oppressed or even known, are no more than vehicles for the larger and axiomatic ideas of their times.[11]

Together these five elements of Black subordination constitute the structure of American racism and explain the continued hierarchization of Blacks as a collectivity in the society as a whole. To change that subordination *all* of the elements of structural racism would have to be eliminated.

Unfortunately, while the civil rights legislation of the 1960s ameliorated the collective condition of American Blacks, it did not destroy the structure of American racism. Indeed, it was a surprise to many to find that legal segregation was simply one part of a complex structure of racial subordination. Robert Carter makes the point well:

Brown's (Brown v. Bd. of Education) indirect consequences, therefore, have been awesome. It has completely altered the style, the spirit, and the stance of race relations. Yet the pre-existing pattern of white superiority and Black subordination remains unchanged; indeed, it is now revealed as a national rather than a regional phenomenon . . . Few in the country, Black or white, understood in 1954 that racial segregation was merely a symptom not the disease; that the real sickness is that our society in all its manifestations is geared to the maintenance of white superiority. . . .[12]

Carter is pointing out the persistence of the two key organizing principles which have historically given form and substance to the structure of racism: hierarchy and collectivism. In an ideal typical sense, hierarchy and collectivism have been the overriding principles buttressing, giving definition to, providing substance for the structure of racism described above. Given this understanding of hierarchy and collectivism as providing the encompassing principle governing intergroup behavior, exceptions are not discounted but help to delineate and underscore the structure from which they diverge. The point is not that there are no individual exceptions but rather that there are no large, secular or public arenas in which race is irrelevant—although it may be more or less salient. Income, geographical mobility, and lifestyle can exacerbate or mitigate but not fundamentally change the encompassing relevance of hierarchy and collectivism for Blacks. Also, it is important to note that while the encompassing principles of hierarchy and collectivism remain salient, the elements of the structure might change and, indeed, in the twentieth century there was a significant transformation of the structure with the elimination of legal segregation and political disenfranchisement and the modification of the nature of economic exploitation of Blacks. The crucial question for our purposes is: what is the relevance of school desegregation as public policy to fundamental transmogrification of the structure of racism? Some historical background is necessary to begin to probe this question.

Richard Kluger's brilliant history of *Brown v. Board of Education* provides us with an intriguing insight into the NAACP decision to pursue a particular kind of strategy in its attack on school segregation and, by extension, on legal segregation.[13] Nathan Margold, who developed the outlines of the initial NAACP strategy in the 1930s proposed that ". . .we boldly challenge the constitutional validity of segregation *if and when accompanied irremediably by discrimination*, we can strike directly at the most prolific sources of discrimination."[14] Margold developed a fresh approach to the major Supreme Court decision upholding segregation (*Plessy v. Ferguson*, 1896) and the major twentieth-century decision specifically upholding school segregation (*Gong Lum v. Rice*, 1927).

"In Plessy," Margold contended "the court had countenanced racial segregation only so long as the separate facilities were equal." But what if the facilities were not equal? And what if a state's schools were habitually operated in a way that failed to provide equal educational facilities for Negroes? Neither of these questions challenged the essential legality of segregation itself. In this sense, Margold was playing it cautiously. His plan, he said, was not "trying to deprive Southern states of their acknowledged privilege of providing separate accommodations for the two races. His target was segregation 'as now provided and administered.' Theoretical equality was splendid, but what would the Supreme Court say if presented with a case in which the theory had never been put into practice?"

So here was Margold's two-pronged weapon with which to attack and eliminate separate and unequal schools. "One prong, in theory, would void segregation laws in several states that had not safeguarded the Negro from unequal school expenditures. The other prong, in theory would outlaw the practice of segregation in states where inequality was habitual and heretofore discriminatory and therefore in violation of equal protection."[15]

The first opportunity to test the Margold theory was the *Murray v. Maryland* case in 1934. No Blacks had been admitted to the University of Maryland Law School since the beginning of 1933 although there were no Maryland state laws that required the segregation of colleges, nor did the charter or rules of the university itself prohibit the admission of Negro students. Segregation was being maintained by custom and by the prejudices of the university administrators. A Black graduate of Amherst College, Donald Murray, sought admission to the University of Maryland Law School but was refused with a letter stating that ". . . under the general laws of this state the University maintains the Princess Anne Academy as a separate institution of higher learning for the education of Negroes. . . ."[16] This missive ignored the fact that neither the Academy nor Morgan College (for Blacks) contained a law school.

In the *Murray v. Maryland* case, argued in Baltimore City Court, the presiding judge's questioning of the President of the University of Maryland was very revealing. Raymond Pearson, the President, quickly stumbled into the trap of trying to assert that patently unequal facilities were in fact equal. He found it extremely hard to defend his position when the differences in laboratory equipment, numbers of Ph.D. holders on the faculty, and expenditures were presented. In making the distinctiveness of segregation against the Negro clear, Pearson was asked whether he would admit Mexicans, Japanese, Indians, and Filipinos to the University as he would admit whites. "If they were residents of the state, they would probably be admitted, yes," said the President.[17]

The performance of the Maryland assistant attorney general was even less impressive than that of the University President. He invoked *Plessy v. Ferguson* in defense of the Maryland custom of segregated schools. But here the brilliance of the Margold strategy paid off—Murray's lawyers had not challenged Maryland's right to establish a segregated educational system, they had simply and powerfully challenged the equality that resulted from the administration of that system. The judge ordered the admission of Donald Murray to the University of Maryland Law School.

The otherwise obscure Murray case is worth the above detailed analysis because the cases which followed it, and which led inexorably to *Brown v. Board of Education*, reflected the general pattern and dynamic of the Murray case. Cases were brought which concentrated on the graduate and professional school level where segregation was most vulnerable because usually not only were facilities for Blacks at that level not equal but they were usually nonexistent. During the era of segregation, most Blacks in the deep south who wanted to pursue professional degrees had to obtain admission to predominantly white schools elsewhere; although for some professional areas, they could attend Howard University.

Victories for the NAACP position were won in a number of cases. In the *Missouri ex rel Gaines v. Canada* 1938 case in which Lloyd Gaines sought admission to the University of Missouri's Law School an important precedent was set. Gaines had been told to apply to Lincoln University where the state planned to build a law school or to go out of state. The court found for Gaines:

The basic consideration is not as to what sort of opportunity other states provide, or whether they are as good as those in Missouri but as to what opportunities Missouri itself furnishes to white students and denies to Negroes solely upon the ground of color. The admissibility of separating the races in the enjoyment of privileges afforded by the state rests wholly upon the equality of the privileges which the laws give to the separated groups within the state. By the operation of the laws of Missouri a privilege has been created for white law students which is denied to Negroes by reason of their race.[18]

Next came *Sipuel v. Board of Regents of the University of Oklahoma* in 1948. The NAACP struggled to extend the *Gaines* decision through the case of Ada Sipuel. Ms. Sipuel sought admission to the University of Oklahoma Law School and had been turned down. Oklahoma allegedly planned to build a Black law school sometime in the future. Again the court held that a Black petitioner was entitled to secure a legal education afforded to others by state institutions.

Sweatt v. Painter 1950 was a significant and qualitative advance building on *Sipuel, Gaines,* and *Murray,* but within the same general framework. In this case, Sweatt sought admission to the University of Texas Law School on the grounds that the Black law school which the state of Texas *had already established* failed to offer him equal educational opportunity. The court agreed:

What is more important, the University of Texas Law School possesses to a far greater degree those qualities which are incapable of objective measurement but which make for greatness in a law school. Such qualities to name but a few include reputation of the faculty, experience of the administration, position and influence of the alumni; standing in the community; traditions and prestige.[19]

Finally, the case which directly set the pattern and laid the ground for *Brown* was *McLaurin v. Oklahoma State Regents* in 1950. In this case, McLaurin had already been admitted to the University of Oklahoma but was segregated within the University. The issue was the stigma of his separation:

Appellant (McLaurin) was thereupon admitted to the University of Oklahoma Graduate School (and) . . . his admission was made subject to "such rules and regulations as to segregation as the President of the University shall consider to afford to Mr. G.W. McLaurin substantially equal educational opportunities as are afforded to other persons seeking the same education in the Graduate College," a condition which does not appear to have been withdrawn. Thus he was required to sit apart at a designated desk in an anteroom adjoining the classroom; to sit at a designated desk on the mezzanine floor of the library, but not to use the desks in the regular reading room; and to sit at a designated table and to eat at a different time from the other students in the school cafeteria.

In the interval between the decision of the court below and the hearing in this court, the treatment afforded appellant was altered. For some time, the section of the classroom in which appellant sat was surrounded by a rail on which there was a sign stating, "Reserved for Colored," but these have been removed. He is now assigned to a seat in the classroom in a row specified for colored students; he is assigned to a table in the library on the main floor; and he is permitted to eat at the same time in the cafeteria as other students, although here again he is assigned to a special table.

It is said that the separations imposed by the state in this case are in form merely nominal. McLaurin uses the same classroom, library and cafeteria as students of other races; there is no indication that the seats to which he is assigned in these rooms have any disadvantage of location. He may wait in line in the cafeteria and there stand and talk with his fellow students, but while he eats he must remain apart.

These restrictions signify that the state, in administering the facilities it affords for professional and graduate study, sets McLaurin apart from the other students . . . Such restrictions impair his ability to study, to engage in discussions and exchange views with other students, and . . . to learn his profession.

We conclude [ended Chief Justice Vinson] that the conditions under which this appellant is required to receive his education deprive him of his personal and present right to the equal protection of the laws. We hold that under these circumstances the Fourteenth Amendment precludes differences in treatment by the state based upon race. Appellant . . . must receive the same treatment at the hands of the state as students of other races. . . .[20]

Finally, in *Brown* v. *Board of Education of Topeka* 1954, the Supreme Court simply extended the *Sweatt and McLaurin* principle that in professional education segregation per se can entail inequality of treatment. Since it had been established in the lower courts that the Black and white schools involved in the

Brown case were, or were being, equalized with respect to buildings, salaries of teachers and other tangible factors, the decision of the court had to rest on the overall, and partially intangible, impact of segregation on public education:

> Segregation with the sanction of law, therefore, has a tendency to retard the education and mental development of Negro children and to deprive them of some of the benefits they would receive in a racially integrated school system.[21]

> We conclude that in the field of public education the doctrine of "separate but equal" has no place. Separate educational facilities are inherently unequal. Therefore, we hold that the plaintiffs and others similarly situated for whom the actions have been brought, are, by reason of the segregation complained of, deprived of the equal protection of the laws guaranteed the fourteenth amendment.[22]

In subsequent decisions, the Supreme Court used the *Brown* precedent to strike down public accommodations segregation. These cases, it should be remembered, increasingly occurred in the wake of an active and forceful civil rights movements. In the *Brown* decision itself, at least one legal analyst believes that Plessy was not expressly overruled.[23] In any case, the point is that the development of case law up to *Brown* followed a particular strategy of showing how the implementation of segregation was faulty and fundamentally unequal. That strategy evolved into demonstrations that state-enforced segregation was inherently unequal. The structure of the system in which the state-enforced segregation in education existed was one in which there was legal segregation and state endorsed political disenfranchisement of Blacks. The strategy which was evolved to attack de jure segregation was a sagacious and appropriate one. The cognitive map which justices have of the society shapes the extent to which arguments make sense, are compelling, sound rational. *Gaines, Sweat, Sipuel, McLaurin* allowed the court to decide on issues involving professional education where the justices had personal experience and knowledge. *Brown* fit nicely into an extant framework.

It should be kept in mind, however, that in 1954, although the country was characterized by a structure of racism which encompassed both north and south, its manifestations were different. In the south there existed the full elaboration of the structure of racism: *legal* segregation; state endorsed political disenfranchisement of Blacks; economic exploitation; cultural marginalization and psychological stigmatization. In the north, in contrast, legal segregation, by and large, ceased to exist in the late eighteenth century and state-endorsed political disenfranchisement in the nineteenth. Informal segregation may have been alive and well as also coercion against Blacks exercising the franchise in some locations, but these were neither legalized nor formal, state endorsed phenomena. *The difference in the two structures was fundamental.*

Because of the pervasiveness and obnoxiousness of legal segregation in the South, it was possible for Blacks and their liberal allies to believe that legal segregation was the problem itself, instead of realizing, it was only the most superficial, though vexing and difficult to dislodge, segment of a much more ingrained structure. The school desegregation cases were absolutely crucial as part of the strategy and process of dismantling legal segregation. In that sense, these cases were an unqualified success and well worth the time and effort put into them. Brown was also important in providing an additional legitimacy to the civil rights movement (keep in mind most laymen believed that the Supreme Court had "outlawed" segregation in the Brown case). In that sense, the school cases were part of a complex web of factors which indirectly led to the transformation of the Southern structure of racism (elimination of legal segregation and state endorsed political disenfranchisement and modification of economic separation as well as to transformation of the Northern structure of racism, specifically, the modification of racial segregation of the labor force. Attempts to extend the principles evolved in the early education cases fought under de jure segregation to cases of de facto segregation quickly became problematical and, indeed, once the structure of racism in the south had been transformed so that both north and south, in essence, shared the same structure of racism as the basis for continued hierarchy and collectivism of Blacks, it even became more difficult to use the same kinds of strategies and arguments in the South.

What was missing was a realization that phenomena which may look the same, such as racially homogeneous schools, may in fact be different because the sociological structure of the society in which the phenomenon is embedded is different. This is not to suggest, I would hasten to add, that school segregation is irrelevant in the North where it mainly exists as de facto rather than de jure segregation. Rather, it is to suggest that the civil rights movement and Black and liberal intellectuals had not really come to grips with the phenomena of northern racism except by analogy with the South. The poverty of analysis was increasingly revealed as a severe problem as the entire country took on the structure of northern racism. A nationwide consensus seems to have emerged against *legal* segregation but since aversion and informal, non-legal, privately based separation was publicly understood as different from legal segregation, it became perfectly consistent to support dismantling of legal segregation and at the same time to oppose bussing and other remedies which threatened informal separation of the races.

SCHOOL DESEGREGATION AS RACIAL PUBLIC POLICY

The foregoing discussion suggests the importance of the school desegregation cases to the dismantlement of legal segregation. But the question remains, what of school desegregation itself—what is its potential for bringing about educational, political, and social change? Nathaniel Jones, writing while NAACP general counsel, believes that the court is the most effective route for increasing educational opportunity for Blacks.[24] He also states:

> Why does the role of the Supreme Court, 25 years after Brown, remain so crucial in undoing school segregation? Why can there not be greater utilization of the political channels or the negotiating process to deal with this problem? For one thing, up to now the Supreme Court has consistently stated that, since Brown, it has never "deviated in the slightest degree" from the principle that school segregation fostered by intentional conduct is remediable in the Federal Court and is not to be left to plebiscites or voter whims.

> However, with few exceptions, when school boards during the past decade voluntarily sought to comply with Brown, they became the target of overwhelming negative political reaction and soon were either driven from office, overridden by referenda or both. Congress' response of late has been to enact crippling anti-bussing amendments.

> The target of Brown was the separate-but-equal vestiges of slavery. That condition still obtains in too many cities all across the land on this, the 25th year of Brown.[25]

Jones seems to suggest that the courts can bring about change in the absence of the will and/or the ability of political and executive branches of government. Jones's discussion, it should be remembered, predates the Reagan administration and the increasingly anti-bussing and to a certain extent anti-school desegregation posture of the Congress. (Congressional failure to support school desegregation became so obvious in the 1970s that Congress was characterized by the U.S. Commission on Civil Rights in its 1979 report as assaulting school desegregation.[26]) But it is politically naive to believe that courts can bring about change in the absence of supportive executive and legislative action?

Even more perplexing is the question what specific kind of social, political, and educational change has been produced by school desegregation and could potentially be produced by school desegregation. This is an extremely complex issue. Even the obvious questions about school desegregation's impact on educational achievement do not have clear and unambiguous answers. For example, it is not clear from the literature that the academic achievement of Black children improves in all or in the majority of currently structured integrated settings. St. John states: "Adequate data have not been gathered to determine a causal relation between school racial composition and academic achievement. More than a decade of considerable research effort had produced no definitive positive findings."[27] In a 1981 assessment of findings on effective desegregation, Robert Crain and Willis Hawley state: "There is simply no satisfactory research on desegregation which would allow one to account, either theoretically or empirically, for why school systems respond the way they do to desegregation and what implications their responses have for their institutional capacity to be effective in terms of the equitable distribution of quality education."[28] Similarly, it is not clear that desegregation produces decreases in prejudiced attitudes. In a cautious review of the literature on the impact of desegregation on racial attitudes, Robert Newby notes that for 'black prejudice toward whites' the studies are about evenly divided between decrease and increase. But for whites, there is a 4:1 tendency in these findings for prejudice to increase towards Blacks.[29]

If it is not clear that school desegregation produces improved achievement and/ or mitigation of racist attitudes, what positive changes do occur? and what additional positive changes could potentially take place? Ronald Edmonds argues that ". . . school desegregation can best be understood when evaluated in a broader sense as an instrument of instructional reform."[30] Class action suits offer what he terms "a tactical last resort" of Black communities that have tried various methods for many years to improve teaching and learning for their children.[31] But all of the emotional reaction and commitment to desegregation occurs not because people see it narrowly as a tactical method to improve teaching and learning but because it is believed, at least in some quarters, to be intrinsically good, and perhaps to be a method for bringing about broad based social change.

SCHOOL DESEGREGATION AND SHIFTING NOTIONS OF THE PUBLIC INTEREST

Thus far, school desegregation has been examined in relationship to the structure of racism and as a form of racial public policy within a more generally defined political and policy setting. Remaining is analysis of school desegregation in relationship to the overall dynamics of change from the 1950s to the 1980s. Clearly, the Brown decision and the civil rights movement were factors which created the political climate for a federal focus on educational equity in the 1960s. Passage of the Elementary and Secondary Education Act was a concrete manifestation of articulated federal government emphasis on educational equity and on equal educational opportunity.

Emphasis on educational equity and equal educational opportunity in the field of education was paralleled in other policy areas by similarly expansive views of the role of government in protecting citizens from environmental and work-related ills; expanding individual potential and opportunity (including work and training programs for people without skills to advance in the marketplace); increasing access and highlighting the problems of groups such as homosexuals, aged, women, and the handicapped and so on. For a short period of time during this era, the notion of public interest seemed substantively to transcend the mere collection of competing private interests. Public discourse during that period legitimized equity as a social priority to an extent which allowed, at least, some legislative action. Indeed government activity during this period can only be understood in the context of general, broadly organized movements lobbying for expanded government action on behalf of disadvantaged groups. Much of this activity came about because of the civil rights movement. The civil rights movement had a profound impact on American society generally and served as a catalyst for the emergence and growth of other movements including the peace movement, women's movement, student movement, ecology movement, gay movement, gray panthers, and so on.

In dialectical fashion, however, this expansion of what was defined as the public interest created its own antithesis which was the demand for ideological, political and public policy shrinkage. That demand for shrinkage, articulated as an encompassed theme in the 1970s, emerged as the dominant ideological thrust under the Reagan administration in the 1980s and was expressed ideologically through demands for a "new federalism."[32] In education the demands for ideological shrinkage, philosophical retreat, and public policy limitation were expressed, albeit inchoately, much earlier in opposition to bussing and to various other plans for school desegregation. Change in federal government educational goals from equal educational opportunity and equity in the 60s and 70s to excellence and freedom of choice for the consumer in the 1980s is a further reflection of a shift in the definition of the public interest. Educational equity and equal opportunity were open-ended goals which were institution challenging *in potential*. Excellence and freedom of choice are more limited in conception. It is not necessary to change structures or institutions to achieve freedom, in the limited definition now being used, and, similarly, excellence can be understood as ultimately an indefinable quality which is most properly pursued individualistically. In an anthropomorphic conception, society can only look on and cheer the individual's achievement. This is quite different from the government, as a representative of society as a whole having the responsibility to aid the disadvantaged and others to achieve equality. Compensatory education, when combined with the goal of equality, involves some focusing of resources on those students with the greatest need. That targeted use of government funds builds a modest redistributive component into public policy.

In a political era in which public ideology had undergone a profound change, one so fundamental that the most basic notions of what the government should and can legitimately do have altered, it is not likely that school desegregation will achieve policy priority. This line of thought suggests the importance of the relationship between public policy and political and ideological climate. *It also situates school segregation as one part of a broader political program and ideological perspective and it focuses our attention on school desegregation as an aspect of political struggle and power conflicts.*

CONCLUSION: SCHOOL DESEGREGATION AND PRAXIS

Understood in the most basic sense, a theory is simply a framework, pattern or model to give direction, meaning, and organization to research. A theory should, at minimum, suggest what the major questions are to be investigated and indicate which aspects of reality are meaningful and significant. It is in that sense that the term "theory" has been used in this essay. As it becomes increasingly clear that the movement for school desegregation has reached an impasse, the need for theoretical analysis becomes all the more pragmatically appropriate and necessary. For educational researchers a more general, conceptual approach to school desegregation is essential for advancing understanding of educational politics, policy formation, and implementation. For activists, similarly, action has to be pursued in light of knowledge of facilitating and constraining factors.

In designating the conceptual elements of a theory, a certain arbitrariness is inevitable as well as the exercise of judgment concerning what constitutes the basic elements of theoretical reality. In exploring themes which I consider central to development of a theory of school desegregation, I suggested that three kinds of conceptual issues were crucial: school desegregation viewed in relationship to the structure of racism; school desegregation as a form of racial public policy reflecting the general dynamics of public policy implementation; and school desegregation as a manifestation of contemporary political and ideological change. Exploration of each of the three themes has enhanced our understanding of school desegregation as part of a broader, more embracing pattern, dynamic, and process of social and political change. Furthermore, each focus has been on race as the primary conceptual element to be explored, elaborated, and analyzed. This approach to a theory of school desegregation, therefore, views desegregation as an example of public policy to redress inequality. This point becomes important because it suggests that approaches to school desegregation that focus on it solely as a form of organizational change are likely to be uninformative and possibly misleading. Instead, the approach in this essay points us toward understanding the structure of inequality and poses fundamental questions: What is the direct and/or indirect relationship of school desegregation to the structure of racial inequality? Indeed, it might plausibly be asserted that school desegregation can usually be seen, not simply as a thing in itself but as a manifestation, expression, reflection of more fundamental ideological, political, economic, and social conflicts in society. The goal, then, is to study school desegregation in such a way that it illuminates these underlying societal dynamics and, conversely, to utilize comparative knowledge about social change in order to enrich our understanding of specific school controversies.

This essay has not attempted to develop a definitive theory of school desegregation but simply to move discussion beyond description of (and moralizing about) events to interpretation of those events in some larger framework. That effort, in turn, focuses our attention on the relationship of school desegregation to long-range policy shifts; the causal or acausal linkage between school desegregation and major social and political changes; the possibility of transmogrification of key institutions and structures through processes generated and initiated by school desegregation efforts; the impact of school desegregation on political values, norms, identities, views of ideological legitimacy; and the importance of school desegregation controversies in shaping the "rules of the political game."

Of course, what is called for here is a "middle-range" theory capable of situating events, people and policies. Middle-range theory itself usually exists within a broader scientific paradigm. In the absence of either middle-range theory or a general paradigm, meaningless data collection occurs, a plethora of interpretations all compete for attention, and no unified opinion exists on what the important research issues are. As Kuhn states:

> If a body of belief is not already implicit in the collection of facts—in which case more than "mere facts" are at hand—it must be externally supplied, perhaps by a current metaphysic, or another science, or perhaps personal and historical accident. No wonder, then, that in the early stages of the development of any science, different men confronting the same range of phenomena, but not usually all the same particular phenomena, describe and interpret them in a different way.[33]

If, as has been argued, school desegregation is best viewed as middle-range theory, the broad gauge theory of which it would be a part would be a more general theory of racial inequality at one level and a theory of social change at the most abstract level. It was suggested above that the traditional structure of racial inequality or racism was composed of five elements: legal segregation, political disenfranchisement, economic separation, cultural marginalization and psychological stigmatization and these five elements were in turn linked to the encompassing principles of hierarchy and collectivism which defined the system. As a form of racial public policy, school desegregation has institutional-challenging potential but it has been implemented in that fashion. Therefore, one line of research is the comparative analysis of various forms of racial public policy in order to elucidate problems of implementing changes in structures of racial inequality. Finally, the relationship of racial public policy to more general policy priorities has to be investigated as well as questions that focus on the kinds of political climates that facilitate or hinder implementation of racial policy change.

The final point that should be made has to do with the range, richness, and utility of a theory of school desegregation. While a theory of racial school desegregation involving Blacks might inform analysts interested in gender or national origin research, it would not be a substitute for developing a structural analysis of those forms of inequality as the basis for understanding gender and national origin school desegregation processes.

Each structure of inequality requires the integrity of autonomous analysis. Comparison, then, entails understanding the similarities and differences among race, gender, and national origin structures of inequality rather than creation of mindless analogies that equate all forms of discrimination with each other. In that sense, a theory of racial desegregation of schools in an important initial step. A comprehensive theory of school desegregation, however, must await the laying of groundwork in a number of disciplines; the analyses of various kinds of structures of inequality; and the melding of policy implementation research focusing on school desegregation with more generalized approaches to social change. This essay has attempted to sketch broadly the outlines of this complex and long-range process.

NOTES

1. See Willis D. Hawley, et al., *Assessment of Current Knowledge About the Effectiveness of School Desegregation* (Nashville Center for Education and Human Development Policy, Institute for Public Policy Studies, Vanderbilt University, April 1981) for a comprehensive review of desegregation studies.

2. Milton Gordon, *Assimilation in American Life* (New York: Oxford University Press, 1964); Nathan Glazer and Daniel Moynihan, *Beyond the Melting Pot* (Cambridge, Mass.: MIT Press, 1963); Edgar Litt, *Ethnic Politics in America* (Glenview, Illinois: Scott, Foresman, 1970) all contain discussions of ethnicity that fail to adequately analyze Blacks.

3. Institutional racism has been used as a model in a number of theoretical works. One of the better discussions of this concept is in Edward Greenberg, Neal Milner, David T. Olson, *Black Politics* (New York: Holt, Rinehart and Winston 1971).

4. See for example William Julius Wilson, *The Declining Significance of Race* (Chicago and London: The University of Chicago Press, 1978, 1980) and Thomas Sowell, *Ethnic America: A History* (New York: Basic Books, 1981).

5. As far back as Gunnar Myrdal, *An American Dilemma: The Negro Problem and Modern Democracy,* 2 vols. (New York: Harper and Row, 1944) Blacks have

been misunderstood as being a caste. Oliver C. Cox, *Caste, Class and Race* (New York: Monthly Review Press, 1948) has an excellent summary and critique of this literature. Cox makes the critical point, still relevant for contemporary proponents of the Blacks as caste position, that although there are similarities between caste and U.S. racism (hierarchy and collectivism in my terms) one cannot speak of one caste but of the *caste system* and *caste ideology*. Louis Dumont, "Caste, Race and Stratification: Reflections of a Social Anthropologist," Appendix A in Louis Dumont, *Homo Hierarchicus: An Essay on the Indian Caste System* (Chicago: University of Chicago Press, 1970) is also an excellent critique of the confusion of caste and racism.

6. Marquerite Ross Barnett, "A Theoretical Perspective on Racial Public Policy," in Marguerite Ross Barnett and James A. Hefner, *Public Policy for the Black Community: Strategies and Perspectives* (Sherman Oaks, California: Mayfield, 1976) pp. 1–55.

7. See Marguerite Ross Barnett, *Symbolic Domination: Stereotypical Images of Blacks in American Culture* (New York: Holmes and Meier, in press).

8. Harold Cruse, *The Crisis of the Negro Intellectual* (New York: William Morrow and Co., Inc. 1967) p. 104.

9. Ibid., p. 105.

10. Joel Kovel, *White Racism: A Psychohistory* (New York: Vintage Books, 1970, 1971) p. 212.

11. Ibid., p. 94.

12. Robert Carter, "The Warren Court: A Critical Analysis," quoted in Derrick Bell, *Race, Racism and American Law* (New York: Little, Brown and Co., 1973) p. 457.

13. Richard Kluger, *Simple Justice* (New York: Alfred A. Knopf, 1976).

14. Quoted in Ibid., p. 135 (Italics Kluger's)

15. Ibid., p. 134.

16. Ibid., p. 188.

17. Ibid., p. 190.

18. *Missouri ex rel. Gaines V. Canada,* 305 U.S. 337. Black's Law Dictionary defines ex rel thusly, "Legal proceedings which are instituted by the attorney general (or other proper person) in the name and behalf of the state, but on the information and at the instigation of an individual who has a private interest in the matter said to be taken 'on the relation' (ex relatione) of such persons who is called 'the relator'."

19. *Sweat v. Pointer,* 339 U.S. 629.

20. *McLaurin v. Oklahoma State Regents,* 339 U.S. 637.

21. *Brown v. Board of Education* (No. 1) 347 U.S. 483.

22. Ibid.

23. Derrick Bell, *Op.Cit.,* states "The 1954 decision in *Brown v. Board of Education,* . . . did not expressly overrule *Plessy v. Ferguson.* The court simply

concluded that in the field of public education the doctrine of 'separate but equal' has no place." (p. 208).

24. Nathaniel Jones, "The Brown Decision: 25 Years Later," *Crisis,* Vol. 86, No. 6, June/July 1979, p. 214.

25. Ibid.

26. U.S. Commission on Civil Rights, *Desegregation in the Nation's Public Schools: A Status Report.* Washington, D.C.: U.S. Government Printing Office, 1979, p. 14.

27. Nancy St. John, *School Desegregation: Outcomes for Children* (New York: John Wiley and Sons, 1975) p. 36.

28. Robert Crain and Willis Hawley, *An Agenda for Further Research on Desegregation Strategies,* Volume II of Willis Hawley, *et al., The Assessment of Current Knowledge About the Effectiveness of School Desegregation Projects op. cit.*

29. Robert Newby, "Racial Balance as a New Form of Injustice," in Marguerite Ross Barnett and Charles C. Harrington, *Readings on Equal Education,* Volume VII (New York: AMS Press, 1984).

30. Ronald R. Edmonds, "Effective Education for Minority Pupils: Brown Confounded or Confirmed," in Derrick Bell, *Shades of Brown: New Perspectives on School Desegregation* (New York: Teachers College Press, 1981) p. 109.

31. Ibid.

32. See Marguerite Ross Barnett, "The New Federalism and the Unfinished Civil Rights Agenda," *Black Law Journal* Summer 1984.

33. Thomas S. Kuhn, *The Structure of Scientific Revolutions* (Chicago: University of Chicago Press, 1962). p. 17.

THE HERITAGE OF AFFIRMATIVE ACTION FOR BLACKS IN AMERICAN HIGHER EDUCATION: SOCIAL RESPONSIBILITY AND INSTITUTIONAL AUTHORITY

Lorenzo Morris

Mounting evidence of the feared "chilling effect" of repeated legal and journalistic challenges to affirmative action has begun to materialize for everyone to see. The national mood, symbolized by the newly installed conservative majority in Washington, has already turned away from the promotion of public programs directed toward disadvantaged minorities. With the 1980 presidential inauguration of Reagan, the nation appeared to be turning completely around and reconsidering past affirmative action initiatives including those already written into law and integrated into established practice. Whether through legislation, judicial reinterpretation, or simply through the discretionary exercise of administrative and private power, recently created equal opportunity programs have lost all but the last threads of support among the mainstream national political leadership. By the force of Executive Order 11246 and by means of continuing litigation under equal employment opportunity regulations, however, affirmative action remains a national obligation. Through employment advertising and the publicized admissions practices of educational institutions, affirmative action retains a high degree of visibility as well as a residue of respectability among the more moderate elements of the new political center, yet, its resilience in the face of legal challenges and its continuation under the harsh light of public scrutiny do not deter the assaults against it.

In less than a decade the prevailing image of affirmative action has been

37

effectively transformed. Initially, it was conceived under the Johnson Administration as a set of programs to hasten and facilitate equal opportunity first for blacks
and then for other minorities. Increasingly, however, that initial concept has been
submerged by the media-popularized image of a burdensome series of regulations
hampering the social mobility of the deserving non-minorities, and of white males
in particular. In the interim, affirmative action eligibility mushroomed from the
initial focus on blacks and native Americans to include Hispanics, some Orientals
and white women. In the course of its extension and its adaptation by diverse
private and public organizations, uncertainty about the meaning of affirmative
action gave way to distrust of its purposes. No one could deny that it grew out of
an intention to buttress equality of opportunity but many came to fear that it
would effectively require equality of results or outcomes for all groups.

As the progeny of democratic individualism, personal freedom and private
initiative, equal opportunity could not be easily reconciled with a policy that
seemed to prescribe the results of individual effort. The critics of affirmative
action also insinuated that the American tradition of meritocracy could only
survive where individual competence and effort were paramount. To them, any
policy which treated people as sociological groups, whether racial, ethnic or
sexual, denigrated individualism. In a wave of historical revisionism affirmative
action was thus transformed from the progeny of equal opportunity to its
antithesis.

The stellar example of American meritocracy, if there could be one, had to be
higher education. In contrast, political institutions had been visibly despoiled by
nepotism, special interests, and secret caucuses, to name just some of its
meritocratic failings. Industry and commerce had been sullied with monopoly,
labor contract restrictions and other restraints on competition. Compared to these
sectors, higher education seemed to be above reproach. The diversity of its
institutions, now more than three thousand, their nationwide distribution, their
variety of educational programs, and, of course, their emphasis on scholarship
were widely thought to assure basic meritocracy.

Given the prevailing capitalist value system, most Americans have not viewed
education as the backbone of the nation's prosperity, but many have seen it as the
foremost defender of the faith and the traditional altar of the individualist's
baptism. In spite of the recurrent conflicts between college radicals and the
military-industrial complex since the 1960s, the ascendence of high technology in
American private enterprise has served to consecrate the union between higher
education and business. At the same time as the technocratic era has brought
visibility to this relationship, it has also exposed the integrity of higher education
to greater questioning. The doubts about the role of higher education were raised
mostly by scholars and representatives of disadvantaged minorities, further
justifying affirmative action in higher education for this peripheral segment of
Americans. In this decade, however, doubts and exposure of this relationship

have been shored up by a protective response from more powerful groups—people who fear the new vulnerability of institutions. These people also resent the implication that their own power is not the product of their dedication to individual enterprise. If American industrialization is the product of individual creativity and tenacity, as innumerable politicians and essayists have claimed, then American technology would seem to be the product of our individual efforts coupled with advanced education.

For the legitimation of power and position to find support in the educational system, race cannot be a basis of selection. Merit-based selection inevitably leads to stratification but it is also supposed to lead to social integration on criteria other than those involving merit—criteria other than racist. The hallmark of the meritocratic perspective, according to Bowles and Gintis, is its reduction of a complex web of social relationships in production to a few rules of technological efficiency (Bowles and Gintis, 1976, pp. 104–5). Education in a technocratic society prepares the way by reorienting individual consciousness of inequality to perceive inequality in terms of such a limited set of rules of differentiation. "The meritocratic orientation of the educational systems," Bowles and Gintis add, "promotes not its egalitarian function, but rather its integrative role: Education reproduces inequality by justifying privilege and attributing poverty to personal failure" (p. 114). Where analysts disagree with the conclusion that social inequality is the likely outcome of American education, most will concede that educational institutions provide academic justification, valid or invalid, for the unequal availability of their resources and credentials to Americans who pursue them. The difference between those who view existing inequalities in education as meritocratically justified and those who view inequalities as unjustified has less to do with their views on merit than with their views on social and educational responsibility for identifying and rewarding the meritorious. The institutionalization of affirmative action, therefore, depends more on the locus of authority in education than on any educational standards which institutional authorities have traditionally sought to protect.

THE IMPACT OF AFFIRMATIVE ACTION

Until affirmative action programs began to make an impact on higher education in the early 1970s, it was widely thought to be an outgrowth of traditional egalitarianism. It was thought to be either a short term adjustment practice through which minorities would be put in a competitive position or a practice that could be amended to fit traditional institutional practices. In the mid-1970s, when the number of affirmative action programs reached their peak, about a quarter of all the 3000-plus American colleges and universities had a special admissions program for minorities. Since higher education employment is in shorter supply than student places, the special admissions programs far outnumber all other kinds of affirmative action. The earlier growth of the admissions programs had the advantage of being "distributive policy," as Theodore Lowi calls it, while faculty positions and some professional school employment could only be integrated through "redistributive policy" (Lowi, 1969, p. 273). In other words, places for students were easily added without changing the structure and overall resources of the institution. Among faculty and professional school students, however, the institutional "pie" was constrained both by resources and institutional norms. These sectors were, therefore, most resistant to affirmative action. When they were eventually drawn into affirmative action programs, the concessions were sparse. In fact, the efforts to extend affirmative action beyond college enrollment seem to have sparked a negative sentiment which tarnished even the most elemental special admissions programs.

Affirmative action programs in higher education did not begin in earnest until the beginning of the 1970s; the Equal Employment Opportunity Act ("EEOC") of 1972 was an important stimulus. Some progress in black faculty employment followed in the next few years but it quickly leveled off. Although the early data on black faculty is seriously limited, apparently blacks held about 3 percent of faculty positions in 1972-73 (A. Bayer, 1973). At least half of these positions were in the 130-plus majority black colleges. By 1975 black faculty employment reached 4.4 percent or 19,915 blacks out of more than 450,000 faculty. Only 2.2 percent of full professors and 2.9 percent of associate professors were black (EEOC). Again, about half of these were at black institutions. The vast majority of blacks at white institutions clustered at the bottom of the tenure ladder or in positions with no possibility for tenure. Discouraging as these figures have been to blacks, the 1977 figures had to be more discouraging. In 1977 blacks were still only 4.4 percent of all faculty. No real progress had been made. In fact, there is virtually no evidence to suggest that any more progressive steps have been seriously undertaken.

As responsive to the national mood as the law, black enrollment had already made its most substantial gains by 1974. By that time blacks were 9.2 percent of all enrollment compared to 7 percent four years earlier. Four years later, however, black enrollment had barely moved; it was 9.3 percent in 1978 (ISEP 1981). The end of measurable progress had already been visible since black enrollment reached its peak at the midpoint of the decade. Black graduate and professional school enrollment, never much more than 6 percent in any category, began declining significantly after 1976. Total black undergraduate enrollment was virtually unchanged in this period, but blacks were disproportionately clustered in lower-status less upwardly mobile, two year colleges.

THE INDEPENDENCE AND AFFIRMATIVE ACTION

By 1976 when black higher education enrollment reached its current peak of 9.3 percent of student enrollment, affirmative action was being publicly juxtaposed to equal opportunity and meritocracy. By then, the 1965 origin of affirmative action had been all but forgotten by non-minorities. The harsher statements of this historical oversight, however, did not emerge until the 1980s. For example, Reagan's EEOC transition team succumbed to historical distortion when it concluded:

> Our legal tradition mandates individual rights not group rights. This has, in fact, been the goal of civil rights organizations for many years. (*The Record*, Jan. 26, 1981: p. 26).

Accordingly, affirmative action is no longer thought to be amenable to educational traditions because it de-emphasizes individual independence which involves "accepting personal responsibility for one's behavior," one's achievements and failures (R. Dreeben, 1973, p. 68). Of course, no individual action in the context of a social organization like a school can be fully independent, but this fact is generally overlooked by the neo-conservatives in education. It is overlooked in large part because American education from elementary school on only emphasizes individual independence as a norm of good behavior. Student performance, in testing and homework assignments, for example, is only measured and rewarded for individual attainment. The child is not only treated as separable from his or her fellow students but also as independent of his/her family and the social and economic background, in the ideal situation. The fact that no child functions independently in school may simply reinforce the normative lesson (R. Dreeben, 1973, p. 68). Group identity and consciousness are only recognized and rewarded in sports, and then the group is recognized as a transitory collection of independent individuals.

Affirmative action, therefore, has had to confront meritocracy and individualism generally and individual independence in particular. In addition, the traditional advocacy of independence and merit has been tied to the values of private rather than public responsibility. Independence in the context of idealized meritocracy encourages private control of education because ideal standards of merit are considered absolute and the operationalization of merit is thought to require technical expertise. Independence at all levels is considered a virtue where decisions are based on expertise rather than consensus.

In capitalist society, of course, the social impetus for private control of education is already there. Yet, educational institutions go further, elevating these important elements of private power to an educational virtue. Ultimately then, affirmative action is pictured as violating the most fundamental principles of American ethics and society: meritocracy and individualism, independence, and private power. Private power, however, refers to institutional rather than individual behavior; it involves the educational process rather than the product (the student). Affirmative action also involves the process. Beyond private power, its link to these other norms, conflictual or supportive, is tenuous at best.

Within American educational traditions, the importance of private control of the educational process depends, for its cultural-social legitimacy, on its link to the pedagogical norms. These are norms, merit selection, etc., which affirmative action is supposed to violate. Admittedly, private power in education is consistent with the national commitment to private enterprise, but that consistency may still be more rhetorical or symbolic than real. The private control of education may be less effective in the promotion of nationally recognized values like meritocracy and individualism than public control.

The bond between the values of independence for students and for institutions is, however, cemented by faculty and administrative views of meritocracy which are often articulated under the rubric of academic freedom. As Gross and Grambsch observe in the two surveys of American universities in 1964 and 1971, faculty and administrative commitment to academic freedom as well as professionalism was stengthened (E. Gross and Grambsch, 1974, p. 74). While these years encompassed the turbulent experiences of campus upheaval from civil rights protest to the introduction of affirmative action, they only reflect a temporary shake-up in the traditional goals of higher education. In fact, sense of social responsibility for students, beyond the transmission of meritocratic values and the reinforcement of professionalism, seems to have diminished. Gross and Grambsch conclude:

Our examination of the goal structure of American universities in 1971 led us to the finding that the top goals involve the protection of academic freedom and the achievement of a variety of support goals related to the careers of faculty and administrators. . . .

When we turned to the feelings about the way things should be, there was some variation, suggesting a guilty conscience about the private concerns revealed by the goal emphasis. (Edward Gross and Paul Grambsch, 1974, p. 73

Whether or not faculty feel guilty about emphasizing their private goals, it is clear that their values on academic freedom will be translated into the pedagogical process and communicated to students. As a report by the Carnegie Foundation for the Advancement of Teaching puts it, "there is a tradition of academic life, centered on the search for truth, that imposes codes of conduct on the campuses that have application in other situations as well . . . [colleges] immerse their students in value-laden experience and teaching everyday" (The Carnegie Foundation, 1978. p. 250).

Unfortunately for affirmative action, greater self-interest on the part of educators is complemented by opposition to external, social, or political intervention in the institutional decision-making process. Inspired by federal action and civil rights upheaval, affirmative action is inevitably associated with external and non-institutional pressures. Even faculty who are supportive of civil rights legislation tend to oppose special admissions for black students in direct relationship to their vocal commitment to academic freedom and professionalism. A study of faculty attitudes by Mingle shows that "when faculty believe that black students should meet the same standards as whites" they tend to be hesitant to support institutional changes:

> According to the study, faculty members who recognized a need for gearing education to the students served were also those who supported black students. White faculty members who emphasized "universalism" and "professional neutrality" usually meant by that emphasis that black students should come to college with the same characteristics as white students (L. Morris, 1979, p. 142.)

Faculty and administrative opposition to affirmative action, as well as off-campus political opposition, are tied to the belief that academic meritocracy can only be protected by those whom traditional academia has certified as meritorious, namely themselves. In other words, the inequities, which most will admit historically characterize selection and promotion in these institutions, are assumed not to have tarnished the beneficiaries of that inequity. The reasons for this assumption are many, but inevitably the assumption results from the optimistic, liberating faith in higher education shared by conservatives and liberals alike. Nearly everyone in policy-making positions seemed to believe in the 1960s that simple access to higher education institutions would be a major, if not definitive, step toward equal opportunity for blacks in all areas of society. Ironically that belief also carried with it the assumption that higher education institutions were intrinsically egalitarian in orientation and ever prepared to promote standards of merit without regard to their prior histories of racial bias. This latter belief was, of course, complemented by the recognition that racism had been largely an influence of the social environment. Yet, the belief in the long suppressed egalitarianism of institutions was never really elevated to the level of logic because educators and politicians never consistently argued that racism had been forced on higher education. On the other hand, some argued that institutions had to accept the racially segregated input of students and personnel which segregated society funneled to them. Institutions were thus subject to the social environment. This argument, however, is not an appropriate justification for the political independence of institutions in the service of meritocracy because it means that institutions are subject to uncontrollable social forces. They would, therefore, need external governmental protection to insure that standards go beyond mere rhetoric.

Consequently, the dual commitment to merit and independence has meant that educators have had to be particularly self-protective and vigilant whenever the social environment was disrupted. First, their own intellectual standards require awareness of the environment, and second, the potential for environmental corruption of those standards always threatens to destabilize relations with public authorities. Either they submit to indeterminant social pressures, accept public "guidance," or resist both. In resisting both, they inevitably generate internal academic dissent like the campus upheavals of 1960s over both civil rights and the Vietnam War. Internal dissent is the corollary of institutional indifference to social change resulting from the longrun inclusion of ideologically diverse students and faculty. A premium on abstract meritocratic standards, real or feigned, leaves institutions incapable of eliminating disruptive social elements. Ultimately, institutionalized political neutrality in a state of political flux breeds partisan conflict both within and outside the institution.

Affirmative action, therefore, is simply one example of a political problem that has characterized American higher education since its inception. Yet, it is a special example because it involves the most overtly political conflict and the most difficult to resolve in the socio-political as well as academic contexts. Still, there is a parallel history of social pressures and political conflicts which has involved higher education institutions in the same kind of political choices and problems, though at a lower level of intensity. Historically, these problems have been resolved without a prior self-conscious evaluation of their consistency with intellectual traditions. Resolutions have been legitimated as irreversible, accomplished facts. The uniqueness of racial inequality, however, on the social, non-academic level makes the resolution of problems of political intervention too sensitive for unconscious bureaucratized adaptation. The stance of institutionalized neutrality showed some positive results in the early seventies but, of course, that was in the short run. The small progress made in the institutionalization of affirmative action was almost immediately shaken by the angry defenders of the tradition of institutional independence (and the protection in the name of merit of whatever happened to be institutionalized).

THE HERITAGE OF RESISTANCE AND ACCEPTANCE

The debate over affirmative action is characterized by indefinite sources of resistance and uncertain goal orientations. In higher education the debate over affirmative action is a natural outgrowth of an historical tension in American education, generally, between states and private responsibility for the articulation of social values. This tension, occurring over a variety of social issues, has been central to the evolution of American education. It emerged first around religious and moral control. In the development of higher education, racial-ethnic issues, however, have been historically pivotal in the overall determination of institutional political goals. The importance of racial issues in educational history has unfortunately not been complemented by transformation in the educational status of blacks. Racial inequality has rather served as the defining frame of reference and catalyst for non-racial, educational development. Only affirmative action poses the threat of making the development of educational, social, and racial changes at once concurrent and inseparable. The tendency of bureaucratic society to compartmentalize social functions makes the intellectually integrative impact of affirmative action even more disruptive for established educators. More than religious issues, affirmative action requires a resolution of the tension between political and institutional responsibility for institutionalized values in education. Effectively, that resolution calls for the reintegration of purpose and practice, of morality and administration, from which higher education has been continually moving away in orientation but not in fact—the tension has remained.

The tension and the critical phases in the development of higher education can be described in terms of five pivotal debates in American education. The first two concern moral responsibility and the segmentation of adminstration in the sense of mind and body. The remaining three also concern moral responsibility, but they are defined by a focus on inequality resulting from racial issues. The historical accommodation to the earlier moral tensions has meant that subsequent political tensions would aggravate and reactivate the unresolved tensions of the past. Moreover, racial issues would become more tenacious as they were translated into the language and polarizations of historically unresolved educational conflicts.

THE ALLOCATION OF MORAL RESPONSIBILITY

With the initial development of public education, an important issue in all areas of education was seemingly resolved, namely the locus of responsibility for morality in public education. That is to say that the issue was effectively resolved only for the Colonial years and the eighteenth century when American society was both homogeneous and rather theocratic by modern standards. In laters years when higher education emerged and all public education became universal, the tensions re-emerged. Nevertheless, as the progeny of elementary and secondary schooling, higher education was spared the explicit political debates over morality.

Early American education was conceived more for social stability and "moral uplift" than for individual upward social mobility. The Protestant Ethic, the driving motive of the capitalistic evolution, was in force when the colonists in the Northeast initiated public education, but the schools had other moral and social obligations. The Protestant Ethic, as Weber describes, was fully embodied in the existing cultural structures, including the church and the workplace (M. Weber, 1958, and R. Collins, 1979, p. 106). The task for schooling was to insure the inculcation of this and other elements of Christian tradition in the young. The productive orientation was implicit, but secondary to the maintenance of basic moral traditions. Accordingly, the Massachusetts Bay colonists passed the "Old Deluder Satan Act" in 1647 to establish common schools for the moral instruction of the young. This instruction inevitably required secular, practical education as well. The colonists feared that children were being led into sinful ways from which they would be saved if they were able to read. Reading was seen as a religious instrument because, of course, the students were expected to read the Bible.

On the other hand, the practical value of education was recognized. The more professional groups of colonists argued that the general lack of skill of the lower class constituted a threat to social stability. In this regard, Randall Collins concludes:

> Traditional Anglo-Protestant culture, in the form of religion and education, was used to create solid middle-class control—indeed, for the new commercial settlers to constitute themselves initially as a locally dominant class. Cultural organizations were their weapon against what they saw as the "barbarism" of their more adventurous and individualistic predecessors. It was this source of demand for traditional culture that gave the clerical class new opportunities, although they would act no longer in the role of undisputed community leaders, but as entrepreneurs selling culture, and thus laying the basis for a public cultural market. (Collins, 1979 p. 108.)

The "cultural market" of which Collins speaks is the loosely regulated supply of and public demand for educational credentials—credentials believed to have some irreducible value for society. The value of these credentials, depended then, as now, on the belief that learning in any form was more valuable when institutionally certified. Implicit in this credentializing process was the rudimentary meritocratic claim that institutions could equitably and efficiently determine the value of individuals' potential contributions to work and society. Unlike modern times, however, credentialism was not problematic because there was no expectation that formal education was necessary for professional or skill development. Merit, both of educated individuals and of educating institutions, therefore, had to be determined in the practical fields of the society and the workplace. Schools were not assumed at the time, unlike the present, to be the singular progenitors and arbitors of merit.

The early fears of lower class instability soon gave way to a defensive reaction by the upper class. They felt the need to protect their hegemony from the growing immigrant populations through a variety of social institutions including schooling. As American communities began to lose their cultural homogeneity in the nineteenth century, the expansion of institutionalized education served to reinforce the status of the traditional middle and upper class groups. Accordingly, Randall Collins observes:

The impetus for the foundation of public elementary schools came primarily from upper-class and upper middle-class professionals, especially ministers, educators, and lawyers. This was the class of religious leaders of earlier days; in the more secular climate of the nineteenth century, they turned to humanitarian crusades, as if to restore their old cultural dominance through moral reforms. The influx of ethnic aliens, beginning with the Irish Catholics in New England of the 1830s and 1840s, gave a special opportunity for cultural entrepreneurship. Public education was but one cause among many. (Collins, 1979, p. 106.)

Beginning with an explicitly moral purpose and an implicit practical/social purpose in the 1600s, supporters of public education quickly began to emphasize the practical value of education. By the end of the 1800s, therefore, the practical aspect was the most salient one in public discussion. Its saliency, however, did not mean that the moral foundation was not well entrenched in the system. A tension between the two purposes thus persisted.

The changing status of blacks in the 1800s aggravated that tension. From a practical standpoint there should have been no objection to the elementary schooling of the former slaves. Yet, the impetus for support of black education by whites came from moralistic organizations and the church. The missionary guidance of black education during Reconstruction is well documented (Franklin and Anderson, 1978). Similarly, black schools in the North emerged with the wave of pre-war abolitionism. White Southerners, by contrast, who did not pursue public education for themselves did so even less for blacks, because their moral-cultural system was relatively stable. Of course, it was threatened by the Northern radicals and by blacks, but it was uncontested within their plantation social systems. It was written into law and preached in church. The essential function of education for them was, therefore, already being served by other institutions.

Blacks in the Reconstruction period were the major institutors of public education because they believed in its practical social value. "It was the liberated Negroes themselves," according to Carter G. Woodson, "who, during the Reconstruction, gave the Southern States their first effective system of free public schools" (Woodson, 1919 reprinted 1968, p. 17). Again here, practicality was understood as the socially integrative function of education. Education for blacks was also thought to be the mode of upward social and economic mobility for the group, but it was probably conceived more in terms of their stability as freedmen than in terms of social revolution. Egalitarianism was no doubt an ulterior motive in their efforts, but it hardly materialized in their plans for schooling. Southern white opposition to elementary schooling for blacks expressed their complex notion of political conservatism in the racist moral sense. Their practicality was expressed in supporting racist moral and political tradition and their disregard for practicality in the societal role of education. The opposition to education for blacks thus reflected the white Southerner's belief that the institution should be instrumental to the moral interest of the inegalitarian state.

By the 1930s and 1940s when higher education became a significant social factor, black participation was scarcely an issue. Higher education had begun to be viewed as a practical vehicle for the development of professionals. Access to it was largely determined by wealth and social position. The institutions served the upper-class by facilitating the execution in the workplace of their inherited social and professional position. Higher education was practical but only for a small subset of society. Meritocracy was an attendent interest in the early years but it was scarcely more of an interest than sports, probably less. Access and promotion by merit was an experiment tried on the very few minorities and poor who penetrated the barriers of prior education, wealth, and social status.

By the end of World War II the societal need for expanded higher education was becoming clear. The military industrial complex had productive needs requiring a large pool of higher skilled and aculturated scientists, and managers. The evolution of society called for more teachers of all types to insure the socialization of the working class and the staffing of bureaucracies (M. Carnoy, 1974, p. 238–39). The emergence of technology both required and reflected a major change in public attitudes toward all levels of education.

SOCIAL PURPOSES VERSUS EDUCATIONAL TECHNOLOGY

In the first half of this century, moral and political concerns were submerged in higher education because there was a fundamental moral consensus among all those familiar with it. As in colonial America, the subset of society involved with higher education were essentially homogenous in culture and social class. The society had to change in other ways before any kind of heterogeneity, or moral issues related to it, could be meaningfully considered.

By the 1950s, when mass higher education had been well established, the moral versus practical tension was supplanted by a tension over the locus of responsibility for social and moral versus practical interests. Fundamentally, the moral questions were simply transformed into questions of *social purpose* to which they had historically been tied anyway. Also with a fundamental conceptual difference, the practical questions could then become *technological* ones. The basic choice of whether educational institutions could and should be responsible for implementing the "good" or defining and defending it remains. When higher education emerged, basic morality was a given. College students and teachers primarily confronted subsidiary moral issues that were open to societal choice within the larger moral/cultural framework. National or social purpose supplanted Christian morality in higher education but the difference between the two was more one of degree than of kind. Both values were defined by powerful social groups in terms of their function in stabilizing social relations. American religious morality was sublimated in quasi-religious expressions of national mission and obligation, what Robert Bellah calls the "civil religion" (Bellah, 1967, pp. 1–21).

The expansionist impetus of higher education became a nationally defined need for more college graduates, but it did not involve the explicit subjugation of institutional missions to national purpose. Institutions had been serving a national purpose within their elitist frame of reference. In the 1950s and 1960s the national government acknowledged their national value by providing institutional funding in line with institutionally defined needs—mainly for physical expansion of libraries. The federal land-grant colleges acts (Morrill Act) of 1860 and 1892 had previously demonstrated the unity of purpose between national, state, and institutional attitudes toward higher education. State governments began to establish colleges and universities in the mid-19th century with the primary motive of replicating the missions and behavior of private institutions. While state and federal funding involved some reorientation of higher education, the reorientation was conceived as largely technical in nature. Louis Hartz appropriately points out: "It is only when you take your ethics for granted that all problems emerge as problems of technique" (Louis Hartz, 1955, p. 10).

Federal and state aid to higher education in the first half of the century came with virtually no strings attached as far as the purpose and structure of the system. Fields of study, like agriculture at some public institutions, were selected for special financial support but this support was designed to follow the established orientation of the institutions. With varying emphases on quality and academic standards, public colleges and universities were conceived on the basis of the traditional models of private institutions.

Two-year institutions may have been an exception but they were small in number until the late 1950s. When the Carnegie Commission on Higher Education recognized that massive access to higher education could benefit the society and respond to a growing demand from lower income groups, it was successful in recommending that states establish and expand public two-year colleges (Carnegie 1970). The number of two-year colleges doubled between the mid 1950s and the end of the 1960s. This expansion represented an important incursion of national policy interests into the otherwise independent system of institutions. It was not disruptive of institutional independence, however, because new, noncompetitive units were created. Second, the inspiration came from the educational community rather than from politicians. Moreover, it was compatible with prevailing concepts of meritocracy because parallel standards were to be extended to cover parallel yet low-level types of credentials. Still, the politics of the situation was a precursor of affirmative action because it entailed the direct assertion of national interests in the process of higher education.

In 1958 the national interests were more explicitly and unilaterally expressed by the passage of the National Defense Education Act (NDEA). The passage of NDEA was the reaction of a traumatized Congress to the suspected military imbalance which the launching of Sputnik, the first satellite by the USSR, was thought to forebode. NDEA was intended to relieve this national sense of foreboding by encouraging college students to pursue the sciences through substantial scholarship assistance. Unlike prior federal financial aid programs, the G.I. Bill and Social Security student benefits, NDEA was a direct federal effort to channel higher education. Prior student aid programs were designed to reward or assist the young or veterans to go to college but they were selected for non-educational reasons. NDEA was the first program to overcome the long-standing opposition to government involvement in higher education. Indicatively, in NDEA, the term "direct" replaced the term "defense." The fear of foreign communism helped to overcome the national fear that government involvement would lead to communist-like control of institutions (N. Thomas, 1965, p. 3).

NDEA and subsequent federal programs established a new precedent by asserting the governmental responsibility and privilege in the determination of some institutional goals—especially the goal of student output in science educa-tion. It also translated into law a national interest in higher education. It did not, however, deprive institutions of their established ultimate authority in any area. It rather redefined the nebulous area of social responsibility as mutually controlled by government and education. Institutionalized social responsibility had been dormant since the colonial period. In asserting a governmental role, NDEA and other financial aid programs concurrently asserted a unique and independent institutional role. Virtually all educational practices were left untouched by government. Effectively, institutions were recognized as the sole arbiters and managers of educational technology. They were freed to attend to the national interests, and to non-conflicting private interests, in any way they saw fit.

With institutions in charge of educational technology and government in charge of the social purposes of education, the world of higher education could theoreti-cally have reached a stable balance of power. There was more tension than stability, however, because educational practices only appeared to be technologi-cal to those outside the institutions and to the blind advocates of independence inside them. Major decisions—from admission policy, curriculum management to faculty governance to name a few areas—involved both technical and value-based decisions (M. Apple, 1979, pp. 127–128).

SOCIAL VALUES WITH TECHNIQUE VERSUS TECHNIQUE WITH SOCIAL VALUES

As a consequence of the externally inspired demand for college credentials and the influx of public and philantrophic financial aid, higher education reached maturity in the 1960s. In the space of twenty years, from 1950 to 1970, nearly every measurable component of higher education doubled or tripled in size—the number of graduate schools, two-year colleges, students, faculty, etc. Only black enrollment took a few more years to make its major gains.

By the time race became an issue in higher education, the ground rules for the governmental and institutional responses were well established. The *Brown* desegregation ruling in 1954 took about fifteen years to impact on phase independent-oriented institutions. Yet their liberal traditions would have suggested a more rapid response except for their allegiance to traditional standards of meritocracy. The validity of established practices in admissions could hardly be challenged without also discrediting their standing as technologically responsible and politically neutral. The implicitly political nature of education, however, surfaced first from students, then from faculty and institutional groups themselves. Most important, the conflict between traditional moral values and racism was unearthed by civil rights upheavals and reevaluated in the light of meritocratic and universalistic standards.

The delay in the response was also important in resisting the territorial imperialism implicit in the *Brown* decision. *Brown* asserted that education was not only inequitable but also technically inferior for blacks under segregated conditions. When colleges and universities got around to focusing on blacks, they did so as if it were an exceptional action aiming at overcoming the societal rather than the institutional injustices. Pre-college education had by then been tagged with the fundamental responsibility. For their part, it was a validation of technological purity, coupled with a reassertion of claims to moral authority. The tension, thus persisted but without much threat of disruption. Governmental policy had in the aftermath of *Brown* not taken the next logical step. It had not asserted any responsibility over the structure or techniques of education at any level. Race, as the bussing decisions indicated, was to be treated as external to institutional practices and racism as an environmental condition. (Morris and Henry, 1978).

Unlike affirmative action policies, desegregation under *Brown* did not call for a change in institutional doctrine or formalized practices. It, therefore, left standards of meritocracy unscathed. In extreme views, it may have threatened independence, but only in the short term could it have affected admissions. In the long term, institutional independence was to be recognized as soon as de jure segregation and its direct effects were remedied; and the remedies were expected in the forseeable future. "All deliberate speed" was thought to be speedy. In 1955, the Supreme Court, while intending to hasten desegregation, showed its deference to educational authorities:

School authorities have the primary responsibility for elucidating, assessing, and solving these [desegregation] problems; courts will have to consider whether the action of school authorities constituted good faith implementation of the governing constitutional principles. . . .

Traditionally, equity has been characterized by a practical flexibility in shaping the remedies by a facility for adjusting and reconciling public and private needs. . . .

(Brown v. *Board of Education of Topeka,*
349 U.S. 294 (1955).
(Cited in T. Dye, 1971, p. 34)

The Supreme Court thus made the interrelationship between educational practices/techniques and social values explicit, but it did not recognize the depth or permanence of the relationship. In its reference to the "psychological harm" raised by segregation, the Court also recognized that blacks had special social needs which education had to address. In submitting these needs to the institutional authorities for redress in the traditional, but desegregated, form, it therefore has reinforced the concept of universalism in educational techniques. The Coleman Report later reiterated the idea that the educational process, once desegregated, was value free (Coleman, 1968). In other words, any cultural or racial values the system had were unnecessary and inappropriate additives to the normal educational process. Institutions were thus thought to be in the center of educational technology which, as technologists, could only be governed by the external inputs and outputs.

In the last analysis, governmental and educational institutions have been assumed to share the same, or non-conflicting, values, but with different priorities. The assumption simply masks the unresolved tension in which each functions as an independent determinant of social values. The bussing issue did not cause institutional transformation because the substance of the policy ends with racial balance at the school door. Other rulings such as those involving tracking like *Hobson* v. *Hansen,* 327 F. Supp. 844 (D.DC.1971) only deal with the most arbitrary and irregular institutional practices.

Accommodation to the tension between the assignment of social values to government and technology to institutions barely survived *Brown*; it could not survive higher education court cases. Since *Adams* v. *Califano,* 430 F. Supp. 112 (D.DC.1977) has come under the Court's purview, public colleges and universities have submitted to federal authority. The tension has thus resurfaced. In order to desegregate, the Courts have had to intervene in the admissions and curriculum areas of these institutions, thereby exercising technical authority. Ironically, state government educational authorities, rather than institutional ones, have been the most vocal and effective in resisting this intervention. Of course, the institutions are governed by the states, but that is not the full explanation. The resistance has hinged on state and institutional claims of good intentions and technical limitations. Specifically, the Southern states involved have talked about established physical plants, traditional student preferences, costs of change and other environment constraints (L. Haynes, 1978). In other words, the Courts moved because the institutions claimed moral agreement and technical immobility. State officials, however, have reasserted the defense of the technical limitation and their domain of independence. More important, the Court could not have initially been expected to go as far toward implementation as it has. In fact, the record of *Adams* shows that repeated litigation has been necessary to get effective action by the Justice Department, the Court's agent.

Ultimately, the direction of *Adams* was turned against traditionally black colleges, as if they had ever been segregated rather than simply separated (Morris 1979, p. 200). In large part, this happened because the desegregation process degenerated to a technical procedure detached from social purpose. The federal government thus abided by the value/practice division of authority even when the distinctly technical authorities were under political-judicial supervision. Americans have attempted to retain the division of authority in spite of the fact that it could not be reconciled with real conditions. That is probably a major factor in the Justice Department's inability to bring closure to the *Adams* implementation process except by fiat. The Reagan administration has therefore resolved to accept previously rejected terms.

Racial inequality forced the tensions out but, unfortunately, they have not been clearly recognized as separable from the racial issue. The inability to regulate higher educational desegregation is a function of the ambiguities in the institutional system. It is also a function of the over-extension of institutional claims to technical responsibility and the traditional denial of public responsibility for social values. The way out of this malaise was, and is, a return to the limited solutions applied to elementary and secondary education, namely, government shifts students paying as little attention as possible to what goes on inside the ivy walls. The minimal additional concern, dictated by the independent nature of higher education and the uniqueness of racial segregation, involves redistribution of special programs among public institutions within each state.

Affirmative action begins where formal desegregation came to an impass, although *Adams* stretched the boundaries. In its concern for racial equality it is an extension of desegregation but in regard to educational authority it is a revitalization of the early American concern for social purposes and public responsibility.

AFFIRMATIVE ACTION AS A RESOLUTION OF POLITICAL-INSTITUTIONAL TENSIONS

The problem with affirmative action is not that it is new to American education nor that it is inconsistent with the institutionalized principles of higher education but rather that it is the traditional second side of the system's historical development. From religion to nationalistic ideology to race, this second side has been gradually submerged in the system. It has never been specified explicitly in the form of responsibility for social values as compared to educational technique, but the distinction has been increasingly rigidified. The rigidity, however, has been most tenable in situations of societal homogeneity and stability. Because race involves the greatest degree of heterogeneity this society has confronted, it has aggravated the tensions involved more than any other issue. As a result, the current stalemate over affirmative action has been overestimated as a racial problem and underestimated as a problem in the qualitative management of higher education.

This is not to say that racial inequality is any less fundamental to patterns of upward mobility than institutional intransigence. On the contrary, affirmative action programs have been more successful in promoting women and other minorities than in promoting blacks. Because racial inequality is pervasive in this society, it is a less specific explanation of the failures of affirmative action in education. The Supreme Court decisions in employment versus those in higher education can serve to illustrate the point. In the medical school admission case, *Bakke,* 438 U.S. 265 (1978), affirmative action won partial support at best while in the employment training case, *Weber,* affirmative action was resoundingly vendicated by the Court (*Weber* v. *Kaiser Aluminum,* 443 US 193 (1979). In *Weber,* the employer was not confined by any administrative traditions or ideological commitments to the state, other than the impersonal maximization of profit. In *Bakke,* however, the institution was judicially constrained to moderate its affirmative action/special admissions programs based largely on the institution's own claims of rationality, meritocracy, and equity in its general admissions process. While referring to Fourteenth Amendment rights of the individual, the Court in *Bakke* illustrated its redefinition of the social significance of race by using Harvard University's affirmative action program; racial differences became "ethnic diversity." Accordingly, Justice Powell gave affirmative action a secondary position in a long established institutional tradition. Unfortunately, institutional interest in diversity grows out of educational techniques and not out of any egalitarian motive:

> Ethnic diversity, however, is only one element in a range of factors a university properly may consider in attaining the goal of a heterogeneous student body. Although a university must have a wide discretion in making the sensitive judgments as to who should be admitted, constitutional limitations protecting individual rights may not be disregarded. . . . As the interest of diversity is compelling in the context of a university's admissions program, the question remains whether the program's racial classification is necessary to promote this interest.
>
> *(Regents of the University of California* v. *Bakke,* 438 US 265, (1978) p. 45)

On one hand, the *Bakke* ruling recognizes social values in higher education. Justice Powell's opinion, as well as those of Justice Marshall and others, concedes that the society's needs for black physicians could be a justification for special admissions if the university had presented evidence to that effect. On the other hand, it assumes a separate dimension of institutional social values through which institutions determine society's educational needs. Their power and authority to make such determinations is viewed as a function of their technological integrity rather than as a function of their subjugation to society or politics.

The Court in *Bakke* thus expressed a transition beyond *Adams* in the distribution responsibility for higher education and social values. *Adams* maintains the value/practice separation by attributing judicial intervention to short-term, racially specific adjustments in the public higher education system. The adjustments were presumably necessary to correct the inability of educational technology to overcome the segregated social environment resulting from historical, non-institutional racism. *Bakke,* however, implies a direct and symbiotic connection between institutional techniques and social values through the designation of an independent set of social/educational values. The Court thus elevated institutional independence and private educational authority to the level of a judicially protected value system.

While less effective, Congress has acted in this same vein. When the major federal financial aid programs were created, direct aid to institutions rather than to students was opposed primarily as a result of the fear of imposing federal standards on institutional practices. Yet, aid to students is largely channeled through institutions. Although the largest programs, Basic Educational Opportunity Grants (BEOG), and Guaranteed Student Loans (GSL) are not campus-based, they are nonrestrictive on institutions and yet responsive to their decisions. For example, BEOG pays half the cost of attendance for low income students without significant demands on the public service orientation or cost-effectiveness of the institution's prices. In 1978 the decision to create the Department of Education had to confront similar Congressional resistance; specifically that the public good in higher education would best be assured by private educators (L. Morris, 1979, pp. 8–15).

Paralleling the courts, Congress began to consider issues at the end of the seventies, which involved institutional responsibility and independence from public authority. When a bill (HR 4949) for the regulation of standardized testing became an issue, it raised enormous controversy in the media but it and similar bills were eventually tabled. The issue of equity in the use of these tests soon gave way to doubts about the appropriateness of regulation. The debate has since been postponed indefinitely as if to say that the private authority of institutions over social and educational equity is too fundamental to be reconsidered. While the Court was more articulate, Congress achieved the same result through indecision.

State legislatures, including California and New York, have passed testing regulations but they centered on the technical and administrative quality of the testing agencies and not on any institutional practices.

CONCLUSION

The last stage in the unresolved tensions between public and private responsibility and between social values and educational techniques appears to be the extension of institutional claims to authority and the delegation of public responsibility. At its inception, affirmative action promised the reassertion of public responsibility for social values. Once that promise began to emerge, there was a retreat to what might be called the technological imperative of institutions. There was a further legitimation of institutional social responsibility. Had the subject of public action been something the society had not traditionally resisted, as it has resisted racial equality, opinion might have gone in a different direction. Apparently, the goal was not sufficiently compelling. As a consequence, affirmative action has been treated as too demanding an imposition on institutional independence. Unfortunately, that imposition has been described as if it primarily concerns standards of merit rather than structures of authority. The resistance to affirmative action is strongest now because it only recently began to be institutionalized. Hostility to its institutionalization results from our national failure to understand institutions. Affirmative action is not understood because public responsibility for education has not been understood.

REFERENCES

Apple, Michael. *Ideology and Curriculum*. London: Routledge & Kegan Paul, 1979.

Bayer, Alan. *Teaching Faculty in Academe: 1972–73*. ACE Research Reports, Vol. 8, No. 2, Washington, D.C.: American Council on Education, 1973.

Bellah, R. Robert. "Civil Religion in America." *Daedelus* 96, 1 (Winter 1967), 1–21.

Bowles, Samuel and Gintes, Herbert. *Schooling in Capitalist America*. New York: Basic Books, Inc., 1976.

Carnegie Commission on Higher Education. *The Open Door College*. New York: McGraw-Hill Book Company, June 1970.

The Carnegie Foundation For the Advancement of Teaching. *Missions of the College*. San Francisco: Jossey-Bass, 1978.

Carnoy, Martin. *Education As Cultural Imperialism*. New York: David McKay Company, Inc., 1974.

Coleman, James. "The Concept of Equality of Educational Opportunity." *Harvard Educational Review,* 68 (1968): 7–22.

Collins, Randall. *The Credential Society.* New York: Academic Press, 1979.
Dreeben, R. "The Contribution of Schooling to Learning of Norms." In *The School in Society.* Edited by Sam Sieber and David Wilder. New York: The Free Press, 1973, p. 68.
Franklin, Vincent and Anderson, James. D. *New Perspectives on Black Educational History.* Boston: G. K. Hall and Co., 1978.
Gross, Edward and Grambsch, Paul. *Changes in University Organizations, 1964–1971.* New York: McGraw-Hill, 1974.
Haynes, Leonard. *A Conceptual Examination of Desegregation in Higher Education.* Washington, D.C.: Institute for Services to Education, 1978.
Hartz, Louis. *The Liberal Tradition in America.* New York: Harcourt, Brace & Co., 1955.
Institute for the Study of Educational Policy. *Equal Educational Opportunity: Status of Blacks in Higher Education, 1975–1977.* Washington, D.C.: Institute for the Study of Educational Policy, 1980.
Lowi, Theodore. *The End of Liberalism.* New York: W. W. Norton, 1969.
Morris, Lorenzo. *Elusive Equality.* Washington, D.C.: Howard University Press, 1979.
Morris, Lorenzo and Henry, Charles. *The Chit'lin Controversy: Race and Public Policy in America.* Washington, D.C.: University Press of America, 1978.
"The Record: EEOC Transition Team's Attack on Affirmative Action." *Legal Times of Washington* (January 1981): 25–26.
Thomas, Norman. *Education in National Politics.* New York: David McKay Company, Inc., 1965.
Weber, Max. *The Protestant Ethic and the Spirit of Capitalism.* New York: Charles Scribner's Sons, 1958.
Woodson, Carter L. *The Education of the Negro Prior to 1861.* New York: G. P. Putnam's Sons, 1915; rpt. 1968.

CASES

Adams v. *Califano,* 430 F. Supp. 112 (D.DC. 1977).
Brown, I., 347 U.S. 483 (1954).
Brown, II., 349 U.S. 294 (1955).
Hobson v. *Hansen,* 327 F. Supp. 844 (D.DC. 1971).
Regents of the University of California v. *Bakke,* 438 U.S. 265 (1978).
Weber v. *Kaiser Aluminum,* 443 U.S. 193 (1979).

THE BOUNDED POLITICS OF SCHOOL
DESEGREGATION LITIGATION

David L. Kirp

Those concerned that the courts are managing the public schools point to race as illustrating the phenomenon. Only through a decision of the Supreme Court was the race and schooling issue placed on the policy agenda, and—except for a brief period during the mid-1960s, when the coordinate branches of the federal government acted in concert—the courts have remained the dominant institutional force in this domain ever since.[1] The courts propose, it is said, and the political branches reluctantly carry out the judicial edicts. Because of this pivotal role played by the judiciary, race and schooling policy is usually perceived as essentially legalist in nature, with little or no political consideration apparent in court decisions.[2]

This article, however, takes the position that despite the dominant position of the courts, the decision-making process blends politics and law. It examines this process from three vantages: the evolution of Supreme Court doctrine since *Brown* v. *Board of Education* in 1954;[3] the interchange at the local level between political institutions and the courts; and the course of specific desegregation suits through the trial courts. At each level, the pattern of interplay between legal and political institutions and values recurs. The development of school desegregation policy emerges as a continuing effort to identify solutions that are at once constitutionally permissible and politically feasible.

Research for this article was supported by grants from the National Institute of Education and the Spencer Foundation. A preliminary draft was presented at a colloquium sponsored by the Harvard Graduate School of Education. The helpful comments of the participants and of William Clune, Robert Kagan, and Mary von Euler are gratefully acknowledged.

THE SUPREME COURT AND SCHOOL DESEGREGATION:
POLITICS AND PRINCIPLE

The Supreme Court decision in *Brown*[4] stands as perhaps the most important ever in its ramifications for the larger society. That decision did no less than set in motion a social revolution and thus contributed to a fundamental alteration of relationships between blacks and whites in the United States. Even as it acted, the Court was necessarily concerned about the political implications of its decision. That concern influenced both the way in which the Court identified the wrong and the scope of the remedy it ordered. In this respect, the Court was at once principled and political.

The ambiguities of *Brown* reveal this duality. Was it segregation *itself* that constituted the wrong, or segregation mandated by law? Was segregation wrong because it distinguished on the basis of race or because it limited the educational futures of black children? While these are nominally doctrinal matters, the Court's lack of clarity in explicating doctrine requires a different reasoning process, which defines the wrong by inspecting what is required by way of remedy.

Judicial decision making with respect to segregation is thus fundamentally incremental: wrong defines remedy, which in turn redefines wrong. The Court moves away from the evil to be undone, not toward some predetermined end. *Brown* sets in motion a decision-making strategy, rather than resolving a problem.

For these reasons, the second *Brown* decision, which addresses the question of remedy, assumes special importance.[5] That opinion is, of course, best rememberd for permitting desegregation to proceed with all deliberate speed. In *Brown II,* the Court also leaves the pace and scope of desegregation to case-by-case determination, providing only loose guidance. Remedy-framing itself as conceived by the Court necessarily and properly takes into account both policy and politics.

The particular factors cited by the Court as pertinent in this enterprise are themselves political in nature: "problems related to administration, arising from the physical condition of the school plant, the school transportation system, personnel, revision of school districts and attendance areas to achieve a system of determining admission to the public schools on a nonracial basis." Some are technical matters that hardly warrant postponing desegregation. Others, such as "the physical condition of the school plant," suggest that, in the Court's view, white school children could not be expected to attend the formerly black schools, despite protestations that black and white schools were in fact equal. The Court left these latter issues to be resolved by political rather than judicial initiative: "School authorities have the primary responsibility for elucidating, assessing, and solving these problems." Only if the political system defaults should judges intervene.

In retrospect, such language sounds pious rather than plausible in its expectation that courts would act only in the face of political default. Between 1955 and 1968, however, this was essentially all the guidance the Supreme Court offered for desegregating the nation's schools. Only in the most exceptional circumstances— as with the outright challenge in Little Rock to the authority of the judiciary—did the Court take action.[6] Even then, Justice Frankfurter was moved to plead for the cooperation of elected officials in achieving desegregation. Success in desegregation meant "working together . . . in a cooperative effort," not the imposition of judicial rule.[7] District court judges consequently enjoyed considerable discretion during these years, and the course of desegregation litigation varied enormously from court to court.[8]

The generalities of *Brown,* coupled with deep political antagonism in the South and a hands-off attitude in Congress, provoked defiance rather than the willing implementation of desegregation that the Court had hoped for. Those district court judges committed to *Brown* began substituting specific requirements for general guidelines. Bolstered by the passage of the 1964 Civil Rights Act,[9] which added congressional support to the judicial arsenal, the Fifth Circuit Court of Appeals developed a sophisticated and highly detailed remedial jurisprudence. In the *Jefferson County* case, it ordered adoption of a freedom-of-choice plan larded with judicially-imposed specifics: the timing and form of the announcement, the nature of equalization efforts among schools, the remedial programs to be offered, the location of new schools, and the reassignment of faculty.[10] The lower courts increasingly exercised their discretionary authority to hasten desegregation.

Beginning with its 1968 decision in *Green v. New Kent County,*[11] the Supreme Court confirmed and further hastened that endeavor. Although these cases narrow the scope of trial court discretion and hence the possibilities of a politically-driven resolution, they still leave considerable room for judicial maneuvering. The persisting ambiguity can be attributed to a deliberate lack of clarity in the opinions themselves.

Consider *Swann v. Charlotte-Mecklenburg Board of Education,*[12] the most influential of these decisions and an opinion that is in some respects highly prescriptive. *Swann* notes the need for the Court to "amplify guidelines . . . defining how far this remedial power extends." With respect to student assignment, the Court identifies the circumstances under which one-race schools are permissible, the need for "frank—and sometimes drastic—gerrymandering of school districts and attendance zones," and the permissible scope of busing. Even as it offered guidance, however, the Court created new, though more limited, zones of discretion for the district court. How can a school district show that a one-race school is "genuinely nondiscriminatory"? How does a court determine whether busing will "impinge on the education process"? The Supreme Court mentioned but did not answer these questions. In leaving these matters to district courts, the *Swann* decision reaffirmed the approach of *Brown II:* "Once a right and a violation of that right have been shown the scope of the District Court's equitable powers to remedy past wrongs is broad, for breadth and flexibility are inherent in equitable remedies."

When the will to do so exists and when circumstances appear to warrant, the Supreme Court can more rightly cabin the lower courts, as it has in reapportionment, criminal process, and abortion cases. "One man, one vote" has a counterpart, for purposes of desegregation, in racial ratios; but these the Court opted not to impose or even to permit. In choosing a different course, the Court should not have been unaware of the political ramifications of its action. *Swann* constitutes a bold move for judicial foray which was bound to evoke controversy. It would be better, the Court apparently concluded, to leave these matters in the hands of the lower courts, whose sense of nuance could be applied in the service of minimizing controversy. If the Court demonstrated its impatience with the progress of desegregation in the South, it was never willing to spearhead a second Reconstruction. Local values, reflected in the fact situations and remedial proposals presented to the lower courts, continued to count for something.[13]

The North was another story. Until the 1970s, the Supreme Court declined to review northern segregation disputes. When it finally decided *Keyes* v. *School District #1, Denver*,[14] the Court resisted imposing a national standard for desegregation despite apparent parallels between the northern and southern situations two decades after *Brown*. The holding in *Keyes*—once deliberate segregation has been shown to exist in a significant portion of a northern school district, a districtwide remedy of the sort prescribed in *Swann* is appropriate—was subsequently hedged round by opinions attempting more precisely to link wrong and remedy.[15] The decisions following *Keyes* do not restrict but instead redirect the discretion of the lower courts. In the second round of the *Detroit* litigation,[16] the Court approved a sweeping remedy which ordered revisions of the student discipline code, creation of vocational schools, teacher restraining, and the like. That opinion appears to license lower court intervention in almost all of a school district's educational and administrative practices. Although such remedies must be related to racial discrimination, discrimination remains diverse, multifaceted, amorphous, and immense; for that reason the district court judge determines the scope of the solution.

From *Brown* to the present, the Court has eschewed a preemptive role. While affirming the necessity of accomplishing racial integration, it has treated the issues in part as educational problems requiring an "educational solution."[17] But it has also recognized the important political aspects of those issues. For the most part, Supreme Court decisions of the past quarter century "pleased, mediated, mollified, or even withdrew";[18] only in the years between *Green* and *Keyes* can they be said significantly to have imposed.

As a whole, the Court's desegregation decisions have shown that "competing moral claims" rooted in constitutional values "must be brokered and negotiated."[19] As political statements, the opinions reaffirm that the Constitution, as

Justice Jackson put it, "does not require self-defeating acts."[20] Yet the decisions are more than political or educational statements. They derive their strength from their constitutional underpinnings, the aspiration to evenhanded treatment embodied in the Fourteenth Amendment. Is it any surprise, then, that district court judges in desegregation cases have found themselves with varied and complicated tasks to perform, obliged to be at once constitutional exegetes, political power brokers, and educational experts.

DESEGREGATION AND THE DISTRICT COURT: MANAGING A POLITICAL PROCESS

In particular locales, school desegregation issues emerge as both political and legal problems.[21] Usually the matter first arises as a political question, in which the parties bargain in an attempt to reach a satisfactory resolution. When that process succeeds, the issue never comes to court. Although the prevailing understanding of desegregation presumes that legal sanctions are required if the effort is to succeed, the facts are otherwise: much desegregation has occurred without a court order.[22]

Even in those instances, however, the possibility of recourse to the courts affects the political bargaining.[23] Civil rights advocates sometimes advance the threat of a lawsuit to increase their bargaining strength; more rarely, the community regards litigation as a confession of failure, an indication either of intolerance or divisiveness inconsistent with its self-perception. In either event, the law is significant. The legalization of a dispute over desegregation through the filing of a lawsuit signals a momentary breakdown in the political process. Bargaining gives way to stance-taking, and interests harden into claims of rights.[24] The transformation does not occur quickly, nor is it taken lightly. Although most northern desegregation suits were filed no earlier than the 1970s, the issue of racial equity in education was framed politically a decade earlier. Recourse to the courts does not signal an end to political involvement, but rather a new stage in the on-going political process. The parties to the desegregation litigation are familiar to one another, and so are the issues over which they differ. Who is to blame for the extant segregation? What should be done about it? The forum, however, is new, as is the introduction of an additional participant, the judge, with considerable formal authority. Because the court can render a legally authoritative resolution of the dispute, the court exercises substantial potential power.

Judicial authority, although substantial, is nevertheless limited by the court's inability to guarantee a solution that works. Desegregation remains a political matter (albeit of a different sort) after judicial resolution of a case. Legal mandates affect the implementation of court-ordered remedies, but implementation itself depends fundamentally on mobilizing diverse community resources, including good will, to achieve the desired outcome. When what is wanted is not a specifiable goal, but a process adaptable to the radical changes that desegregation brings, the subtler persuasive arts are likely to accomplish more than a legal decision standing by itself.[25] Courts cannot unilaterally run school systems.

The more narrowly the court defines successful implementation, the more possible it is to achieve; thus, there has been a tendency by the courts to convert implementation of a systematic policy change into an order for compliance with a narrow rule.[26] A court interested in asserting its own power might focus on racial mixing, which is easier to implement than an order mandating adjustments in the organization, financing, or instructional mission of the schools. But even a school district that implements a racial balance order must take into account whether residents will vote with their feet by leaving and thus perpetuate racial imbalance.[27]

If a racial balance order can rarely be readily implemented by unilateral authoritative decision, this is even truer of the broader remedial orders that have more recently become commonplace. Because courts depend on the cooperation of the disputants for implementation of a remedy, they have been led to establish a political bargaining relationship designed to achieve agreement between the parties. Yet the bargaining process also differs significantly from that of everyday politics. Permissible outcomes are defined by the judge's understanding of what is constitutionally permissible. The court will not accept any agreement, but only an agreement consistent with the teachings of *Brown* and its progeny. If the judge holds views about the educational substance of a good outcome, these too are interjected into the bargaining process.

Desegregation cases thus reveal not a single mode of judicial behavior but a range of judicial stances. The politically oriented mediator-judge stresses agreement as the primary concern, assuming a relatively passive role. The legalist judge, persuaded that the elaboration of authoritative principles in the context of a specific situation fully describes the judicial task, does not enter the political domain. For very different reasons, the judge motivated by particular educational concerns may behave similarly, looking to the parties primarily for after-the-fact support. In many lawsuits, each of these considerations is apparent.

Greater judicial activism will occur when no consensus readily emerges from the bargaining. The court will of necessity find itself shaping political relationships, refusing to accept existing configurations as unalterable. In such circumstances the court is likely to structure the bargaining process iteratively. The decision itself is not forever fixed but may well be modified in light of subsequent experience; the decree itself becomes a political document, not a final order, as amenable to adjustment as the political environment that produced it.

Lower courts have long known that the political nature of desegregation cases restricts the authority of the judge. More than a decade ago, the district judge in the Washington Parish, Louisiana, case described the work of courts as "an attempt by civic- and social-minded judges to add legal precepts to the force of moral, social and political principles in the effort of the responsible sectors of our society to eradicate the divisive and ruinous prejudces between the citizens of this nation."[28] The court's contribution is supplementary and not primary, hortatory and not directive. As the district court in the Lansing litigation declared, courts "cannot order people to be charitable to one another in their daily affairs. The law provides impetus, sets limits, corrects abuses—it is an external conscience. But the change of heart must come from within."[29]

This widely shared perception has led the courts to urge compromise in the belief that the real parties at interest, the general populace, will be more likely to accept an agreement than respond to an order. Even courts that have been rebuked for overreaching their authority have typically, in the early stages of litigation, attempted to mobilize support for a plan at once politically agreeable and constitutionally permissible. In Pasadena, Judge Real's insistence that racial balance in the schools remain in effect for his lifetime was reversed by the Supreme Court, which used the occasion to limit the scope of the trial judge's remedial discretion.[30] In contrast, the first remedial order in the Pasadena case was couched in general terms, intended to accelerate a desegregation planning process already well under way within the school district.[31] In Boston, Judge Garrity's decision to place South Boston High School in receivership is widely viewed as the most dramatic example of unilateral judicial action. Yet the Boston court had relied first on the district itself, then on a panel of masters chosen for their political astuteness, to devise a workable plan for the city.[32] In general, these decisions do not speak of uncompromisable rights but instead concern themselves with divergence among interests, when some balancing is both legitimate and appropriate.

It is during the remedial phase of litigation that courts have the greatest scope for political maneuver.[33] If one conceives of the initiation of litigation as interrupting an ongoing political process, that process often resumes when a resolution acceptable to the parties and the court is formulated.[34] This enterprise, too, is often iterative: the court issues an order, notes the responses of the parties, and then issues a subsequent, usually more precise, order.

The trial court does not order compliance with a preestablished standard, the judge behaving much as a Socratically-inclined law professor in leading the parties to the "right" answer. On the contrary, within the limits established by the law, there is no single right answer. Thus, in the context of the particular case, just as in the development of doctrine at the appellate level, the court's desire is to proceed incrementally, basing its decisions on precedent. Artful dodging by appellate courts and avowedly tentative orders by trial judges serve much the same purpose. What the trial court wishes to achieve is less a good outcome than the inauguration of a decision-making apparatus that will continue even after the order is entered.

This is only one mode of judicial behavior, and its details are altered by circumstance. When the parties are in essential agreement even before the lawsuit is filed, the gentle declaration of legal norms may prompt agreement.[35] In some instances, school boards have depended on courts to order them to do what they would *like* to do but lack political courage to accomplish on their own. In these cases, the imposed remedy usually represents a solution agreed to by the parties and endorsed by the court.[36]

Courts elsewhere have been more activist. In Atlanta the court relied first on a court-appointed citizens' committee and subsequently on the parties to promote a settlement, in both instances shielding delicate negotiations from public scrutiny.[37] The Dallas judge identified by name outside groups that in his judgment ought to aid in the effort at resolution; he thus helped bring into being, and relied on the recommendations of, a group that represented the diverse interests of the Dallas citizenry.[38] In each of these cases, the court expressed its preference for negotiation over adversary relations.

The perception that the formulation of a remedy is a process also increases the likelihood of settlement. Judge Doyle noted that the Denver remedy "won't be too final. . . . I think it's going to be temporary-final. . . . It doesn't look to me like we're going to wrap this up in one fell swoop."[39] In Las Vegas the trial court permitted a one-year experiment with a free-choice integration plan; only after it failed to achieve substantial integration was a more extensive plan put into effect. The court of appeals approved this step-by-step approach. "The present decree," it said, "is the beginning, not the end, of the remedial process. No doubt it will be modified and adjusted in the light of progress made in the elimination of the effect of segregation."[40] In these suits the court is not announcing unalterable law but rescuing a principle out of compromise.

The cases in which the court has appointed masters may represent the clearest instances of promoting a negotiated remedy.[41] The master, who is usually retained after the parties themselves have failed to resolve the matter satisfactorily, serves as an alternative mechanism for incorporating political considerations in the deliberations. Because the master is not a judge, he is free to engage in the kind of negotiation that a court may find too time-consuming or too much at odds with its usual functions. In almost all cases in which the court has placed reliance on masters, they have sought, as the several masters in the Boston case put it, to "desegregate and defuse," developing a solution when possible from agreement among the parties.

Although both parties are typically asked to draft proposals, the courts have relied primarily on the district's plan, and this too encourages compromise. This practice of asking the wrongdoer to propose the terms of a remedy is somewhat unusual. The conventional explanation points to the special expertise of the district and the appropriateness of drawing upon that expertise for practical guidance in prescribing a remedy. To some extent, the explanation is sensible: a school district should know how to promote racial mixing with the least disruption of neighborhoods or should be aware of what changes in pedagogical practice ought to accompany desegregation. Yet insofar as formulation of a remedy demands rejection of current practices, the school district may be the worst agency to assume responsibility for the job.[42] Though knowing how the system currently operates, the district may lack the perspective needed to determine how to alter it. Moreover, the district will probably do as little as it has to in order to satisfy the court. When the urge to minimize prevails, the plan which emerges in response to the court order will be less good, by the criteria of rationality, than what an outside expert might produce.

Yet dependence on the school district encourages negotiations between the parties. Sometimes the interchange is expressly called for, as when the court asks the litigants to participate jointly in planning; and in any event, the fact that the plaintiffs as well as the court will evaluate the district's proposal tacitly promotes the same end.

At this stage of litigation, the district court may invite the participation of a number of outsiders—citizens' groups, intervenors with a thin claim to involvement, representatives of minority viewpoints—not represented in earlier phases of the suit. Their involvement makes the lawsuit an even more political forum. Because each of the parties to this process, including the judge, has something to gain from consensual resolution, a classic bargaining situation develops.

Courts in a number of instances have attempted to enlist other government agencies in this enterprise to broaden the scope of the process. In *United States* v. *State of Missouri*[43] local school districts were required to cooperate in preparing an area-wide solution. The trial court also permitted a sixteen-month delay so that state officials could study nine proposed plans; a revised plan, submitted by the state, won eventual approval. The appeals court in *Omaha* ordered the participation of the school district, plaintiffs, the state education department, and an interracial committee.[44] The Coney Island court sought assistance from federal, state, and local housing agencies.[45] In Indianapolis Judge Dillin openly urged suburban school districts to participate in a rather modest busing plan: "If the suburban schools would accept 15 percent new minority students from the Indianapolis Public Schools," he declared, "this would solve the problem, preserve their local autonomy, and end this case."[46] The remedial order in the Delaware suit was even more directly drafted with legislative intervention in mind: the decree would not go into effect, the court declared, unless Delaware failed to propose its own plan.

Co-optation is what the court intends in each of these instances. A willing school board or state legislature is far less likely to attempt to subvert, or grudgingly to manage, a solution when the remedial burden has not been unilaterally imposed. Thus, the courts often accept a remedy that does not fully satisfy the *Swann* desegregation criteria if it meets the minimum constitutional obligation and is acceptable to the government agency obliged to put it into effect.

Such a process assumes that the parties to the dispute will cooperate. When they do not, bargaining fails. School districts or state agencies may opt out, either because they perceive their ideological commitments as absolutes—claims of right and not defenses of an interest—or because they resist the court's assumption of responsibility for negotiation, perceiving in that act an inappropriate combination of functions.

The cases illustrate these rationales for nonbargaining. The court's request that the school district develop a plan consistent with broad guidelines evoked outright defiance in Boston, a sham effort in Denver and Cleveland; without collaboration, the court had to rely on school district conscripts and outside resources.[47] Defendants' refusal to cooperate sometimes stems from fear that helping to plan a solution may jeopardize their capacity to oppose any remedy in an appeal case.[48] In such situations, the court's double role as decision maker and mediator creates confusion. The political participants may wonder why they are doing the judge's work for him or her, or, if this is not the work of the judge but rather the responsibility of a variety of government agencies, why framing a solution should be judicially mandated.

Appellate review limits the scope of bargaining in another way by providing judicial oversight of both culpability and remedy. Even when the parties prefer a consensual remedy to one imposed by the court, they may disagree on its terms. The school district may well prefer no remedy, and if it appeals the decision with this end in view, plaintiffs are likely to counter by promoting their original remedial suggestions. Alternatively, plaintiffs may seek appellate review to obtain a remedy more ambitious than that adopted by the trial court. When either scenario occurs, the bargaining process disintegrates. For bargaining to succeed, all parties must prefer implementation of the agreed-upon solution to any court order.

The wide variation in court orders from one city to the next also reveals the fundamentally political nature of the bargaining process. The decisions seem responsive to variations among districts; they honor community idiosyncracies. Moreover, considerable differences exist among the several desegregation decisions of a single judge.

Of greater importance, the orders generally demand less racial mixing than a strict application of the Supreme Court's remedial standard would dictate. The courts have consistently sought approaches other than strict racial balance to achieve a unitary school system. The Coney Island court, responding to a proposal of the local school board, ordered a junior high school, the focus of the suit, converted into a school for the gifted. Reacting to school district suggestions, the Dallas court adopted magnet schools as the basis of its solution. The Denver court responded to widely voiced community concerns about the demise of neighborhood schools by ordering that students be bused for only a half day, the only aspect of the decision reversed on appeal. The order in Boston left whole sections of that city unaffected by busing. The Memphis court mandated "a balance" between what is referred to as practicalities and "constitutional require-ments."[49] The San Francisco decision permitted the school district to select its own plan, which promised less complete relief from racial isolation than one proposed by the NAACP, which offered more racial mixing at the price of less community involvement and support.

Within the relatively broad range of discretion left by the Supreme Court decisions, the outcomes of the cases have been quite distinct, and in good part, that distinctiveness results from the workings of a constrained political process managed by the court. The exercise of equity jurisdiction is supposed to result in an idiosyncratic justice, where results are tailored to the particulars of the situation. To some considerable extent, this appears to be what has happened in desegregation litigation during the past decade. This outcome is at least partly traceable to the ways in which judges have managed these controversies.

The traditional legalist conception of litigation, which stresses the application of reason and precedent in developing and extending legal norms, powerfully influences thinking about how courts do and should behave. Whatever the actual bases of a judge's decision, this legalist refrain is routinely heard. And legalist concerns in fact delimit the scope of trial court's actions, shaping the structure of the suit and the form of remedy.

There is a sharp distinction between law and politics in the conventional view. Law consists of authoritatively derived norms not subject to compromise be-tween legal interests. Politics, in contrast, involves brokering among interested parties to reach a result that is not so much right as widely preferred. Law is a rational analytic enterprise, in this conception, whereas politics honors the pragmatic. When judges take it upon themselves to engage in institutional reform,[50] they do so with apparent reluctance, for such efforts test the bounds of law. In *Hobson* v. *Hansen,* a desegregation case that in the scope and particular-ity of judicial intervention serves as a model of institutional reform decrees, Judge J. Skelly Wright sought to reconcile the comprehensiveness of his opinion with a commitment to judicial restraint: "It would be far better indeed for these great social and political problems to be resolved in the political arena by other branches of government. But these are social and political problems which seem at times to defy such resolution. In such situations, under our system, the judiciary must bear a hand and accept its responsibility to assist in the solution *where Constitutional rights hang in the balance.*"[51] That last phrase is the key. Courts, in Judge Wright's view, do not as a rule break political logjams. Only when political means fail to honor constitutional rights do courts have license to intervene.

Yet bounding constitutional rights is not easy, especially when the legal source is a constitutional provision as vague and elastic as the Fourteenth Amendment. That amendment manifests a commitment to equality as powerful as it is vague; and judicial decisions elaborating upon and extending the amendment elicit a train of further expectations. "Judicial activism feeds on itself," Professors Harold Horowitz and Kenneth Karst have said. "The public has come to expect the Court to intervene against gross abuses. And so the Court must intervene."[52]

This attitude is at once familiar and problematic. *Must* has to be regarded as rhetorical, for judges often intervene first and rationalize later. But something more than rationalization is involved in desegregation as in other constitutional realms. Even when courts act in ways that appear quintessentially political, as in removing the headmaster of a Boston high school, or suprapolitical, as is banning antibusing meetings in Denver, they take great pains to relate what they are doing to a received tradition.

Activism is linked with legal traditionalism in myriad ways. At times the decision's relation to desegregation precedents is obscure, representing judicial behavior that has its source and inspiration elsewhere. In the Indianapolis case, for instance, the trial court appeared bent on ordering a metropolitan remedy, persisting even after the Supreme Court had sharply constrained such orders. At the least, the district court pushed at the limits of the legally permissible. Yet Judge Dillin saw it otherwise: "It is my absolute and positive duty to follow the law and desegregate the Indianapolis public schools. . . . If I die tomorrow, someone else would have the same duty and I don't know that they could do it differently."[53]

This stress on the continuity of process is a vital proposition for the judge to maintain. If those affected by court opinions accept this legalist view of the judiciary, support is easier to achieve; it is, after all, the process and not the outcome for which support is ultimately asked. A contrary perception is more likely to evoke resistance. Yet more than camouflage is involved in reliance on legalism. The rhetoric also reveals that the court's self-perception is legalist, and that perception affects what the court will do. Obeisance to legal norms is a significant part of the judicial process, for the limits imposed by law shape the lawsuit in a variety of ways. They restrict intervention to those with a stake in the controversy whose views are inadequately represented by the original parties; intervention for political purposes by those on either side of the controversy is sharply discouraged.[54]

Legalist concerns also constrict the scope of questions that a court will entertain. In the midst of desegregation disputes between black plaintiffs and a school district, other groups with distinct but assertedly related grievances have sought to participate in the litigation. Although courts have generally permitted expansion of the scope of the suit when the connection is convincing—as when the would-be intervenors represent limited-English-speaking students for whom desegregation is an inadequate remedy[55]—they have not routinely permitted these suits to become forums for educational policy. For that reason, even activist courts have rebuffed efforts to interject the claims of the handicapped into desegregation litigation.

The significance of legalist concerns is also manifest when legal and educational policy questions, or legal and political questions, collide. Judges frequently formally eschew taking any responsibility for educational matters. Their doing so assumes particular significance when, as in the Little Rock suit, the judge perceives a choice between educational and legalist concerns:

> The Court also realizes that the money that the District is going to spend for transportation will have to come out of funds that otherwise would be spent for increased salaries, educational supplies and materials, and for other conventional and desirable educational purposes. There is nothing the Court can do about that. At this time at least the duty of the District to comply with the requirements of the Supreme Court, the Court of Appeals, and this Court in the matter of integration must take priority over ordinary educational considerations.[56]

When political issues are explicit, judicial affirmation of the primacy of constitutional values is commonplace. Judge Real, hearing the Pasadena case, dismissed public opinion as irrelevant to the deliberations: "I have a constitutional duty to decide cases not the way people want them [decided] but the way I feel is proper to decide them."[57] As Judge Doyle in Denver noted, "The shape of the Constitution is not dependent upon the way the people vote . . . so I expect that the voice of the people is entitled to some consideration, but if it's in conflict with the Constitution of the United States, why, it's not going to carry any weight. It can't, in a court of law. The law is something else."[58]

The Wilmington litigation illustrates to what extent legalist concerns shape a lawsuit.[59] Because that case involved the creation of a metropolitan school district, it might be regarded as an adventure in judicial policy making that exceeds the legally permissible; that, at least, was the view of those who sought the impeachment of the district court judge, arguing that "the likelihood of a revolutionary change in the Delaware public school system [brought about by the desegregation suit] has interfered with the function of that system."[60] Yet this perception misrepresented the task that the court set for itself, a bounded legalist task: "to order a remedy which will place the victims of the violation in substantially the position which they would have occupied had the violation not occurred."[61] Application of that standard led the court to insist on metropolitan area relief: "The entire northern New Castle area must be treated as one community in terms of its population characteristics, because that is the way it was perceived and treated by the State and its citizenry."[62]

At each stage in the proceedings, legalist concerns shape the suit, minimizing the policy-making role of the court. One suggested approach involving urban-suburban school clusters was rejected because in the court's judgment it was "fraught with complex problems unsuited for judicial determination." Another proposed plan "plac[ed] the Court in the ongoing position of general supervisor of education in New Castle County. In the event of disagreements over curriculum patterns or textbooks, the Court or a master would have to step in." The court resisted judicial creation of several new districts because there was "little guidance from state or federal constitutional guarantees." The court did not mandate a countywide district because that would involve "a major shift in Delaware school policy."[63] The court's order was designed to intrude least upon the political workings of the system; and it explicitly permitted the state legislature to develop its own alternative plan.

Some courts are far less affected by legalist standards. In Atlanta, for instance, the district court strove to provide what was "practical."[64] And in St. Louis the court approved a consent agreement that, by requiring almost no desegregation, clearly failed to meet the constitutional standard set by the Supreme Court.[65]

The influence of legalism varies from case to case, but it is almost always substantial. Cases in which the legalist mode predominates do not reflect merely the elaboration of a constitutional standard remote from political considerations; the constitutional yardsticks are too vague, the context too intrusive, for that. In many desegregation cases the concerns of law, politics, and educational policy are interdependent.

Educational Policy Concerns

Decision making in desegregation cases is also affected by educational policy issues that are more or less intimately related to race. Until the 1970s, courts defined the scope of desegregation suits narrowly. The focus was exclusively on factors influencing racial mix, such as pupil attendance zones.[66] But racial balance alone has come to seem an imperfect remedy for the problems brought to light in a desegregation suit. The discrimination that the courts have identified extends beyond purposeful discrimination to encompass substantive questions of curriculum, student discipline, and educational innovation; it also affects the structural apparatus of the system, the presumed racism of the educational institution itself.[67] In some instances, these concerns have formed part of a more comprehensive remedy. When the extraordinarily high proportion of black pupils has made racial mixing infeasible, attention to the substance and structure of the educational program may be the *only* nonformalistic response to discrimination.

Once a trial court has undertaken to remedy racial discrimination, it makes little sense to confine that remedy to numerical balancing. For one thing, the wrong itself has deeper roots; for another, a decision responsive to the relationship between educational and racial concerns is more likely to evoke the kinds of reform required to make nondiscrimination a reality.

Most cases follow this pattern of linking race and education. Some judges, however, regarding desegregation suits as a vehicle by which to excoriate current practices and propose new ones, have rendered decisions quite apart from the views of the parties to the dispute and with little heed to the connection between the policy issue being addressed and the nature of the constitutional wrong. This behavior poses problems of both substance and form. To be sure, the breadth of educational policy issues that a desegregation dispute touches upon makes it difficult to define the scope of the required remedy. It is hard to think of an issue *not* affecting, and affected by, race. But if the courts are to be regarded as something other than "school superintendents who enter office by a slightly different route,"[68] attention needs to be paid to the limits of the court's inquiry.

The failure to involve the parties in negotiation over educational programs is a second source of concern. There exists no single "best" educational solution to the problem of race and schooling; the choice is largely a matter of strategy, and the courts do not monopolize competence in that realm. On the contrary, to the extent that the educational components of a remedy address themselves to how well it will work in practice, there is every reason to leave these matters largely to the parties who have a deeper understanding of the practicalities. When courts have in effect functioned as school superintendents, they have introduced an extraneous element into the constitutionally-bounded bargaining process.

The Detroit case offers a classic example of this problem. After the Supreme Court had rejected a remedy linking Detroit with the surrounding suburban communities, the trial court was ordered to devise a solution that involved the city.[69] It is not the scope of the remedy, but the process by which it was reached that distinguishes Detroit. Although the sweep of the court's order is impressive—including provision of a new guidance program, establishment of an arm of the school bureaucracy to improve relations with the community, bilingual education, and a reform of the educational testing program—it is not unique. Other cities, among them Boston and Denver, have received similarly comprehensive orders. What differentiates Detroit is Judge DeMascio's approach to the task. The court mandated improved educational programs in lieu of greater racial mixing, voicing its unwillingness to treat "school children . . . as pigmented pawns to be shuffled about and counted solely to achieve an abstraction called 'racial mix.' "[70] In this effort, its concern was educational benefits, not constitutional rights. This solution did not emerge from negotiations between the two parties. Although Judge DeMascio shared the details of the plan with district officials prior to releasing his opinion, it was his plan, not the board's. Indeed, whereas the amount of racial mixing ordered was less than the school board itself had proposed, the educational policy changes were far more extensive than the parties had anticipated. "The court was as enthusiastic about revitalizing the educational process as it was reluctant to desegregate it."[71]

In Boston, the court sought to involve the parties in the framing of a solution, but its decision—particularly with respect to the elements that linked the school district with the area's universities, colleges, industries, and cultural institutions—went well beyond what the parties had in mind. That decision was intended as a prescription for excellence in a district perceived as a shambles. "Both Judge Garrity and his experts apparently believed that the quality of instruction in Boston Public Schools had been so poor for so long that a redistribution of resources would not guarantee the plaintiff class the equal protection they were entitled to under the law. In order to provide equal protection, the Judge and his experts believed it was necessary to upgrade the entire system of education in Boston."[72]

It may be that these courts devised a remedy similar to what a healthy political system should have adopted on its own. And they may well have acted as they did only because they perceived the existing political order as bankrupt and hoped to restore a well-functioning school district. But it is doubtful that the court, using such an approach, has any realistic chance of achieving this end. The educational dilemmas are real enough, but they have not readily responded to other sorts of ministrations, and there is no reason to think that the court alone—as distinguished from the court acting in tandem with the parties—can do much better. The hope to improve educational quality, regularly expressed in these opinions, echoes *Brown*'s encomium to education. But "quality" is an elusive notion and can be manipulated to mean whatever the judge would have it mean. Concerns for quality are sometimes tied to the quest for a politically acceptable settlement. At other times, the judge speaks without heed to the parties' views. Quality and desegregation are sometimes linked, while elsewhere courts reluctant to order racial mixing regard them as fundamentally opposed.

Each belief—that racial mixing will generate improved education or, conversely, that quality education is better secured without the disruptive effects of massive desegregation—constitutes a plausible premise for policy. It is not their substance that is problematic but rather the fact that these views are urged by courts, without either the legitimacy derived from constitutional interpretation or the quite different legitimacy that can emerge from institutional interdependency of the parties. These *ex cathedra* policy statements amount to no more than a declaration of what the good life might entail; and although judges, like the rest of us, are entitled to hold views on such matters, there is no justification for their conversion of those sentiments into legally binding decisions.

Legitimacy, Participation, and Constitutional Values

Neither legalism nor practical politics by itself but instead some combination of the two bargaining "in the shadow of the law,"[73] prevails in desegregation litigation.[74] The legal standard set forth by the court signals "the general direction to be pursued and a few salient landmarks to be sought out or avoided";[75] within the scope set by law, political interchange managed by the court takes place. The process is political in that it stresses institutional policies rather than specifiable grievances, negotiable interests rather than unyielding entitlements. In some circumstances it is political in a second sense: the process functions iteratively, as a sequence of mutual adjustments in which the court guides the parties to reach an agreement within the bounds fixed by the applicable substantive law.

At neither the appellate nor the trial level are courts so single-mindedly committed to the resolution of controversies through the reasoned or principled application of the Constitution as is conventionally supposed.[76] Yet legalist considerations do matter greatly. Judicial decisions do not merely mask personal predilections and political preferences.[77] Instead, a process of interchange drawing on both principled and pragmatic considerations seems very much at work, both between the parties and the court and among the branches of government.[78]

The courts have largely succeeded in developing a new mode of decision making with noteworthy effects on social policy. But what licenses judges to act in this fashion? Certainly not the traditional conception of adjudication, which sharply distinguishes judging from politics; from that perspective, these novel activities encroach on the authority of the coordinate branches and threaten to upset the constitutional equilibrium.[79] The courts themselves have sought to maintain this conception: even as they act politically, they emphasize continuity with past legalist behavior. While the courts goad a political process, they issue orders; while they seek to balance interests, they refer to rights.

We tend to forget just how adaptive the federal judiciary has always been in acting within a constantly shifting political context. In the judicial quest for relevance, rights have often been rooted in contemporary realities and beliefs. And the consequences of court decisions are significant, as the justices themselves well understand. During the oral argument in the *Brown* case, Justice Frankfurther inquired: "Does anyone know . . . where we can go to find light on what the practical consequences of these decisions have been?"[80] Consequences may not be of much interest to the legal positivist who views court opinions as commands, but they are of vital concern to a judiciary as deeply enmeshed in the political discourse as the federal courts. Attending to consequences indicates a need for adaptability, which, in turn, strengthens the effectiveness of the court in the face of altered circumstances. In the context of desegregation, the newly perceived relationship between restructuring institutions and undoing discrimination, and the concomitant necessity for framing remedies that extend beyond racial balance, may be said to warrant the judicial adaptiveness evident in these decisions.

Yet, as a justification for this new mode of activity, the court's need for adaptiveness proves too much. The court cannot simply assume any posture or confront any question as long as the outcome promises to be efficacious. Were it otherwise, there would be neither place nor need for majoritarian government. Hence the core question: *How can the judiciary reconcile the need to act effectively with the importance of retaining the qualities that distinguish it from the coordinate branches of government?*

While no bright line demarcates the activities of the courts, judicial decision making is distinctive in two respects. First, the decisions themselves emerge from interchange between the court and those directly affected by the issue; they derive from actual controversies, and not from the desire to undo abstract mischiefs. Second, those decisions are based on the positive law, not on the judges' beliefs.

Institutional reform litigation, and specifically the desegregation cases, may be understood as an attempt to preserve these distinctively judicial attributes, even as the form and nature of the litigation evolve. Consider first the process of decision making. The scope of the cases makes the actual participation of all affected a practical impossibility; that, of course, is the rationale for class actions. But even within the courtroom, representative participation amounts to scarcely more than a conceit.[81] The class itself has no formal notice of the litigation. Divergent voices within the larger class—those who might be interested in securing black separatism, for example, or exempting Hispanic students from the decree—are discouraged, for they introduce complications not readily resolved in the adversarial setting.

In adapating the process of adjudication, shaping a more political resolution of the controversy through negotiation, the court is attempting more fully to honor the range of affected interests. When the court crafts a remedy, it attempts to involve affected outsiders and to augment the dialogue of the courtroom. This negotiation offers a forum to those who were likely to have been excluded from the give-and-take prior to the lawsuit—the racial minorities who suffered the consequences of nonrepresentation. Judicial solicitude for the constitutional wants of "discrete and insular minorities"[82] is a familiar explanation for court intervention, but it assumes renewed significance in these cases. When the participation succeeds, when court-initiated negotiations in fact revitalize a pluralist system of decision-making, it unclogs for minorities the channels of government, giving them some say over their own lives.[83]

Process matters greatly in the constitutional scheme of things. As John Hart Ely has written, the Constitution "is overwhelmingly concerned . . . with ensuring broad participation in the processes and distributions of government."[84] But the Constitution does not address only the nature of representation; it encompasses broad substantive rights as well, among them the right to equal treatment. The Fourteenth Amendment's substantive command serves as the basis for the desegregation cases. Constitutional language is, of course, not tightly bounded, its generality seems appropriate to a value as durable and as public as equality.[85] The breadth of the constitutional provision permits judges to take note of ever more subtle forms of inequity. It also licenses attention to the strategic elements of remedy, taking into account such factors as the complaisance of the school district, the feasibility and acceptability of the alternatives, and the need to address not only the manifestations but also the source of the threats to equality.[86] Equal protection is not, however, a limitless concept; nor can it be equated with perceptions of the good society. The history of desegregation cases reveals, for the most part, a judiciary earnestly attempting to link the specific remedy with the constitutionally defined wrong being redressed.

Finally, the process of participation and the substance of decision do not occupy separate spheres. When the basis for decision—here, equality—is in flux, and when the litigants desire consensus, then the effort to assure opportunities for participation enhances the legitimacy of the outcome.[87] Within constitutional limits, equality means what those affected agree that it means. In process and substance, justice is idiosyncratic. Its meaning evolves with changes in circumstance and with altered understandings of the value of equality.

NOTES

1. For fuller discussion of this history see David Kirp, "School Desegregation and the Limits of Legalism," *Pubic Interest,* 47 (1977), 101; and Gary Orfield, *Must We Bus? Segregated Schools and National Policy* (Washington, D.C.: Brookings Institution, 1978).

2. For a critique of what is seen as misplaced legalism, see Lino Graglia, *Disaster by Decree: The Supreme Court Decisions in Race and the Schools* (Ithaca, N.Y.: Cornell Univ. Press, 1976).

3. 347 U.S. 483 (1954).

4. For a discussion of this history see Richard Kluger, *Simple Justice* (New York: Knopf, 1976).

5. 349 U.S. 294 (1955).

6. Cooper v. Aaron, 358 U.S. 1 (1958).

7. *Id.* at 20 (Frankfurter, J., concurring).

8. For a general treatment see Jack W. Peltason, *Fifty-Eight Lonely Men* (Urbana: Univ. of Illinois Press, 1961).

9. 42 U.S.C. §2000.

10. U.S. v. Jefferson County Board of Education, 1372 F.2d836 (5th Cir. 1966); *aff'd* 380 F. 2d 385 (5th Cir. 1967) (en banc). See also Note, "The Courts, HEW, and Southern School Desegregation," *Yale Law Journal,* 77 (1967), 321.

11. 391 U.S. 430 (1968).

12. 402 U.S. 1 (1971).

13. For a general treatment see Gary Orfield, *The Reconstruction of Southern Education* (New York: Wiley, 1969); and Beryl Radin, *Implementation, Change, and the Federal Bureaucracy: School Desegregation Policy in HEW, 1964-1968* (New York: Teachers College Press, 1977).

14. 413 U.S. 189 (1973).

15. See Dayton Board of Education v. Brinkman, 433 U.S. 406 (1977); but compare Dayton Board of Education V. Brinkman, 439 U.S. 1357 (1979).

16. 433 U.S. 267 (1977).

17. 418 U.S. 717 (1974) (White, J., dissenting).

18. J. Harvie Wilkinson III, *From Brown to Bakke: The Supreme Court and School Integration* (New York: Oxford Univ. Press, 1979), p. 310.

19. Wilkinson, p. 308.

20. Terminiello v. Chicago, 337 U.S. 1, 37 (1949) (Jackson, J., dissenting).

21. The politics of race and schooling is more fully treated in David Kirp, *Elusive Equality: The Evolution of American Race and Schooling Policy* (Berkeley: Univ. of California Press, forthcoming).

22. See Millicent Cox, *A Description of School Desegregation since 1965* (Santa Monica, Calif.: Rand 1979), for a survey of school district experience.

23. Compare David Kirp, "Race, Politics, and the Courts: School Desegregation in San Francisco," *Harvard Educational Review*, 46 (1976), 572, with Kirp, "Race, Schooling, and Interest Politics: The Oakland Story," *School Review*, 87 (1979), 355.

24. For a general treatment see Paul Peterson, *School Politics, Chicago Style* (Chicago: Univ. of Chicago Press, 1976).

25. See Mark Yudof, "Implementation Theories and Desegregation Realities," *Mississippi Law Review* (forthcoming). For a more general view, see Richard Elmore, "Organizational Models of Social Program Implementation," *Public Policy*, 26 (1978), 185; Paul Berman, "The Study of Macro- and Micro-Implementation," *Public Policy*, 26 (1978), 157; and Richard Elmore, "Backward Mapping: Implementation Research and Policy Decisions," *Political Science Quarterly*, 94 (1979), 601.

26. Research on the impact of judicial opinions often succombs to this temptation. See, for example, Stephen Wasby, Anthony A. D'Amato, and Rosemarie Metrailer, *Desegregation from Brown to Alexander: An Exploration of Supreme Court Strategies* (Carbondale: Southern Illinois Univ. Press, 1977); Theodore Becker and Malcolm Feeley, eds., *The Impact of Supreme Court Decisions* (New York: Oxford Univ. Press, 1973).

27. On the causes of white resistance to and flight from desegregation, compare Michael Giles and Douglas Catlin, "Mass-Level Compliance with Public Policy: The Case of School Desegregation," *Journal of Politics*, 42 (1980), 722, with David O. Sears, Carl P. Hensler, and Leslie K. Speer, "White Opposition to Busing: Self-Interest or Symbolic Politics?" *American Political Science Review*, 73 (1979), 369. Also see Albert Hirschman, *Exit, Voice, and Loyalty* (Cambridge, Mass.: Harvard Univ. Press, 1970).

28. 276 F. Supp. 834, 846-7 (E.D. La. 1967).

29. NAACP v. Lansing Board of Education, 429 F. Supp. 583, 631 (W.D. Mich. 1976).

30. Pasadena Board of Education v. Spangler, 427 U.S. 424 (1976).

31. See Mitchell Feigenberg, "Pasadena," in David Kirp, Nancy Borow, Mitch-

ell Feigenberg, Tim Gage, Elliot Marseille, and Dorothy Robyn, *Judicial Management of School Desegregation Cases* (Washington, D.C.: National Institute of Education, 1979), p. 41.

32. Ralph Smith, "Two Centuries and Twenty-Four Months: A Chronicle of the Struggle to Desegregate the Boston Public Schools," in *Limits of Justice: The Court's Role in School Desegregation,* ed. Howard Kalodner and James Fishman (Cambridge, Mass.: Ballinger, 1978), pp. 25; 84-85.

33. See Owen Fiss, "The Supreme Court, 1978 Term, Foreword: The Forms of Justice," *Harvard Law Review,* 93 (1979), 1. Political considerations also affect who has a legally cognizable interest and what facts are deemed relevant. But legalist concerns are most important during these stages of the litigation. Fact-finding and rule-applying during the liability stage of the suit make the legal status of the parties clearer, affecting both their perceptions of legal right and their bargaining power.

34. See, for example, Robert Goldstein, "A *Swann* Song for Remedies: Equitable Belief in the Burger Court," *Harvard Civil Rights-Civil Liberties Law Review,* 13 (1978), 1.

35. See Dorothy Robyn, "St. Louis," in Kirp et al., *Judicial Management.*

36. See, for example, Nancy Borow, "Minneapolis," in Kirp et al., *Judicial Management;* compare Kirp, "Race, Politics, and the Courts."

37. See Nancy Borow, "Atlanta," in Kirp et al., *Judicial Management.*

38. See Tim Gage, "Dallas," in Kirp et al., *Judicial Management.*

39. Supreme Court of the United States, October Term, 1971, No. 71-507, Appendix Vol. 4, Hearings, May 11, 1970, p. 1609 a.

40. Kelly v. Guinn, 456 F. 2d 100, 110 (9th Cir. 1972).

41. That combination may also be found in other institutional reform cases. See David Kirp and Gary Babcock, "Judge and Company: Court-Appointed Masters, School Desegregation, and Institutional Reform," *Alabama Law Review,* 32 (1981), 313.

42. For a discussion of these organizational issues, see, for example, Karl Weick, "Educational Organizations as Loosely Coupled Systems," *Administrative Science Quarterly,* 21 (1976), 1; James March, "American Public School Administration: A Short Analysis," *School Review,* 86 (1978), 217; Seymour Sarason, *The Culture of the School and the Problem of Change* (Boston: Allyn and Bacon, 1971).

43. 363 F. Supp. 739 (E.D. Missouri 1973); mandate conformed to, 388 F. Supp. 1058 (.E.D. Missouri 1975); *aff'd* in part, *rev'd* in part 515 F. 2d 1365 (8th Cir. 1975); appeal after remand, 523 F. 2d 889 (8th Cir. 1975).

44. U.S. v. Omaha, 521 F. 2d 530 (8th Cir. 1975); remanded on other grounds, 433 U.S. 667 (1977).

45. See James Fishman, "The Limits of Remedial Power: *Hart* v. *Community School Board 21,"* in Kalodner and Fishman, p. 115, n. 32.

46. Quoted in William Marsh, "The Indianapolis Case: *United States* v. *Board of School Commissions,"* in Kalodner and Fishman, p. 353.

47. See Elliot Marseille, "Denver," in Kirp et al., *Judicial Management;* also Smith, "Two Centuries."

48. See Dorothy Robyn, "Wilmington," in Kirp et al., *Judicial Management.*

49. Northcross v. Board of Education, Memphis City Schools, 341 F. Supp. 583 (597) (W.D. Tenn. 1972).

50. For discussions of institutional reform litigation, see, for example, Donald Horowitz, *The Courts and Social Policy* (Washington, D.C.: Brookings Institution, 1972); Archibald Cox, *The Role of the Supreme Court in American Government* (New York: Oxford Univ. Press, 1976); Fiss, "The Supreme Court, 1978 Term"; Abram Chayes, "The Role of the Judge in Public Law Litigation," *Harvard Law Review,* 89 (1976), 1281; Theodore Eisenberg and Stephen C. Yeazell, "The Ordinary and the Extraordinary in Institutional Reform Litigation," *Harvard Law Review,* 93 (1980), 465; Michael Rebell and Arthur Block, *Educational Policy-Making and the Courts* (Washington, D.C.: National Institute of Education, 1979).

51. 269 F. Supp. 401, 517 (D.D.C. 1967).

52. Kenneth L. Karst and Harold W. Horowitz, "Reitman v. Mulkey: A Telophase of Substantive Equal Protection," *Supreme Court Review,* 1967, p. 39.

53. *Indianapolis Star,* 14 Aug. 1973, p. 1.

54. See Marsh, "The Indianapolis Case," in Kalodner and Fishman, p. 343, n. 124. Quoting the Indianapolis judge: "[This court will not assume] the additional burden of dealing with sham issues put forward in the interest of political opportunism. . . ." (Marsh, p. 328).

55. See Peter D. Roos, "Bilingual Education: The Hispanic Response to Unequal Opportunities," *Law and Contemporary Problems,* 42 (1978), 111; and Orfield, *Must We Bus?*

56. Clark v. Board of Education, 328 F. Supp. 1205, 1217 (E.D. Ark. 1971).

57. Hearings, Civil Action 68-1438-R, (Spangler v. Pasadena Board of Education), U.S. District Court, Southern California, 1970, p. 419.

58. Hearings, Civil Action C-1499 (Keyes v. School District #1), U.S. District Court, Colorado, July 22, 1969, p. 755.

59. See Robyn, "Wilmington," Kirp et al., *Judicial Management.*

60. Robyn, "Wilmington," p. 99.

61. Robyn, "Wilmington," p. 51.

62. Robyn, "Wilmington," p. 52.

63. Robyn, "Wilmington," p. 53-55.

64. Hearings, Civil Action 6298, (Calhoun v. Cook), U.S. District Court, Northern Georgia, December 28, 1972, pp. 42-43.

65. Robyn, "St. Louis," in Kirp et al., *Judicial Management.*

66. See Frank T. Read, "Judicial Evolution of the Law of School Integration

Since *Brown v. Board of Education,*" *Law and Contemporary Problems,* 39 (1975), 7.

67. Mark Yudof, "School Desegregation: Legal Realism, Reasoned Elaboration, and Social Science Research in the Supreme Court," *Law and Contemporary Problems,* 42 (1978), 57.

68. U.S. v. Hendry County School District, 50 F. 2d, 550, 554 (5th Cir. 1974).

69. See Elwood Hain, "Sealing Off the City: School Desegregation in Detroit," in Kalodner and Fishman, p. 223.

70. Bradley v. Milliken, 402 F. Supp. 1096, 1101 (E.D. Mich. 1975).

71. Hain, "Sealing Off the City," in Kalodner and Fishman, p. 292.

72. Susan Greenblatt and Walter McCann, "Courts, Desegregation, and Education: A Look at Boston." *Schools and the Court: Desegregation.* Vol. 1 ERIC Clearing House on Educational Management, 1979.

73. Compare Robert Mnookin and Lewis Kornhauser, "Bargaining in the Shadow of the Law: The Case of Divorce," *Yale Law Journal,* 88 (1979), 950.

74. For empirical discussions of these cases see M. Kay Harris and Dudley P. Spiller, Jr., *After Decision: Implementation of Judicial Decrees in Correctional Settings* (Washington, D.C.: Government Printing Office, 1977); Note, "The Wyatt Case, Implementation of a Judicial Decree Ordering Institutional Change," *Yale Law Journal,* 84 (1975), 1338; Note, "Judicial Intervention and Organizational Theory: Changing Bureaucratic Behavior and Policy," *Yale Law Journal,* 89 (1980), 513.

75. Chayes, "The Role of the Judge," p. 1300.

76. The classic statement of this proposition is Wechsler, "Neutral Principles of Constitutional Law," *Harvard Law Review,* 73 (1960), 1. See also Lief Carter, *Reason in Law* (Boston: Little, Brown, 1979).

77. Thurmond Arnold, "Professor Hart's Theology," *Harvard Law Review,* 73 (1960), 1299. See Theodore Benditt, *Law as Rule and Principle* (Stanford, Calif.: Stanford Univ. Press, 1978), pp. 22-32.

78. Compare Alexander Bickel, *The Least Dangerous Branch: The Supreme Court at the Bar of Politics* (Indianapolis: Bobbs-Merrill, 1962).

79. See, for example, Robert F. Nagel, "Separation of Powers and the Scope of Federal Equitable Remedies," *Stanford Law Review,* 30 (1978), 661; Alexander Bickel, *The Morality of Consent* (New Haven, Conn.: Yale Univ. Press, 1975); Gerald F. Frug, "The Judicial Powers of the Purse," *Pennsylvania Law Review,* 126 (1978), 715.

80. Quoted in Becker and Feeley, *Impact of Supreme Court Decisions,* p. 1.

81. See Derrick Bell, "Serving Two Masters: Integration Ideals and Client Interests in School Desegregation Litigation," *Yale Law Journal,* 85 (1976), 470.

82. U.S. v. Carolene Products Company, 364 U.S. 144, 152 (1938).

83. See John Ely, *Democracy and Distrust* (Cambridge, Mass.: Harvard Univ. Press, 1980). For a skeptical treatment of how well pluralist politics function to

safeguard the rights of minorities, see William Gamson, *The Strategy of Social Protest* (Homewood, Ill.: Dorsey Press, 1975); and Theodore Lowi, *The Politics of Disorder* (New York: Basic Books, 1971).

84. Ely, *Democracy and Distrust,* p. 87.

85. For a discussion of "public values" in the place of constitutional adjudication, see Fiss, "The Supreme Court, 1978 Term."

86. See Note, "Implementation Problems in Institutional Reform Litigation," *Harvard Law Review,* 91 (1977), 428.

87. See Lawrence Tribe, "The Emerging Reconnection of Individual Rights and Institutional Design: Federalism, Bureaucracy, and Due Process in Lawmaking," *Creighton Law Review,* 10 (1977), 433; Hans Linde, "Due Process of Lawmaking," *Nebraska Law Review,* 55 (1976), 197.

II.
GENDER DESEGREGATION

WOMEN AND PUBLIC POLICY:
AN OVERVIEW

Jo Freeman

During the last two decades there has been a revolution in public policy toward women. Beginning with passage of the equal pay act in 1963 and the prohibition against sex discrimination in employment in 1964, Congress has added numerous laws to the books which have altered the thrust of public policy toward women from one of protectionism to one of equal opportunity. While implementation leaves much to be desired, and equal opportunity by itself will not eradicate women's secondary position in society, the importance of this fundamental change should not be underestimated.

Parallel to this development the Supreme Court has fundamentally altered its interpretation of women's position in society. Until 1971, the judicial approach to women was that her rights and responsibilities, opportunities and obligations, were essentially determined by her position in the family—her role as a wife and mother. Women were viewed first and foremost as members of a dependent class whose individual rights were subservient to that class position. From this perspective virtually all laws which classified by sex were Constitutional. Today most such laws have been found unconstitutional. The remaining laws and practices that treat the sexes differently are subject to more searching scrutiny than in the past, and the Court is particularly disapproving of rationalizations for them that encourage dependency.

A brief overview of the laws and judicial interpretations which have affected the position of women amply illustrates the way in which their family status formed the basis for their social status. Not surprisingly, laws on women are most frequently found under the rubric of "family law." The basic principle of family law derives from Blackstone's codification of the English Common Law. This provided the primary precedent for American judicial interpretation of the marital relationship. That relationship was succinctly summed up by Justice Black in 1966 when he defined it as resting "on the old common-law fiction that the husband and wife are one . . . [and] that . . . one is the husband."[1] The fundamental basis of the marital relationship is that husbands and wives have reciprocal, not equal, rights. The husband must support the wife and children, and the wife must render services as a companion, housewife, and mother in return. While this doctrine is largely unenforceable in an ongoing marriage (the courts have held that they should not intervene in an intact relationship[2]) and only occasionally applied in divorce,[3] the courts have found it so fundamental to public policy that contracts before or during marriage altering the nature of these reciprocal duties have been held illegal.[4]

While the division of labor in the marital relationship has never been success-fully challenged in the courts, most of the traditional disabilities of the married woman were chipped away by the activities of feminists in the 19th century. The substantive and procedural disabilities incurred by women upon marriage in that century were sufficient to make them legally nonexistent. When Edward Mans-field wrote the first major analysis of *The Legal Rights, Liabilities and Duties of Women* in 1845, he summed up:

> It appears that the husband's control over the person of his wife is so complete that he may claim her society altogether; that he may reclaim her if she goes away or is detained by others; that he may use constraint upon her liberty to prevent her going away or to prevent improper conduct; that she cannot sue alone; that he may maintain suits for injuries to her person; and that she cannot execute a deed or valid conveyance without the concurrence of her husband. In most respects she loses the power of personal independence, and altogether that of separate action in legal matters.[5]

The passage of many married women's property acts eventually

> granted married women the right to contract, to sue and be sued without joining their husbands, to manage and control the property they brought with them to marriage, to engage in gainful employment without their husbands' permission, and to retain the earnings derived from the employ-ment.[6]

Nonetheless, a plethora of minor and major disabilities remained prior to the start of the current feminist movement. There have been many changes in the last decade, but the rights and responsibilities of married men and women have yet to be equalized.[7]

As the courts have made clear, the traditional concern of public policy with a woman's family role formed the basis of her legal existence.[8] One of the earliest cases of sex discrimination to reach the Supreme Court was instigated by Myra Bradwell who had been refused a license to practice law by Illinois. The court ruled against her in 1872 and a concurring opinion by Justice Bradley explained that

> The constitution of the family organization, which is founded in the divine ordinance, as well as in the nature of things, indicates the domestic sphere as that which properly belongs to the domain and functions of womanhood. The harmony, not to say identity, of interests and views, which belong, or should belong, to the family institution is repugnant to the idea of a woman adopting a distinct and independent career from that of her husband. . . .
>
> It is true that many women are unmarried and not affected by any of the duties, complications, and incapabilities arising out of the married state, but these are exceptions to the general rule. The paramount destiny and mission of women are to fulfill the law of the Creator, and the rules of civil society must be adapted to the general constitution of things, and cannot be based upon exceptional cases.[9]

This rationale has persisted until the last few years. What it reflects is a refusal to see women as individual people apart from their identity as members of a class with a specific social role. Most of the similar state and Supreme Court cases on women used language which did not talk about the rights of individual persons under the Constitution, but the rights of "the sex." The judges have not discussed the rights of citizens but the rights of "women as citizens." The Constitution nowhere mentions the rights of "women as citizens" or even differentiates beween different rights of different citizens, but judicial opinion has established such a differentiation.[10]

This was especially evident in the long fight at the turn of the century to pass protective labor legislation in an attempt to curb sweatshop conditions. Originally intended to apply to men and women, the Supreme Court declared a violation of the right to contract those laws which applied to both sexes, but in 1908 allowed those that applied only to women on the grounds that woman's

> physical structure and a proper discharge of her maternal functions—having in view not merely her own health but the well-being of the race—justify legislation to protect her. . . . The limitations which this statute places upon her contractural powers . . . are not imposed solely for her benefit, but also largely for the benefit of all. . . . The reason . . . rests in the inherent

difference between the two sexes, and in the different functions in life which they perform.[11]

With this precedent, the drive for protective legislation became distorted into a push for laws that applied to women only—on the principle that half a loaf was better than none. While this policy was also favored by male labor leaders who saw the "protection" of women as a way to limit competition, it is safe to say that the Supreme Court contributed significantly to the proliferation of state protective laws for women only. The court has long since rejected the thinking that prevented protective legislation for men, but it expanded its 1908 decision to restrict the activities of women further. The specific case was concerned only with protecting women from strenuous labor but it has been cited in support of the barring of women from juries,[12] of different treatment in licensing occupations,[13] and of the exclusion of women from state-supported colleges.[14]

The attitude that women's family role made sex a legitimate basis for classification was expressed by the court as late as 1961 when it upheld the conviction of a Florida woman by an all-male jury for murdering her husband by assaulting him with a baseball bat. When she argued that the state law's provision that women were not required to serve on juries unless they registered such a desire with the clerk of the circuit court virtually ensured their elimination from the jury pool and thus violated her Fourteenth Amendment rights, the court replied that

Despite the enlightened emancipation of women from the restrictions and protections of by gone years, and their entry into many parts of community life formerly considered to be reserved to men, woman is still regarded as the center of home and family life. We cannot say that it is constitutionally impermissible for a State, acting in pursuit of the general welfare, to conclude that a woman should be relieved from the civic duty of jury service unless she herself determines that such service is consistent with her own special responsibilities.[13]

It was not until after the start of the current feminist movement that the courts began to display a different attitude. The initial cases exhibiting this turn-around were those generated by Title VII of the 1964 Civil Rights Act, which prohibited discrimination in employment on the basis of race, color, religion, national origin, or sex.[16] Subsequently, when many employers continued to refuse to hire or promote women to some jobs on the grounds that their working conditions violated state protective laws, women often took them to court. Typical was the judgment of the Fifth Circuit in 1969 when it refused to adopt a "stereotyped characterization" that few or no women could safely lift 30 pounds:

Title VII rejects just this type of romantic paternalism as unduly Victorian and instead vests individual women with the power to decide whether or not to take on unromantic tasks. Men have always had the right to determine whether the incremental increase in remuneration for strenuous, danger- ous, obnoxious, boring or unromantic tasks is worth the candle. The promise of Title VII is that women are now to be on equal footing.[17]

The promise of Title VII was not made by Congress with full knowledge of what it was doing. When the 1964 Civil Rights Act was being debated, one of the most controversial sections was that prohibiting discrimination in employment. In one of many ploys by its opponents, Rep. Howard W. Smith of Virginia proposed a floor amendment to add "sex" to the protected groups. While this provision was strongly supported by the women of the House, especially Rep. Martha Griffiths (D-Mich.) who claims she intended to make such a proposal herself, most of the House liberals opposed it, as did the Women's Bureau of the Labor Department. Nonetheless, neither side felt strongly enough to spend more than a few hours in debate (the "sex" amendment had never come up in committee) and little of this was serious. Instead, both Smith and the liberal opponents played the provision for all the laughs it was worth and the ensuing uproar went down in congressional history as "Ladies Day in House."[18]

Looked at from the perspective of two decades, the prohibition of employment discrimination on the basis of sex is one of the most profoundly redistributive decisions of our century. According to Lowi, redistributive policies are the most far-reaching and least understood of the different types of public policies. They involve the redistribution of social resources from one major group to another.[19] Given the highly sex-segregated nature of the job market,[20] much of it due to direct discrimination, accomplishment of the idea embodied in Title VII would significantly change the employment opportunity structure of our society in favor of women.

The opportunity structure would be altered even more radically if the idea of affirmative action, as required by Executive Order 11246 amended by Executive Order 11375, would actually see fruit. This order, which prohibits discrimination on the basis of race, color, religion, or national origin by all holders of federal contracts (covering one-third of the labor force), was issued by President Johnson on September 24, 1965 as the latest in 25 years of executive orders on racial discrimination by federal contractors. While the addition of "sex," in Executive Order 11375, was not made until over two years later, it was done relatively effortlessly, in large part owing to the precedent of Title VII. The executive branch sought to bring its policies into conformity with those of Congress.[21]

If we ignore for the moment issues of implementation, the nonchalance with which this major redistributive decision was made by both the executive and legislative branches raises the question of how this could happen. There was no organized women's movement in 1964, not much of one in 1967, and little pressure from other women's organizations. Only the most naive would assume either that the men of the Eighty-eighth Congress and the Johnson administration were sufficiently sympathetic, or the women sufficiently powerful, to effect this policy with minimal opposition.

True, the Equal Pay Act had finally passed Congress in 1963 preceded by hearings on the economic problems of women. But not only is the Equal Pay Act barely if at all redistributive, it is more indicative of congressional negligence than interest. First proposed in 1868 at the National Labor Union Convention, equal pay did not become a federal issue until World War I, when many women were encouraged, even required, to move into jobs that had formerly been held by men during the national emergency. Since women traditionally worked for less money than men, the two to four million women suddenly added to the work force created a concern that they would depress wage rates and that men would be forced to work at lower rates after the war. Actions were taken to preclude this by requiring that women replacing men be given equal pay. Some of this momentum carried over after the war, and in 1919, Montana and Michigan enacted the first state equal-pay laws. It was many years before others followed their lead. World War II saw a repeat of what had happened in the first war, and the introduction of the first equal pay bills into Congress. But it was not until 1945 that a major bill with broad coverage was debated and it took "eighteen years of persistent, unsuccessful efforts to get an equal pay bill to the floor of Congress"[22] before the federal government was added to the roster of nineteen states that prohibited wage differences on the basis of sex. Even this law applied to only 61 percent of the labor force.

Throughout all the early agitation for equal pay, the major concern of Congress and the supporting unions was the "prevention of women's wages from undercutting the wages of men."[23] Women's unions and feminists supported equal pay out of dedication to principle and feelings of working-class solidarity but always with the proviso that there would be training programs for "working girls" to provide women with the same opportunities as men to earn decent wages.[24] For the most part they never achieved decent wages because male unions continued to exclude women from membership and apprenticeship programs while employers,[25] when faced with a choice between male and female employees, chose women only if they would work for lower wages. Then as now equal pay was irrelevant without equal job opportunity. If anything, the Equal Pay Act "*increased job security for men* by discouraging the replacement of men with lower paid women."[26]

Thus, it was left to Title VII and Executive Order 11375 to begin, almost unnoticed, a major revolution in public policy. Why it was initially unnoticed, at least by those who passed it if not by those who were affected by it, lies in the disregard that women have normally experienced from political leaders and in the routine nature of the addition of "sex" to the pantheon of prohibited discriminations.

It is practically a truism among political scientists that most policy making in the United States is incremental. Great decisions are rarely made; in fact they are often strenuously avoided by our legislators. Instead policy changes are made incrementally, adding a little bit here and there. Congress had been debating and passing legislation to curtail race discrimination in employment since the 1930s.[27] What the early legislation lacked was a means of enforcing this prohibition. The most controversial aspect of Title VII was not the idea of prohibiting discrimination, but that of creating an independent enforcement agency, the Equal Employment Opportunity Commission (EEOC). And, needless to say, while the EEOC did come into existence with Title VII, it did so without any real enforcement powers (until amended by another incremental change in 1972).[28]

Adding "sex" to "race, color, religion and national origin" as a category of prohibited discriminatory practices, was, from the perspective of white, male legislators in the early 1960s, only another increment. Women may have comprised more than half the population and at that time more than one-third of the labor force, but it was Congress' failure to be cognizant of this fact and not their sensitivity to it that permitted sex discrimination to be prohibited so easily. In fact, the only people apparently aware of what the addition of the word "sex" might mean were some women, in and out of Congress, who approved of it, and blacks with their white supporters, who were quite hostile to the idea. In their view, women were well off and should not be allowed to compete with minority groups for a share of the slim federal pie.[29]

Ironically, it was overcoming the hostility of civil rights activists, not Congress, that was the first major battle of the new feminist movement. In fact, this hostility was a major contributor to the formation of the movement. From the very beginning, the EEOC sought to ignore the sex provision as much as possible. The first executive director, Herman Edelsberg, even stated publicly that it was a "fluke" that was "conceived out of wedlock." He felt, "men were entitled to female secretaries."[30] Not everyone within the EEOC, however, was opposed to the sex provision. Two of the five EEOC commissioners and at least one of its lawyers argued that it would be taken more seriously if there were "some sort of NAACP for women" to put pressure on the government. As government employees they could not organize such a group but they spoke privately with those whom they thought could do so, including Betty Friedan and many members of the state commissions on the status of women. Partly as a result of their urgings, the National Organization for Women (NOW) was formed in 1966 and directed a good portion of its initial energies toward changing the guidelines of the EEOC.[31]

Even before NOW's organizing conference in October 1966, the temporary steering committee had fired off telegrams to the EEOC urging it to change its ruling that help-wanted advertisements listed under seperate male and female columns were not a violation of Title VII. In the following months, NOW added two more demands: (1) that the *bona fide occupational qualification (bfoq)* exemption of Title VII[32] not be interpreted so as to permit employers in states with "protective labor legislation" to use those laws as rationales for denying equal job opportunity; and (2) that the *bfoq* specifically not be interpreted to allow airline requirements that stewardesses must retire upon marriage or reaching age 32. While the EEOC ruled favorably on the latter demand, the first two issues were resolved by the courts years later. After much "waffling," the EEOC finally decided on August 14, 1968 that sex-segregated want ads were illegal but found itself powerless to enforce that ruling until the Supreme Court acted five years later.[33]

The EEOC's initial attitude toward "protective labor legislation" was contrary to that of most feminists, and in line with that of organized labor. While these laws differed from state to state, the bulk of them limited the hours a woman could work, usually to 48 per week, and the amount of weight she could lift on the job, generally to 35 pounds. Feminists had long opposed these laws, arguing that their major use was to prevent women from earning overtime pay, from being promoted to jobs in which overtime might be required, and from gaining access to jobs which occasionally require lifting more weight than the limit.[34] Most labor unions, including the women within their leadership ranks, had long supported these laws, believing that they were a necessary protection for women. The EEOC supported this perspective and refused to investigate several complaints made by women when their denial of job opportunities was justified by employers on the basis of state protective laws. Many women took their cases to court where the decisions were repeatedly in their favor. Concomitantly, the attorneys general of several states ruled that their states' protective laws were succeeded by Title VII and therefore void.[35] As a result, the EEOC was forced to change its interpretations to keep them in accord with judicial rulings, and by 1969 "concluded that such laws and regulations . . . will not be considered a defense to an otherwise established unlawful employment practice."[36]

These court rulings not only changed the EEOC guidelines but paved the way for passage of the Equal Rights Amendment. The ERA was the only feminist-supported proposal which had a long political history, and opposition, behind it. First proposed in 1923 by the National Women's Party as a means to eradicate sex-specific laws, it was introduced into every subsequent Congress. The Senate passed it in 1950 and 1953, but only with the addition of the "Hayden rider" that the amendment "shall not be construed to impair any rights, benefits, or exemptions now or hereafter conferred by law, upon persons of the female sex."[37] Such an amendment was anathema to feminists, but demanded by organized labor as they did not want protective labor legislation undermined.

By 1970, however, not only had numerous court decisions preempted this argument by voiding protective labor laws in favor of Title VII, but extensive research was beginning to disclose that labor laws applying to women only probably caused them greater harm than benefit. Thus, at the very time the emerging feminist movement was turning its attention to ERA, its only major organized opposition was fading from the field.

In February of that year, roughly two dozen NOW members disrupted hearings on the eighteen-year-old-vote amendment being held by the Senate Judiciary Subcommittee on Constitutional Amendments to demand that hearings be scheduled on the ERA. At the same time the official Citizen's Advisory Council on the Status of Women endorsed the ERA and issued a definitive legal analysis originally written by a founder of NOW. As momentum gathered, the Senate Judiciary Subcommittee called hearings on the ERA in May, and the White House released the report of the President's Task Force on Women's Rights and Responsibilities with its endorsement of the ERA. Then at the 50th anniversary conference of the Women's Bureau on June 13, Secretary of Labor-designate James D. Hodgson added the Labor Department's endorsement. The Women's Bureau and the Labor Department had traditionally opposed the ERA out of deference to organized labor.[38]

The pivotal move, however, had occurred two days before when Rep. Martha Griffiths (D. Mich.) filed a petition to discharge the House Judiciary Committee from further consideration of the amendment as it had not been considered during the previous twenty years. Griffiths was one of the few members of Congress who had both the interest and resources to make such an audacious move. This rarely used procedure requires the signatures of a majority (218) of House members and is generally opposed as upsetting the routine procedures of Congress. Griffiths was not only a longtime supporter of women's bills, but had sat for several years on the powerful Ways and Means Committee. In this position she had accumulated a lot of political favors which she had not used up for home district bills. Consequently, she was not only able to get the requisite number of signatures, but they included most of the chairmen of the standing committees, people who normally disapprove of such petitions. The House passed the ERA in August, as the result of a strenuous lobbying campaign by several women's organizations. The Senate proved more obdurate, and added a rider to permit prayer in public schools. This killed the amendment for the Ninety-first Congress.

The Ninety-second Congress saw the beginning of an enormous 15-month campaign by a potpourri of feminist, women's, establishment, and liberal organizations covering most of the political spectrum, allied with women in several congressional offices and administrative bureaus. Two to three dozen volunteer lobbyists virtually lived in the halls of Congress for the duration, and Congressman Tip O'Neill (D.-Mass.) was quoted as saying that the ERA generated more mail than the Vietnam War.[39]

During this time the ERA's strongest opponent, the AFL-CIO, ceased its active opposition. This change was a result of the voiding of protective labor laws by Title VII, and the efforts of the director of the Women's Bureau to convince women unionists to support the ERA. Consequently, by the time the ERA was sent to the states for ratification, on March 22, 1972, its opposition consisted largely of the John Birch Society, the Communist Party, the National Council of Catholic Women, and only a few members of Congress.

For the first year the ERA appeared to have clear sailing as twenty-eight states quickly ratified it. Then, in January 1973, a national "Stop ERA" campaign surfaced, headed by noted right-winger Phyllis Schlafly. Her initial efforts were not taken seriously by the pro-ERA organizations, but when only a few more states ratified it in the next couple years they gradually realized they could not take support for granted. They also began to realize that "Stop ERA" was not an isolated movement, but part of a resurgence of right wing sentiment which additionally opposed busing to achieve racial integration in the schools, and the legalization of abortion.[40]

These realizations did not bring immediate action by feminist groups. At the time the ERA was sent to the states, the movement had not yet made an impact in southern and rural states, and these were more than the one-quarter needed to prevent passage of a constitutional amendment. As the movement had always been highly decentralized, looking upon national direction of local activities as something to be avoided, the coalition that passed the ERA on the national level could not be easily replicated in the states, and the national coalition did not have the foresight and support to recruit and train "outside agitators" for those states that could not generate sufficient resources within. Not until 1977, with three states to go and only two years left to gain them, did the women's movement begin a nationally coordinated effort.

Regardless of the outcome of the ERA, the two-year final battle to get it through Congress had some very beneficial side effects. Primary among them was the climate it created in Congress that there was serious constituency interest in women's rights. The ERA was probably the easiest of all the legislative issues to generate mail about from a wide cross section of the population. Once the question of the value of "protective" legislation was out of the way, courtesy of Title VII, there was something vaguely immoral about the inequitable application of the Constitution. Since there was as yet little organized opposition to women's rights legislation in general, this mail created the impression that there was strong support for the whole policy area. As Clausen points out, there is no simple explanation of congressional decision making. Of the five major policy areas he analyzed, he found that constituency pressure was the most significant in the area of civil rights and liberties.[41] While his analysis was done before there were women's rights issues, it is reasonable to assume that as they are basically civil rights issues, and as there was minimal opposition from the parties and the major interest groups, they would follow the same pattern.

The other major side effect of the ERA struggle was the establishment of liaisons between feminist organizations and congressional staff. The ERA lobbying effort both provided an excellent excuse to establish working relationships with and to educate staff, and facilitated the discovery of sympathizers among them. The incipient network this created made it easier to know whom to approach for information and/or support for other bills.

With this impetus, the Ninety-second Congress passed a bumper crop of women's rights legislation—considerably more than the sum total of all relevant legislation previously passed in the history of this country. In addition to the 1972 Equal Employment Opportunity Act and the ERA, there were: (1) Title IX of the Education Amendments Act which prohibits sex discrimination in federally aided education programs; (2) the addition of sex discrimination to the jurisdiction of the U.S. Commission on Civil Rights; (3) a Child Development Act that would have provided free day care for children in families of four or more with an annual income of less than $4,300, and a sliding fee scale for families with higher incomes, if it had not been vetoed by Nixon; (4) an amendment to the Revenue Act that allowed parents with combined incomes of up to $18,000 per year to make income tax deductions of up to $400 a month for child care; and (5) a plethora of anti-sex discrimination provisions to several federally funded programs including health training, revenue sharing, Appalachian redevelopment, and water pollution.

For our notoriously slow-moving Congress, this is a very impressive achievement. When one considers the ninety-five years it took for equal pay to go from idea to act, and the decades spent fighting for civil rights legislation, it barely seems possible. Even if one allows for the strenuous lobbying and letter-writing campaigns, and the lack of an organized opposition, the relatively easy manner in which the women's liberation movement achieved higher legislative gains so quickly requires some explanation.

The answers lie with several major assets that the movement had which have never been properly credited for its success. The first was the incipient network of supporters referred to earlier. This network provided the movement with easy access to many key points of decision making—a major goal of any interest group. Most such groups, especially if they emerge from dissident social movements, spend years developing sympathetic contacts on key committees and in key agencies. Because of the many women in government in a position to give information, if not always to make decisions, who were potentially sympathetic to the feminist cause, the movement had to invest comparatively little time in acquiring access. Together, the women in government and those in feminist and related groups formed a ready "policy system"—a phenomenon common to any significant policy area.[42]

The second contributing factor is incrementalism. Virtually all of the relevant legislation in the early 1970s involved amendments to or parallels of minority civil rights legislation. Minority civil rights organizations have spent decades trying to enact into law bills which the women's movement achieved in only a few years. Other, predominantly white, interest groups have spent equally long amounts of time trying to achieve their legislative goals. In effect, the civil rights movement broke the ground for the feminist movement. It created both a precedent for and a model of action in the area of sex-discrimination. Once the main redistributive decision had been made about the addition of sex discrimination as an area of federal policy, all that was really necessary was pressure to apply it consistently.

Third, politicians are always looking for ways to please their constituents that will not cost them support from other quarters. Since half the voters in their districts are women, and there were, in the early 1970s, no major differences of opinion among those groups claiming to represent women's interests, it was easy to persuade legislators that a vote for the feminist position would please their female constituents without incurring the wrath of other groups. The momentum begun by the Ninety-second Congress was sustained by subsequent Congresses. In the late 1970s dozens of bills passed Congress prohibiting sex discrimination in virtually all Federal programs—particularly those which also prohibit discrimination on the basis of race, religion, and national origin.

Later Congresses, however, saw some divergence from the pattern of incrementalism, as well as the first serious successes by a growing opposition. The Ninety-third Congress saw passage of the first law prohibiting sex discrimination for which there were no parallel prohibitions for race: the Equal Credit Opportunity Act. The disabilities women experienced in obtaining credit were first brought to national attention at the 1972 hearings of the National Commission on Consumer Finance.[43] It became clear at these hearings that outmoded assumptions made it more difficult for single women to get credit than men, and virtually impossible for a married woman to obtain credit in her own name—even when she was the major provider of her family's financial support. Creditors were also unwilling to count a wife's income to determine eligibility when a married couple applied for credit jointly.[44]

Although credit discrimination had not previously been prohibited on the basis of race, this area was otherwise similar to those for which discrimination was prohibited in the Ninety-second Congress. There was a "policy vacuum," i.e., few established positions and no real opposition. Even the credit industry was aware that its practices eliminated from borrowing consideration people it would otherwise consider credit-worthy. It confined its lobbying to minimizing the paperwork requirements of the law.[45] No public expenditures were required. Women's groups were able effectively to mobilize support and technical expertise through use of the "policy system." Those women and couples most likely to benefit from additional eligibility for credit were those most likely to be politically active or to contribute to campaigns.

Although the initial bill was introduced by Rep. Bella Abzug (D.-NY), the bill which was eventually passed was sponsored by a Republican senator from a southern state—William R. Brock (Tenn.). At the time he was a presidential hopeful, and no doubt thought his sponsorship of such a bill would bring him the support of women's groups on what was essentially a conservative issue. Precisely because he was a conservative, his unswerving support was crucial to the eventual passage of the bill, despite opposition from some unexpected quarters. The source of this opposition was a female Democratic member of the House— Lenor Sullivan (Mo.)—who was chair of the subcommittee scheduled to hold hearings on the bill. She refused to hold hearings on the grounds that the most appropriate legislation should prohibit discrimination against all groups. This obstacle was overcome through some parliamentary maneuvering, and the final bill passed overwhelmingly. Two years later prohibitions of discrimination on the basis of race, religion, and national origin were added to the act.

The same Congress saw the other major departure from the pattern of incrementalism in the passage of the first laws aimed directly at eliminating sex-role stereotyping, not just prohibiting discrimination. The Women's Educational Equity Act provides grants for the design of programs and activities to eliminate stereotyping and to achieve educational equity. The funding is not extensive (and of the initial products from these grants only a few look promising) but the mere existence of such a program represents a federal commitment to social changes of which the policy makers are probably not aware. Support for eliminating sex-role stereotyping in vocational education was added two years later.

Of somewhat less significance than the Women's Educational Equity Act, but reflecting a similar departure from simple incrementalism, were laws to create a National Center for the Control and Prevention of Rape and an amendment to the Foreign Assistance Act requiring that particular attention be given to "programs, projects and activities which tend to integrate women into the national economies of foreign countries."

As a general rule, equalizing access to various institutions and prohibiting discrimination may assist sex-role changes but does not really instigate them. A major exception to this are those policies which gradually integrate women into the military. Women have served intermittently in the armed forces for most of this century, but their participation has been highly restricted. Until 1967 there was a quota on women of two percent of the armed forces, and the requirements for their enlistment were hgher than those for men.

With the passage of the ERA by Congress in 1972, the abolition of the draft in 1973, and the continuing decline in the birth rate which was depleting the supply of young men, the Pentagon decided to expand women's participation. The military then began what has been the only truly successful affirmative action program for women. In only four years women's participation in the armed forces increased to five percent, the occupations open to female enlisted personnel expanded from thirty-five percent to eighty percent, and the proportion of women assigned to traditionally male jobs quadrupled."[46]

Most of these changes were achieved administratively, but a few required amending the relevant statutes. Thus, the ages at which men and women could enlist were equalized in 1974, women were admitted to the military academies in 1975, and benefits for spouses were equalized by a Supreme Court decision in 1973. Since most of the restrictions on women's participation in the armed forces are not incorporated in the law, the Pentagon has been able to pursue its policy changes without congressional approval.

Yet these policies are not anticipated to lead to a female participation rate of greater than seven percent, and while women can legally serve in most combat positions—in fact they are trained for many—there is no expectation that they will actually be put in these positions in the foreseeable future. Needless to say, the reinstitution of the draft, or another war, could radically change the current projections.

Objections to the possibility of drafting women or putting women in combat have been a significant argument in preventing ratification of the ERA. Detractors have ignored the fact that while the ERA would require women to be drafted if men were, it would not require that women actually face combat. Women can currently by drafted into combat positions if Congress and the military so desire. Yet this issue was raised again when the ERA returned to Congress for the first time in seven years. It returned because the National Organization for Women was afraid that the seven-year deadline for ratification would arrive on March 22, 1979 without the necessary three-fourths of the states having voted their support. Consequently, NOW asked Congress to extend the deadline.

Such a request was totally unprecedented. Of the twenty-six amendments to the Constitution, only five of those proposed in the last sixty years have had deadlines—always seven years—before which the states had to ratify. The deadlines were always met, and since there was no vocal opposition to the ERA in the early 1970s, the inclusion of such a deadline in this proposed amendment was not an issue, until it became apparent that it probably would not be met.

The idea of extending the deadline was actually conceived by two feminist law students in Los Angeles who were writing a term paper. They reasoned that if Congress had set the deadline, Congress could extend it, and furthermore, since the deadline was specified in the enabling resolution, not the proposed amendment itself, extension should only require a majority vote, not the two-thirds required for constitutional amendment. They brought their idea to the attention of the editor of the *National NOW Times,* who lived in Los Angeles; she sold it to NOW president Ellie Smeal, who in turn persuaded Rep. Elizabeth Holtzman (D.-N.Y.), a member of the House Judiciary Committee (which considers constitutional amendments) that it was feasible. Everyone else thought it was absurd.

Despite initial negative reactions by representatives, journalists, and other opinion makers, logic and lobbying eventually prevailed. In its attempt to extend the deadline, NOW essentially tapped the anger of an enormous number of women who felt the movement was declining after having achieved only some of its goals, but who felt personally powerless to do anything about it. NOW channeled this anger and energy into letters and marches on Washington. On July 9, 1978, the anniversary of the death of Alice Paul, author of the ERA, NOW organized a march of 100,000 women on the Capitol, despite so little advance publicity that many feminists did not know it was being planned. Three months later, after the House had passed the extension but when it appeared that the Senate would adjourn without doing so, NOW brought over 5,000 people into Washington on five-days notice to rally at and lobby in the Senate. Less than two weeks later the Senate passed the extension. In the interim NOW had maintained a fully staffed lobbying operation on the Hill, with local chapters collecting signatures on petitions and encouraging people to write letters.

This originally impossible victory proved to be a pyrrhic one. First of all, to gain the necessary votes, NOW compromised its initial demand of a seven-year extension into one of three years, three months, and eight days. (June 30, 1982 was agreed on to meet the exigencies of state legislative schedules.) NOW organizers knew that they would probably not get the remaining three states to ratify by lobbying alone. There just were not any "undecideds" left among the current state legislators. This meant that success required an electoral strategy: pro-ERA forces would have to identify and defeat enough "antis" in marginal districts to gain the votes necessary when each state legislature met again. In the United States, it is very hard to make significant changes in the composition of a legislature in only one election, unless there is an issue of overwhelming importance. The states that had not ratified are by and large conservative states. Thus, while an electoral strategy might work over the period of two or three elections, trying to achieve it in only one was a real gamble and one that lost.

Second, the spin-off effects of the original ERA campaign were not duplicated by the campaign for the extension; in fact it may have had the opposite result. Instead of viewing the outpouring for the ERA extension as generalized support for the entire women's rights policy area, members of Congress appeared to interpret it as indicating that women will sacrifice other issues in exchange for support on the ERA.

This attitude, and the reasons for it, were particularly evident when Congress debated President Carter's proposals for reorganizing the civil service. The only major proposal to be defeated was that modifying the preference given to veterans when they seek civil service jobs. The proposed modification would not have abolished the preference for hiring veterans; it would merely have restricted it to a one-time use within 15 years of discharge (and this was a compromise from the original proposal of 10 years). Since 98 percent of all veterans are male, this gives men a decided advantage over women when competing for civil service positions. As the statistics indicate, veterans' preference has resulted in significantly fewer women (and minorities) being hired or achieving high grades than would have been the case had they competed on equal terms. Women comprise 41 percent of those who pass the entry-level professional and administrative exam, but only 27 percent of those who are hired. Male veterans comprise 20 percent of those who pass but 34 percent of those actually hired. Women constitute 41 percent of the civilian labor force, but only 30 percent of the civil service. Veterans are 25 percent of the labor force, but hold 48 percent of all federal civil service jobs. Since many veterans are career military officers, retired after only 20 years with excellent pensions, training, and experience, they hold 65 percent of the three highest grades in the civil service, while women hold only three percent.

The modification proposals were defeated, despite strong administration backing, because the veterans' organizations opposed them vigorously; and NOW's attention was diverted to the ERA extension. While the other national feminist groups strongly supported modification of veterans' preference, they were not able to educate and mobilize their members on this issue sufficiently to have an impact.

Increasingly successful opposition to feminist positions also emerged around abortion and is likely to spread to other issues. The pro-choice movement preceded and was independent of the women's movement, but once abortion was recognized as an important feminist issue, the overlap among supporters of each movement has been enormous. Similarly the anti-choice movement, which emerged with pro-choice victories in the late 1960s, and crystalized with the January 1973 Supreme Court decision abolishing most abortion laws, began independently of the anti-ERA forces but has merged significantly with them.

Since the Supreme Court's decision was a constitutional interpretation, it would take a constitutional amendment to change it totally. Anti-choice congressmen have proposed several, but none of them has gotten out of committee. The strategy of the anti-choice groups has therefore focused on whittling down the use of abortion.[47] Most of their efforts have been on the state level, as it is state laws that regulate medical procedures. On the national level, they have focused on eliminating the use of federal funds to pay for abortions. Thus amendments have been passed to prohibit the use of foreign aid or family planning funds for abortions, and to deny them to military personnel or Peace Corps volunteers. But the biggest battles, and the most significant results, have been over the use of Medicaid funds for abortions. Medicaid pays for health care of those individuals and families considered to be living in poverty. Each year, funds for Medicaid must be made available by Congress as part of their budgetary appropriations for the departments of Labor, and Health, Education, and Welfare (now Health and Human Services). Each year there has been an amendment prohibiting the use of these funds for abortions. The first year this amendment failed to pass. But in 1976 funds were denied for abortions except in cases of rape or incest or for those necessary to save the life of the mother. Legal action charging that this was discriminatory against poor women—the only ones who depend on Medicaid for health care— was initially successful. But when the lower court's decision was appealed to the Supreme Court, it held—to the surprise of pro-choice forces—that while the government could not prohibit abortions, it was not required to pay for them. Every vote over Medicaid appropriations since then has seen eligibility defined still more narrowly. Today Medicaid pays for virtually no abortions.[48] Most abortions are still covered through private health care plans, but without them abortions are available only to those who can pay for them.

Although encroachments on the availability of abortion have been the major success of antifeminists, this is not their only area of attack. Their greatest concerns, and feminists' greatest failures, are on almost any issue that touches on the family. In fact, even before abortion became a national issue, laws to provide child-care services were vetoed by two presidents on the grounds of their "family-weakening implications." Since then, Congress has been less than enthusiastic about promoting federally sponsored child care.

These failures point out the biggest challenge to developing future public policy affecting women: breaking the tradition that a woman's obligations and opportunitites are largely defined by her family circumstances. While most of the legislation, administrative decisions, and court rulings of the last decade have ignored women's family status, they were able to do so because the particular issues were economic ones, and in a time of an expanding economy and expanding welfare rolls, it seemed expeditious, even conservative, to enhance a woman's right to support herself.

But if present trends continue, the next few years should see more and more women competing with men and each other for fewer and fewer jobs. The lack of jobs and the declining birthrate may well lead national policy makers to decide, as they did in the Depression, to restrict employment opportunities to "one per family." (This was proposed in the public service employment component of Carter's welfare reform program, but was not passed by Congress.)

It is still assumed that the principle economic unit is the two-parent family, *one* of whom is the primary wage earner, with the other a dependent. It is this assumption that feminist theory must challenge. Feminist proposals must recognize that all adults should have responsibility for the support of themselves and their children, regardless of their individual living situation, and that all are entitled to policies that will facilitate carrying out this responsibility regardless of sex, marital, or parental status. Acceptance of this idea would require an entire reconceptualization of women's role in the labor force, of what is a family and of what our social obligations to it are.

The current attitude toward the employment of women can best be characterized as supporting "equal employment opportunity." Though much improved over earlier views, this one asserts that women who are like men should be treated equally with men. It accepts as standard the traditional male lifestyle, and that standard in turn assumes that one's primary responsibility should and can be one's job, because one has a spouse (or spouse surrogate) whose primary responsibility is the maintenance of house and family obligations. Women whose personal lifestyle and resources permit them to fit these assumptions, could, in the absence of sex discrimination, succeed equally with men.

Most women cannot, however, because our traditional conception of the family, and women's role within the family, make this impossible. Despite the fact that only twenty percent of all adults live in units composed of children plus two adults, only one of whom is income producing, our entire social and economic organization assumes that this is the norm. Consequently, couples who share family responsibilities, or singles who take them all on, pay a price for deviancy.

The fact that a majority of the population is paying this price has brought about some reforms, but a total reorganization is necessary.

This reorganization must be one which abolishes institutionalized sex-role differences, and the concept of adult dependency. It needs to recognize the individual as the principle economic unit, regardless of what combinations individuals choose to live in, and to provide the necessary services for individuals to support themselves and their children. In pursuit of these goals, programs and policies need to make participation by everyone in the labor force to the full extent of their abilities both a right and an obligation. They should also encourage and facilitate the equal assumption of family responsibilities without regard to sex, as well as develop ways to reduce conflict between the conduct of one's professional and private lives.

Unfortunately, there does not exist in either the government or the women's movement any means to translate these ideas into specific policies, coordinate their passage, or oversee their results. With few exceptions, policy development is generally a patchwork of individual ideas, group preferences, and chance events. It is rare that one sees an attempt at long-range strategy by any interest group or institution; the few groups that do develop such strategies rarely have the resources to carry them out. This means that those policies on women most likely to appear in the future are those that build on the precedents of the past, and not all these precedents are ones likely to transform sex roles or change the traditional division of labor.

Given that antidiscrimination as a focal point will only take the movement so far, the reactive nature of policy formation, the lack of coordination among feminist groups, and the general anti-intellectualism of American society, the likelihood is all too great that we will enter another blind alley like that of "protective labor legislation." As should be clear from its history, protecting women from some of the working conditions that men faced seemed like a good idea to most at the time, but in the long run only served to hinder women's progress. Not only did such policies encourage sex segregation of jobs, but they also discouraged even those employers who might have been willing, or pressured, to put women in the occasionally more strenuous but always better paying jobs.

While the outlines of the next blind alley can already be seen, few people are pointing it out. This blind alley is one which sees the married couple as the basic economic unit. It starts from the assumption that it is socially desirable for one class of adults to be economically dependent on another, and seeks to reform some of the difficulties and uncertainties that dependency might create. The classes I am referring to are those of "breadwinners" and "dependent spouses." While in theory members of either sex can be members of either class—or even change classes occasionally—in practice the sex of each class is largely predetermined, as is the fact that few men will opt to be dependent spouses if they can avoid it. Since the high divorce rate and the greater longevity of women make it very likely that those who choose to be "dependent spouses" will not always be spouses, policies are emerging to facilitate a transition. Such a transition is necessary, but transitional programs should be ones which eventually eliminate the need, i.e., eliminate the class of "dependent spouses." They should not be programs which permanently transfer dependency from "breadwinners" to society in general, nor should they encourage dependency for a major portion of one's life by extolling its benefits and minimizing its costs. Instead, transitional policies should educate women to the reality that they are ultimately responsible for their own economic well-being, and are entitled to the opportunities to achieve it.

Needless to say, the consequences of revising our policies to focus on the individual rather than the family as the basic economic unit, deliberately eradicate the sexual division of labor in both the family and the work force, establish equal participation in the labor force as a right as well as an obligation, and institutionalize the support services necessary to achieve the above, would not be felt only by women. Such policy changes would reverberate throughout our economic and social structure. Thus, one should not anticipate their achievement in the near future. But one will not be able to anticipate their achievement at all until the ideas are raised and the need for change understood. To do this the women's movement needs to return to its origins and begin the process of questioning and consciousness raising over again.

NOTES

1. *United States* v. *Yazell* 382 U.S. 341 (1966) J. Black dissenting.

2. *McGuire* v. *McGuire* 157 Neb. 226, 59 N.W. 2d 336 (1953).

3. Citizen's Advisory Council on the Status of Women, *The Equal Rights Amendment and Alimony and Child Support Laws* (Washington, D.C.: U.S. Government Printing Office, 1972), cites cases and statistics indicating that alimony is rarely given (in less than 2 percent of the cases) and then usually only for a few years. Child support is similarly honored more in the breach than in the action. According to one study, 62 percent of those fathers ordered to pay child support are out of compliance within a year, and 42 percent never make any payments. Stuart Nagel and Lenore Weitzman, "Women as Litigants," *Hastings Law Journal 23* (1971): 190.

4. A good discussion of this is to be found in Lenore J. Weitzman, "Legal Regulation of Marriage: Tradition and Change," *California Law Review 62* (July-September 1974): 1259-63. The relevant cases include *Miller* v. *Miller* 132 Misc. 121, 228 N.Y.S. 657 (Sup. Ct. 1928); *Graham* v. *Graham* 33 F.Supp. 936 (E.D. Mich 1940); *Vock* v. *Vock*, 365 Ill. 432, 6 N.E. 2d. 843 (1937); *Norris* v. *Norris*, 174 N.W. 2d 368 (Iowa Sup. Ct. 1970); *Garlock* v. *Garlock*, 279 N.Y. 337, 18 N.E. 2d

521, 522 (1939); *Mathews* v. *Mathews*, 2 N.C., App. 143, 162 S.E. 2d 697, 698 (1968).

5. Edward Mansfield, *The Legal Rights, Liabilities and Duties of Women* (Salem, Mass: Jewett and Co., 1845), p. 273.

6. Leo Kanowitz, *Women and the Law: The Unfinished Revolution* (Albuquerque: University of New Mexico Press, 1969), p. 40.

7. Women's Bureau, U.S. Dept. of Labor, *Handbook on Women Workers* (Washington, D.C.: U.S. Government Printing Office, 1975), ch. 9.

8. Jo Freeman, "The Legal Basis of the Sexual Caste System," *Valparaiso Law Review 5* (Spring 1971): 211-12.

9. *Bradwell* v. *Illinois*, 83 U.S. (16 Wall.) 130, 141-142 (1872) (J. Bradley, concurring). See also *Ex Parte Lockwood*, 154 U.S. 116 (1893).

10. Blanche Crozier, "Constitutionality of Discrimination Based on Sex," *Buffalo University Law Review 15* (1935): 723.

11. *Muller* v. *Oregon*, 208 U.S. 422 (1908).

12. *Commonwealth* v. *Welosky*, 276 Mass. 398, 414, 177 N.E. 656, 664, (1931), *cert. denied*, 284 U.S. 684 (1932).

13. *Quong Wing* v. *Kirkendall* 223 U.S. 59, 63 (1912); *People* v. *Case*, 153 Mich. 98, 101, 116 N.W. 558, 560 (1908); *State* v. *Hunter*, 208 Ore. 282, 288, 300 P. 2d 455, 458 (1956).

14. *Alldred* v. *Heaton*, 336 S.W. 2d 251 (Tex. Civ. App.), *cert denied*, 364 U.S. 517 (1960); *Heaton* v. *Bristol*, 317 S.W. 2d 86 (Tex. Civ. App.), *cert. denied*, 356 U.S. 230 (1958).

15. *Hoyt* v. *Florida*, 368 U.S. 57 (1961).

16. 42 *U.S.C.* 2000e.

17. *Weeks* v. *Southern Bell Tel.*, 408 F. 2d 288, 236 (5th Cir. 1969).

18. For a thorough documentation of this event, see Carolina Bird, *Born Female: The High Cost of Keeping Women Down* (New York: David McKay, 1968), ch. 1. For a blow-by-blow account of the floor happenings, see *Congressional Record*, House, February 8, 1964.

19. For an analysis of his three major categories of public policy—distributive, regulatory, and redistributive—see Theodore J. Lowi, "Distribution, Regulation, Redistribution: The Functions of Government," in *Public Policies and Their Politics*, ed. Randall B. Ripley (New York: W. W. Norton, 1966), pp. 27-40.

20. Edward Gross, "Plus Ça Change . . . ? The Sexual Structure of Occupations Over Time," *Social Problems 16* (1968): 198-208; Francine D. Blau, "Women in the Labor Force: An Overview," in *Women: A Feminist Perspective*, ed. Jo Freeman (Palo Alto, Calif.: Mayfield, 1975), pp. 211-26.

21. Jo Freeman, *The Politics of Women's Liberation* (New York: David McKay, 1975), pp. 193-94.

22. Bessie Margolin, "Equal Pay and Equal Employment Opportunities for Women," *New York University Conference of Labor 19* (1967): 297; see also

Morag MacLeod Simchak, "Equal Pay in the United States," *International Labour Review 103*, 6 (June 1971).

23. Elizabeth Baker, *Technology and Women's Work* (New York: Columbia University Press, 1964), p. 412.

24. Alice Henry, *Women and the Labor Movement* (New York: George H. Doran, 1923), p. 129; Edith Abbott, *Women in Industry* (New York: D. Appelton, 1910).

25. Gail Falk, "Sex Discrimination in Trade Unions," in *Women: A Feminist Perspective*, ed. Jo Freeman (Palo Alto, Calif.: Mayfield, 1979), pp. 254-76.

26. Caruthers Gholson Berger, "Equal Pay, Equal Employment Opportunity and Equal Enforcement of the Law for Women," *Valparaiso Law Review 5* (Spring 1971): 331.

27. The principle of equal job opportunity was first passed by Congress in the Unemployment Relief Act of 1933, (48 *Stat.* 22). It provided "that in employing citizens for the purpose of this Act no discrimination shall be made on account of race, color, or creed."

28. See Freeman, *The Politics of Women's Liberation*, pp. 177-84. Prior to 1972, the EEOC could only investigate and conciliate complaints. Afterwards, it had the option of taking recalcitrant violators to court.

29. For an example of this thinking, see U.S. Commission on Civil Rights, *Jobs and Civil Rights*, by Richard P. Nathan, Clearinghouse Publication No. 16 (Washington, D.C.: U.S. Government Printing Office, April 1969), pp. 50-55.

30. Herman Edelsberg, at the New York University 18th Conference on Labor, cited in *Labor Relations Reporter 61* (25 August 1966): 253-55.

31. Freeman, *The Politics of Women's Liberation*, pp. 54-55.

32. Sec 703(e) of Title VII reads: "it shall not be an unlawful employment practice for an employer to hire . . . on the basis of his religion, sex or national origin in those certain instances where religion, sex or national origin is a bona fide occupational qualification reasonably necessary to the normal operation of that particular business." The EEOC has interpreted this exemption narrowly.

33. *Pittsburgh Press Co.* v. *Pittsburgh Commission on Human Relations*, 93 S.Ct. 515 (1973).

34. Susan Deller Ross, "Sex Discrimination and Protective Labor Legislation," in *The Equal Rights Amendment*, Hearings before the subcommittee on Constitutional Amendments of the committee on the Judiciary, U.S. Senate, pp. 5-7 May 1970, p. 408.

35. Equal Employment Opportunity Commission, *Laws on Sex Discrimination in Employment* (Washington, D.C.: U.S. Government Printing Office, 1970), p. 10.

36. Commission guidelines of 19 August 1969.

37. 96 *Cong. Rec.* 872-3 (1950); 99 *Cong. Rec.* 8954-5 (1953).

38. Freeman, *The Politics of Women's Liberation*, pp. 209-13.

39. Ibid., pp. 213-18.

40. Most abortions were legalized by a Supreme Court decision in January 1973 that laws restricting abortions in the first trimester and most in the second trimester were an unconstitutional violation of the right to privacy. *Roe* v. *Wade*, 410 U.S. 113, *Doe* v. *Bolton*, 410 U.S. 179.

41. Aage R. Clausen, *How Congressmen Decide: A Policy Focus* (New York: St. Martin's Press, 1973), p. 221.

42. Ralph K. Huitt, "Congress, the Durable Partner," in *Lawmakers in a Changing World*, ed. Elke Frank (Englewood Cliffs, N.J.: Prentice-Hall, 1966), p. 19; Douglass Cater, *Power in Washington* (New York: Random House, 1954), p. 22; Ernest S. Griffith, *The Impasse of Democracy* (New York: Harrison-Hilton Books, 1939), p. 182.

43. Joyce Gelb and Marian Lief Palley, "Women and Interest Group Politics: A Case Study of the Equal Credit Opportunity Act," *American Politics Quarterly 5* (July 1977): 331-52.

44. National Commission on Consumer Finance, *Consumer Credit in the United States* (Washington, D.C.: U.S. Government Printing Office, 1972), pp. 498-99.

45. Gelb and Palley, "Equal Credit Act," p. 336.

46. Martin Binkin and Shirley J. Bach, *Women and the Military* (Washington, D.C.: The Brookings Institution, 1977), ch. 2.

47. Nadean Bishop, "Abortion: The Controversial Choice," in *Women: A Feminist Perspective*, ed. Jo Freeman (Palo Alto, Calif.: Mayfield, 1979), pp. 64-80.

48. Ibid.

THE CONTINUING PROCESS OF RETHINKING
GENDER IDENTITY

Susan Riemer Sacks

How does a human being know that it is a girl or a boy? How does the child develop a sense of being either female or male? How does the child learn what it means to be a girl or a boy? How does one learn that she or he is related to other same-gender persons? What is feminine or masculine? What does that mean? What is femininity or masculinity? What do they mean? How is a child socialized to behave "in accordance" with being a girl or boy? Feminine or masculine? Finally, why do human beings make the dichotomy girl/boy, woman/man, feminine/masculine?

These questions govern our thinking about the topic of human development of gender identity and identification with others of one's gender. To make the discussion cogent, we need to share a common terminology for this paper. Social scientists have tended to use "sex" and "gender" interchangeably or to distinguish them as biological vs cultural labels. Use of "gender" terminology makes us pause to think about the implications of being labelled from birth as "girls" or "boys." The major theoretical formulations regarding gender development will then be examined, and finally influences of biological, psychological, and cultural factors will be considered.

THE TERMINOLOGY

Sex has been used in the research literature to designate the biological status of a person as being female or male. The term is used here to refer only to reproductive and love-making activities.[17]

Gender is the cultural and social classification of a person as possessing feminine or masculine qualities. Like sex, gender has been studied as a dichotomous split, either feminine or masculine. Gender includes the following components: *Gender attribution* is the process by which one classifies another as female or male. *Gender assignment* is a special case of gender attribution; it takes place at birth and is the designation by doctor, midwife, or parents as "baby girl" or "baby boy." Gender assignment is usually based on the inspection of external genitalia, "the prime insignia."[37] Once the assignment of gender has been pronounced, attribution of gender by others to the infant and the implicit attitudes involved in this attribution remain overall gender consonant.

Even in the case of children born with ambiguous genitalia, once assigned, the child almost always develops an unambiguous gender identity as girl or boy. Thus, while genitalia are an important aspect of gender, they are not, in and of themselves, sufficient as a total explanation of gender attribution.

Core gender identity is the sense of "I am female," or "I am male." One's core identity is *self attribution* of gender, the feeling that one is a girl or a boy. It is not dependent on how others identify the person, but is one's own biological self-designation. How is one's core gender identity ascertained? We ask: "Are you a girl *or* a boy?" The nature of response to such a question is partially determined in the formulation of the either/or question.

Gender role identity is the sense of "I am feminine," or "I am masculine." One's gender role identity is the self-designation of psychological femaleness or maleness, the degree to which one incorporates the activities and behaviors seen as "appropriate" for her/his gender according to societal standards.

Gender role behavior is the set of expectations about "appropriate" behaviors for persons of one gender or another. A person is "born into" the female or male category and is expected subsequently to perform the female or male role and to behave in accordance with the prescriptions and proscriptions of that gender. Persons are often defined by their gender role behaviors. A stereotype is a set of beliefs about the characteristics of the occupants of a role.[17]

To understand the relationship between assignment (girl/boy), identity (feeling like a female or male), and role (behaving like a female or a male), we first attribute gender. Kessler and McKenna[4] argue that dichotomous gender attribution is a social construction, a means for ordering perceived reality. We divide the world into two categories, female and male, and that dichotomy controls decisions about one's gender assignment, identity, and role. The compelling significance of genital attribution equaling gender attribution leads to identity and role and is critical for human development in a society which essentially devalues the feminine and values the masculine. A challenge to the two-gender structure, traditionally grounded in biology and considered invariant, centers on understanding that gender is a construction of the culture and that gender identity is continually evolving throughout one's life span.[29]

Rethinking the meaning of dichotomy is crucial to conceptualizing gender identity as a process. The concept of life and death, the ultimate dichotomy, is being challenged legally and morally today. When is someone really dead? When the heart stops? When the brain stops? When the monitor ceases? Conceptualizing a living-dying continuum opens the possibility in our thinking for the existence of a gender continuum.

Let us keep this in mind as we examine the major theories for development of gender identity.

TRADITIONAL THEORETICAL EXPLANATIONS FOR GENDER DEVELOPMENT

The three major formulations—the psychoanalytic, social learning, and, cognitive theories—share the assumption that there are two discrete genders, female and male, and that they are natural and proper. Furthermore, there are two dichotomous gender roles, feminine and masculine, which are the expression of the two genders.

Psychoanalytic Theory

Expounded first by Freud[13] and continued by his disciples, this approach espouses a biological deterministic interpretation of gender development. In brief, the child's gender identity is dependent on the evolution of a specifically sexual consciousness of self as female or male. In this theory sexuality is the core meaning of both biological and cultural gender. Person notes that gender orders sexuality and then at least for men genital sexuality becomes the mainstay of masculine gender; women's gender identity can be maintained in other ways.[29]

Identification was central to Freud's theory of development. The child between three and five, becomes 1) aware of her/his genitals and 2) makes a self attribution of gender: "I have a penis, I am a boy" or "I do not have a penis, I am a girl." With this recognition begins 3) the Oedipal fantasy involving genitals and the parents. The child 4) identifies with the same-gender parent, internalizes the attitudes and role behaviors of that parent, and hopes to "win" the opposite gender parent. Eventually the child achieves 5) the "appropriate" gender role.

Genital identity was equated with gender identity. Contemporary researchers in the psychoanalytic tradition have incorporated socio-cultural influences. Stoller and others have found that pregenital identification for girls and boys with the mother is central to gender identity.[38] Gender role development evolves from parent-child interactions and the fostering of "appropriate" behaviors, especially independence and assertiveness, and from the replication and reproduction of roles and functions.[10,29] In this theory, gender identity is attained by the resolution of libidinal motivations, and the intrapsychic *integration* of the symbols and attitudes of one's gender assignment. This guarantees cohesive gender identity.

Social Learning Theory

Expounded by Mischel and Bandura,[24] gender identity is developed through a learning process based on reinforcement and imitation. The sequence involves: 1) the awareness by parents, and others in the child's environment, of the child's gender assignment. The child then 2) imitates or identifies with the actions, attitudes, and responses of the same-gender parent and later with same-gender peers. Through direct or indirect reinforcement, verbal or non-verbal, the child 3) learns to discriminate gender-type behaviors, and to generalize them to other situations. Once learned, the child performs gender-type behaviors.

Gender identity develops through rewards which follow "appropriate" behavior: "I want rewards, I am rewarded for doing girl(boy) things, therefore, I want to be a girl(boy)."[18] There is some disagreement in the data over whether or not parents reward girls and boys differentially. This will be discussed later. For the social learning approach, gender role development is fostered by imitation and modelling, and the content of the reinforcement, either positive or negative, is more significant than the gender of the model. Gender identity proceeds from external environmental forces as the child learns to behave as others behave, and as she or he is reinforced for the behaviors.

Cognitive Learning Theory

First presented by Kohlberg, the cognitive-learning theory explains the development of gender identity by incorporating principles from Piaget's work: that the child plays an active role organizing the world in accordance with the child's level of cognitive functioning, and the child's understandings are qualitatively different from the adults'. The acquisition of gender identity assumes this sequence: "I am a girl(boy), therefore I want to do girl(boy) things, therefore the opportunity to do girl(boy) things (and to gain approval for doing them) is rewarding."[18]

Kohlberg[18] and others[21] have generated considerable evidence to support the cognitive-learning theory. Sometime between eighteen months and two and one-half years, the child can identify its own picture when included in a group of pictures of other children. By three years, about eighty-eight percent of children label themselves correctly as "a girl" or "a boy." The child is using "girl" as she might use her name "Laurie" or any other label. According to cognitive theory, the three-year-old child has learned the label for a "correct" gender identity, but she or he cannot yet classify her/himself with others of the same gender, nor does the child know what being a girl or boy means.

Between three and five, children are actively organizing their world and their way of classifying things in it. By four, children tend to assign gender labels to dolls based on length of hair or clothing, not by genitalia. One four year old, when asked by his mother whether the new baby he had visited next door was a boy or a girl, replied, "I couldn't tell, it wasn't dressed."

During the period of conceptual growth from four to seven, the child develops an awareness of genital differences along with the concept of self-anatomical constancy. This development is a gradual process of the child's active interaction with its environment. The child must understand the principle of conservation (from Piaget,[5] for example, that equal amounts of water in different size containers are still equal), in order to comprehend that her vagina or his penis is a permanent part of the body. Usually by six years of age, the child conceptualizes gender as anatomy, fixed and irreversible; it is then that gender identity is achieved. This means that the child knows her or his identity and understands that she or he will always be a girl or boy. Until then the child bases its self-gender category on the gender-type attributes in its repertoire—hair length, clothes, toys—and believes that by changing clothes one can change gender.

Briefly stated, cognitive learning theory suggests that between two and three years children learn gender self-labelling. During the next two years they learn to generalize the labels to each other. Self attribution of gender does not indicate constancy of gender identity, according to Kohlberg.[18] Constancy of gender identity can only be attained when the child has achieved the cognitive developmental stage of conservation; when the child is certain of the "principle of invariance" of physical objects.

Once the child knows its gender identity, the child has the capacity to classify others as being of the same gender. At this point, connotations of gender roles become incorporated in the child's thinking. Kohlberg suggests that the masculine role becomes valued for its power, aggression, and strength, and the feminine role for "niceness" and attractiveness. The characteristics attributed to the masculine role have been assessed as socially prized qualities; those of the feminine role as not prized or culturally valued qualities.[7]

Young children, even at five, seek reinforcements dependent on gender-typed values. Boys show consistent same-gender preferences over a range of toys and activities; girls tend to vary, in fact often preferring other-gender toys and activities. Perhaps the inconsistency of girls' choices coincides with awareness of the valuing of, and the inherent interest derived from, "boys' toys" and games. The point here is that once gender role is established the child tends to identify with the same gender parent and to behave accordingly.

Cognitive learning theory explains learning of gender identity and gender role as part of the rational learning process of childhood. The child is intrinsically motivated and actively seeks to acquire "appropriate" gender role behaviors to help organize and understand the world.

The table below summarizes, in the terminology of this chapter, the steps in gender development according to the three theories discussed. It is important to observe in each theory that the steps in the acquisition of gender differ and the process for acquisition is different.

Table I

THREE THEORIES OF GENDER DEVELOPMENT

Psychoanalytic	*Social-Learning*	*Cognitive-Developmental*
1. genital awareness = gender identity (fantasy process)	1. others' awareness of genitals (reinforcement process)	1. others' awareness of genitals (labeling process)
2. identification with same gender parent	2. identification with same gender parent	2. gender identity
3. gender role identity	3. gender role identity	3. gender role identity
	4. gender identity	4. identification with same gender parent

Other Theories

Others have proposed variations of the theories of gender identity. The process of gender identity and gender role development is so complex that no one mechanism—identification, imitation, reinforcement, or cognitive learning—fully explains the acquisition of gender. There seems to be fairly general agreement that core gender identity (I am female; I am a male) is established in childhood, but the aspects of gender role identity (I am feminine, I am masculine) need not be "fixed" and may continue to evolve throughout adulthood.

The child's knowing that she is a girl or he is a boy at three does not demonstrate that the child knows what it will *mean* to be a woman or a man. In their theoretical formulation Kessler and McKenna[17] suggest that when the child understands that transformations do not change the object's physical characteristics, the child begins to share the adult rules for gender construction. By six or seven, when the child knows that gender is an invariant characteristic of her/himself, gender identity is established. They argue that the social construction of gender itself, like skin color one of the few human characteristics invariant from birth, must be reexamined in the context of dichotomizing reality into two genders.

Evidence indicates that at three, children's preference for gender-type toys and activities is not dichotomized.[21] By six, children tend to express gender-type preferences consistently. Toys and activities take on gender fixed and dichotomized categories. At four and a half my son told me, "You can't be a doctor; mommies are nurses." For him, this was a statement of immutable fact. By eleven or twelve, children differentiate between anatomical attributes and role attributes. They understand that the former remain basically fixed, and that behaviors and feelings are components of the concept of gender role which are not invariable in the same way.

In studying attribution of gender, Kessler and McKenna[17] asked three groups of children—preschool, kindergarten, and third grade—to draw a picture of a girl and a boy. The children were shown the three groups of drawings one month later. Accuracy of gender attribution increased with age. The eight and nine year olds identified their own drawings and those of their own group with greater accuracy than did four or six year olds who examined their own depiction or those of their peers. The most interesting finding was that children in each age group attributed gender correctly for the drawings of their own peers. This seemed to indicate that the cues which operated for four year olds were shared by other preschoolers, but not necessarily by kindergartners or third graders. The same held within each of the other two groups.

When asked why a drawing was a girl or a boy, preschool and kindergarten children gave response such as "His hands" or "He's big" without characterizing the features. Sometimes they said, "It just is." Once the gender was attributed to the figure, the child was asked for a reason for the classification. The researchers concluded the child's reason displayed the factual status of gender, as the child constructed the facts. The child was not concerned with giving a "good reason," but simply related her or his reason. While "the hands" would not be a "good reason" to adults because it is not a dichotomous or generalizable feature for gender attribution, it was perfectly "logical" for the child. Children treated size and hair length as dichotomous identifiers just as adults use genitalia.

The use of children's drawings and their identification of their own figures provide evidence for their thinking. Goodnow, after decades of studying children's drawings, maintains that they represent "visual thinking."[15] Her analyses indicate that children's drawings are a form of problem-solving. Children are thinking when they draw a figure; though their reasons for gender attribution may not be the same as the cues they use, they are sharing their interpretation of their reality. It is not until the child has incorporated the concept of dichotomous gender invariance based on genitalia that the child and the adult use the *same* rules for constructing gender attribution.

The children's identification of their drawings tends to support the cognitive learning theory of gender development. However, their responses elucidate the learning of cultural valuing of attributes of gender. Eventually, children learn to give "good reasons" for identification by gender. Their interpretation of "fact" is modified to fit the cultural structure of a two gender world.

Kessler and McKenna suggest that we form a belief in two genders to begin with as much on the basis of behaviors as on biology.[17] The attribution of dichotomous behaviors is not necessarily the way women and men or even children behave. Yet we are no more gender-blind than we are color-blind. We still ask–"What'd you have?" and we continue to interpret behavior and make differential attributions regarding motivations based on gender even knowing that the genders behave in similar ways.

Gender attribution leads to "discovery" of biological, psychological, and social differences which will now be examined. Research on human similarities and differences contributes to the understanding of the development of gender role identification and behavior: How the child learns what it *means* to be a girl or a boy, feminine or masculine.

INFLUENCES ON GENDER DEVELOPMENT

Biological Influences

Are there characteristics which are genetically controlled and predispose a child to learn a particular behavior? Psychoendocrine research has provided some data to indicate that some behavioral or tempermental proclivities may be influenced by prenatal hormonal environment,[1] although most dispositions may be modified by social influences. The gender of assignment and rearing is rarely modified after three years, except in the case of transsexuals. (For a full discussion, see Kessler and McKenna[17] and Stoller.[38])

Biology determines anatomical differences between females and males. At conception the genetic gender of the fetus is established. The basic structure is female, X chromosomes. For a male fetus to develop a Y chromosome, androgens must be present; the androgen hormones influence the development of external and internal genitalia, as well as the central nervous system.

Money and Ehrhardt[26] studied twenty-five androgenized girls with a matched control group. During pregnancy in the 1950s the mothers of these girls were given progestine (which acted like androgen) to prevent miscarriages. Essentially, the hormones influenced the development of masculinized daughters, some infants with penises. The penises were removed surgically at birth; the internal reproductive organs were female; some additional hormonal treatment at puberty ensured development of secondary gender characteristics.

Money and Ehrhardt studied these girls to ascertain if prenatal androgens affected their behaviors.[26] They found that the girls who had been fetally androgenized displayed more tomboyish behaviors, though not physical aggression, than the control group. The group, as compared to the controls, preferred trucks to dolls, functional dress, and showed little interest in "mothering" younger children. The group chose careers over marriage, as contrasted with reverse interests for the controls. Money and Ehrhardt concluded that prenatal hormonal treatments influenced the brain and subsequent behaviors of the androginized group. Both female and male fetuses exposed to synthetic progestins tend to be "ultra-masculine" according to Money. Researchers at Rutgers[31] have found estrogens taken during pregnancy are associated with group dependency and a disposition for the child to be a "joiner."

Research in the area of biological influences continues. There is some indication, especially in the work of John Money and his colleagues, that hormonal differences may predispose certain neural pathways to receive certain "information."

This area of research combined with differences in performance on measures of aggression and visual-spatial tasks has led some scientists to conclude: "male superiority (with respect to mathematical ability) is probably an expression of both endogenous and exogenous variables."[4] Conclusive answers to questions of biological contributions to gender development remain for further investigation. Awareness and an understanding of the constancy of external genitalia are central to the gender identity process; evidence of hormonal influences on gender role development and behavior is still being gathered and its conclusiveness assessed.[39] The very idea that active behavior, tomboyishness, playing with trucks and so on is identified and referred to as masculine while nurturing is referred to as feminine suggests that the culture has constructed them as such.

Psychological Influences

A world dichotomized in two genders must be a world in which scientists can discover differences according to gender. The challenge is to differentiate those beliefs that create the social construction of gender and are based on reliable "evidence" and those which are based on the generalized stereotypes and yet become so deeply embedded as to be self-fulfilling prophecies.

Evidence indicates greater variability *within* gender than *between* genders.[22] More differences exist among girls and women and among boys and men than between girls as a group and boys as a group. Furthermore, developmentally girls and boys are more similar than they are different.

It is difficult to draw definitive conclusions from research on gender difference and its relationship to gender development. In the examination of studies of gender differences, researchers note that even repeated findings of gender differences do not indicate necessarily the *origin* of the difference.[21,27] In addition, as noted earlier in this chapter, the underlying assumptions inherent in scientists' questions, i.e., are you a girl or a boy?, controls the parameters of the response. In other instances, observers' judgments are influenced by their perception of the gender of the participants in a study. For example, college student observers viewed a video-tape of a nine-month-old child. For difference observers, the child was given a girl's name or a boy's name. When the observers believed the infant to be a boy, its strong reaction to a jack-in-the-box was labelled *anger*; when the observers believed the infant a girl, they assessed the reaction as *fear*.[21] It is almost impossible when reading research studies to measure the effects of the gender belief system of the observer. The study cited above should serve to indicate the power of judgments made "in the eyes of the beholder." These cautions regarding research on gender differences and the power of the two gender dichotomy must be kept in mind.

To summarize briefly, the child acquires a growing understanding of gender role expectations as she or he experiences increasingly broader contacts, from immediate family, relatives, teachers, peers, to adults in other environments (shop-keepers, bus drivers, medical people). The pattern of this development is:

1. Children first hold fairly stereotyped notions of gender roles.
2. Children view gender "inappropriate" behavior as wrong; they hold their peers in tow.
3. After about nine years of age, children follow "appropriate" behaviors by custom, not moral force; boys exercise fewer deviations, though girls may be tomboys.
4. As children develop cognitively, their ability to expand the categories of gender role behavior expands. Unfortunately, this expansion becomes ultimately limited by the limitations and attitudes of cultural beliefs.
5. Developing flexible conceptions of gender "appropriate" behavior may be particularly difficult for children in our society—unless there is continuous efforts by parents and teachers to encourage a balance for both girls and boys of self-assertiveness and a concern for, and relations with, others. Block suggests that integration in girls and boys of both agency, self-assertion, and communion, mutuality and interdependence, through active socialization process would broaden and enrich each child's human potential.[6]

Summary of results of differentiated behaviors along gender lines indicates that on the average:

1. Preschool children tend to prefer activities and toys that are gender-typed.
2. Preschool age children tend to choose same gender playmates even before three years of age.
3. Style of play differs: boys tend to exhibit more aggression than girls and their play is rougher.
4. Girls, at the age of about four, increasingly use rules of procedure, "taking turns," during playtime.
5. Boys, at the age of about four, become increasingly more gender-typed than girls and avoid as "sissy" those activities and toys labelled as such by peer mates.

(For detailed discussion, see Maccoby and Jacklin[22] and Maccoby[21].)

This summary identifies areas where research findings have indicated differences between girl and boy children. On the other hand, they do not indicate the origin or cause for the differences.

Parents' Role

Do parents treat children in such a way as to shape them toward gender "appropriate" behaviors? Are some behaviors rewarded and others sanctioned? Maccoby and Jacklin's review of socialization patterns in parental behavior indicated very few differences.[22] Nevertheless, stereotypes of gender influence adults' perceptions of newborn infants.[33] Thirty pairs of parents were interviewed during the first twenty-four hours postpartum. The infants did not differ in weight, length, or Apgar scores. Yet daughters were rated as pretty, little, and soft, while sons were rated as robust, strong, and large-featured compared to each other. Both mothers and fathers physically handle their own new infants similarly: being close, gentle, responsive.[28]

As the infant gets older, different styles of interacting do emerge; mothers tend to do more caretaking, diaper changing and feeding, while fathers do more playing, tossing, and wrestling. Block notes that boys are encouraged to achieve and compete, and to control feelings; girls are encouraged to be dependent and caring, and verbal about feelings.[6] These encouraged characteristics can have far-ranging implications for restricting the potential behaviors of both girls and boys. In contrast, adults of both genders who rate high in psychological androgyny accept gender "appropriate" and "not appropriate" roles without difficulty or self consciousness, and share, for example, child-caring tasks.[2,3]

As indicative of the dichotomous messages of child-rearing practices, most parents do feel that it is important for their children's clothes and toys to be gender identifiable by others. Further, parents do discourage, particularly sons, from activities considered "appropriate" for girls. On the Marlo Thomas album "Free to Be You and Me" there is a song entitled, "William Wants a Doll." Five-year-old William's desire for a doll "to hug and hold" is the epitome of taboo. He is called a "sissy" by his friend, a "jerk" by his cousin. His father buys the classics: a basketball and a baseball glove. Finally, the grandmother explains that William wants a doll so that he may learn the care that his child will need someday. As the song ends, William's grandma buys him a doll.

Parental anxiety regarding indications of homosexual tendencies in their sons, as perceived as demonstrated by home-making, dressing-up, and doll play, evoke powerful parental restrictions on young boys' play. Nevertheless, in preschool classes for two- and three-year-olds, all activities—dolls, trucks, cooking, and blocks—are engaged in by children regardless of gender when teachers foster play and promote the activities as components of the total learning process.[8,12,36] Maccoby and Jacklin conclude that "at least not many behaviors are strong enough to elicit clear differential reactions from caretakers" (p. 232).[22]

Do parents and teachers label the two gender roles differently? It appears that parents and teachers do perceive different "natural" characteristics for the two genders, i.e. "Just like a little boy." Aggression is seen as "natural" for boys and dependency as "natural" for girls. Nevertheless, adults believe it is important for both boys and girls to possess similar characteristics. Studying sixty-four prospective parents from three different birth delivery environments (home birth, maternity centers, hospital), Sacks and Donnenfeld found that over eighty-five percent of parents in each group valued as important for both sons and daughters:[35]

> to have good manners
> to be responsible
> to have good sense and judgment
> to have interests and talents and,
> to be able to make decisions.

Eiduson studied 200 parents about to have children, equally divided among unmarried couples, single mothers, living groups, and nuclear two-parent family structures.[11] The families in the study participated for three years, and Eiduson reported that:

> 1. Fathers do not participate in child caretaking as much as they had anticipated in the pre-birth data: in all groups fathers contribute the bulk of income.
> 2. Mothers still perform domestic and child caretaking, but fathers do help with former (laundry, shopping).
> 3. Mothers remained chief nurses, diaperers, groomers, and feeders. Fathers, when they were involved, were observed rough-housing, going for a walk; mothers taught, played, and cuddled.
> 4. Families with expressed gender-role egalitarian philosophies were no different from others with respect to toys, activities and dress for the children: all were essentially "unisex."
> 5. The child was a child, and any differences in socialization, eating, toileting, or discipline were not a function of the child's gender.
> 6. In general and regardless of gender, parents were openly affectionate with the children, encouraged independence, and fostered cooperation.
> 7. Finally, studying the data for gender differences among the 200 children revealed similar psychological, social, physical, and nutritional development for boys and girls from infancy to age three years.

In summary, even in families choosing alternative living structures, parental values and philosophies do not appear to influence child-rearing practices during the early childhood years. From this and other studies, the years three to six, rather than infancy, may be crucial for parents who wish to implement egalitarian gender role preferences in their child-rearing practices. It is during the period from three to six, when children's gender identity formulation is consolidating, that parents' and preschool teachers' flexibility with respect to gender role "appropriateness" could make a difference. Children encouraged to explore their fullest potentials would not be bound by gender "appropriate" behaviors, socially constructed on the basis of gender stereotypes.

Overall, Maccoby and Jacklin conclude that there is remarkable uniformity in the socialization of young children.[22] The picture may shift, as scientists gather more data on the role of parental influences in childrearing, especially fathers and siblings. At this point, it appears only that boy children have more intense experiences of socialization both from parents and from teachers. They tend to be restricted from gender "inappropriate" activities more frequently than girls, and receive more frequent interactions—punishment, praise, encouragement—from both parents and teachers. Boys evoke more concern regarding their behavior and performance, and whatever the explanation for this may be, the greater amount of socialization pressure which boys experience over girls must have consequences for the development of their gender identity and gender role behaviors.

Gender role sterotyping and the consequent internalization hurt both girls and boys. Girls learn to repress energy and curiosity and to conform to the "appropriate" roles as conveyed in family, school, books, mass media, and peer groups. Boys learn to fill the role "boys will be boys" or suffer the consequences of deviating from the expected, the norm. Making flexible the role-limiting characteristics would create freedom for children to grow.

This brief review of the psychological factors influencing gender role identity and behavior leads to suggested areas for further research:

1. Empirical research on the influence of same and other gender siblings and the gender composition in the family structure could elucidate our understanding of gender identity development.

2. Considerably more work is called for on the influence of fathers as co-parents and on gender role development. Are fathers more lenient with daughters? More demanding with sons? How similar or different are fathers compared to mothers as nurturers?

3. Will parents who choose alternative life styles translate their values to non-gender specific child-rearing practices? Will these children then differ with respect to gender identity and gender role identity from those "traditionally" reared?

4. More research is needed to ascertain why girls and boys between six and twelve years engage so frequently in same-gender activities. Is their gender identity so fragile during these years that it cannot withstand "testing" by mixing?

5. Life span and human development research should address questions of gender identity changes. As a person no longer needs to be identified as an

egg or sperm carrier for reproductive purposes, core gender identity may modify to incorporate other gender attributes. Chromosomes and carrier characteristics may be replaced by other identifying characteristics.

But, such research issues which seek differences on a two gender dichotomy make *difference* an irreducible concept. As Chodorow states, the focus on gender differences denies "those *processes* that create the meaning and significance of gender" (p. 67).[10] The fundamental research agenda must be a *re*examination of the construction of gender inherited by, and sustained in, our culture with a focus on understanding how gender differences are produced and, consequently, reproduce gender inequalities. We must shift our vantage point and reexamine the fundamental premise of the construction of a two gender world. In a non-gender organized culture, we have little evidence that biological or psychological gender differences would be identified as salient.

Other Influences

The position presented in this chapter is that neither individual gender identity formation nor gender role development occurs devoid of the social climate. The environment for gender formation, in fact the notions regarding gender itself, is the production and reproduction of the thinking of the society. When concepts of femininity and masculinity cease to be value weighted and the constraints of gender are eliminated, people will be free to be uniquely human, to develop their full capacities.[3] Then autonomy *and* attachment, agency *and* communion, can be integrated and individually expressed. Girls and boys beyond three years will *not* be forced to internalize differentially valued "appropriate" behaviors and thus not carry into adulthood conflicts about being assertive, competent girls and nurturant, help-seeking boys.[34] Children clearly become aware of being girls or boys gradually. Their early play involves switching back and forth in gender identity and role. Sometimes they play "mommies," sometimes "fire chief." When gender role behaviors are not narrowly sanctioned, formation of gender identity is not confounded by limitations on "appropriateness" of roles.

A broad construction of humanness contributes dignity to differences. If a man person chooses to become a nurse, he is no less a male; if a woman person chooses to become a surgeon, she is no less a female. Possessing the competencies and interests to select a career in deviation from the expected gender role occupation need not conflict with one's gender identity. The point is that gender identity is elastic with respect to the components of one's being which it encompasses. Since nursing and medicine in this country have been so traditionally gender restricted, choosing a perceived "across-gender" occupation tests one's sense of gender identity. One's gender identity as female or male person may be expanded, made more complex, but the person makes the choice *within* her/his concept of female or male identity. "That the children might be most nobly born, and reared in an environment calculated to allow the richest, freest growth, they had deliberately remodeled and improved the whole state" (p. 102)[14].

The question "What'd you have?" presents the cultural dichotomy: If it is a girl, then . . . ; If it is a boy, then . . . . It helps the questioner call upon her or his repertoire of "appropriate" reactions and responses. It governs which behavior the adult will elicit. Over all, parents and adults *tend* to treat girl and boy infants and children simply as children, but they also tend to permeate their environments with gender related symbols of dress, toys, reinforced activities, verbal and non-verbal interactions, and handling. In some subtle and sometimes not easily measureable ways, adults envision and value a two gender social order.

If gender is understood as a social construction and the dichotomous view of gender is questioned, adults can question the narrow, limiting and constrictive concepts of gender role which are the product of dichotomized thinking. A non-gender world would eliminate the caution from mothers to daughters by Rich:

"You can be anything you really want to be"—*if* you are prepared to fight, to create priorities for yourself against the grain of cultural expectations, to persist in the face of misogynist hostility. Interpreting to a little girl, or to an adolescent woman, the kinds of treatment she encounters because she is female, is as necessary as explaining to a nonwhite child reactions based on the color of her skin" (p. 248)[32].

NOTE

Another version of this article appeared as chapter 1 of Janet Muff, ed., *Socialization, Sexism, and Stereotyping: Women's Issues in Nursing,* St. Louis: C.B. Mosby Co., 1982

REFERENCES

1. Baker, S.W. 1980 Biological influences on human sex and gender, SIGNS, Journal of Women in Culture and Society, vol. 6, (1): 80.
2. Bem, S.L. 1975 Sex-role adaptability: One consequence of psychological androgyny, Journal of Personality and Social Psychology, 31: 634.
3. Bem, S.L. 1976 Probing the promise of androgyny. In Kaplan, S.G., and Bean, J.F. (editors), Beyond sex-role stereotypes: Readings toward a psychology of androgyny, Boston: Little, Brown and Company.
4. Benbow, C.P. and Stanley, J.C. 1980 Sex differences in mathematical ablity: Fact or artifact? Science, 210: 1262.
5. Biehler, R.F. 1981 Child development: An introduction (ed. 2), Boston: Houghton Mifflin Co.

6. Block, J.H. 1973 Conceptions of sex role: Some cross-cultural and longitudinal perspectives, American Psychologist, vol 28, (6): 512.

7. Broverman, I., Broverman, D., Clarkson, F., Rosenkrantz, P., and Vogel, S. 1972 Sex role stereotypes: A current appraisal, Journal of Social Issues, 28: 59.

8. Carmichael, C. 1977 Non-sexist childraising, Boston, Beacon Press.

9. Chodordow, N. 1978 The reproduction of mothering: Psychoanalysis and the sociology of gender, Berkeley, Cal.: University of Calfornia Press.

10. Chodorow, N. 1979 Feminism and difference in psychoanalytic perspective, Socialist Review, vol 9: 66, July-Aug.

11. Eiduson, B. T. 1980 Changing sex roles of parents and children. *In* The child in his family: Preventive child psychiatry in an age of transition, E. J. Anthony and C. Chiland, eds., New York: John Wiley & Sons.

12. Frazier, N., & Sadker, M. 1973 Sexism in school and society, New York: Harper and Row.

13. Freud, S. 1952 A general introduction to psychoanalysis, New York: Washington Square Press, Inc.

14. Gilman, C.P. 1979 Herland, London, England, The Woman's Press Ltd.

15. Goodnow, J. 1977 Children drawing, Cambridge, Ma.: Harvard University Press.

16. Hyde, J.S., & Rosenberg, B.G. 1980 Half the human experience: The psychology of women, second edition, Lexington, Ma.: D.C. Health and Co.

17. Kessler, S.J., & McKenna, W. 1978 Gender: An ethnomethodological approach, New York: John Wiley & Sons, Inc.

18. Kohlberg, L. 1966 A cognitive-developmental analysis of children's sex-role concepts and attitudes. *In* The development of sex differences, Maccoby, E. ed., Stanford, Stanford University Press.

19. Lynn, D.B. 1969 Parental and sex role identification: A theoretical formulation, Berkeley, Cal., McCutchan Publishing Corp.

20. Lynn, D.B. 1974 The father: His role in child development, Monterey, Cal., Brooks/Cole Publishing Company.

21. Maccoby, E.E. 1980 Social development: Psychological growth and the parent-child relationship, New York, Harcourt Brace Jovanovich, Inc.

22. Maccoby E.E. & Jacklin, C.N. 1974 The psychology of sex differences, vol 1, Stanford, Cal., Stanford University Press.

23. Miller, J.B. (editor) 1973 Psychoanalysis and women, Baltimore, Penguin Books Inc.

24. Mischel, W. 1966 A social-learning view of sex differences in behavior, *In* The development of sex differences, Maccoby, E., ed., Stanford: Stanford University Press.

25. Money, J., & Ehrhardt, A.A. 1968 Prenatal hormonal exposure: Possible effects on behavior in man. *In* Endocrinology and human behaviour, Michael, R. P., ed., Oxford: Oxford University Press.

26. Money, J., & Ehrhardt, A. 1972 Man and woman/Boy and girl. Baltimore: Johns Hopkins University Press.

27. O'Leary, V.E. 1977 Toward understanding women, Belmont, Cal.: Wadsworth Publishing Co., Inc.

28. Parke, R.D., & Sawin, D.B. 1976 The father's role in infancy: A reevaluation, The Family Coordinator, 25:365.

29. Person, E.S. 1980 Sexuality as the mainstay of identity: Psychoanalytic perspectives, SIGNS, Journal of Women in Culture and Society, vol 5, (4): 605.

30. Pleck, J.H. 1975 Masculinity-femininity: Current and alternative paradigms, Sex Roles, 1:161.

31. Restak, R.M. 1979 Birth defects and behavior: A new study suggests a link, The New York Times, Jan. 21, IV:9.

32. Rich, A. 1976 Of woman born, New York: W. W. Norton & Co.

33. Rubin, J.Z., Provenzano, F.J., & Luria, A. 1974 The eye of the beholder: Parents' views on sex of newborns, American Journal of Orthopsychiatry, vol 44, (4): 512.

34. Sacks, S.R., & Eisenstein, H. 1979 Feminism and psychological autonomy: A study in decision making, Personnel and Guidance Journal, 57: 419, April.

35. Sacks, S.R., & Donnenfeld, P. 1984. Parental choice of alternative birth environments and attitude toward child-rearing philosophy. Journal of Marriage and the Family 46(2): 469-475.

36. Stacey, J., Béreaud, S., & Daniels, J. (editors) 1974 And Jill came tumbling after: Sexism in American education, New York: Dell Publishing Co., Inc.

37. Stoller, R.J. 1974 Facts and fancies: An examination of Freud's concept of bisexuality (1973). *In* Women and analysis, Strouse, T., ed., New York: Grossman Publishers.

38. Stoller, R.J. 1975 Sex and gender, vol II, New York: J. Aronson.

39. Wittig, M.A. 1976 Sex differences in intellectual functioning: How much of a difference do genes make? Sex Roles, 2(1): 63.

A FEMINIST PERSPECTIVE IN LAW AND PRACTICE:
THE WOMEN'S EDUCATIONAL EQUITY ACT

Mary Ann Millsap and Leslie R. Wolfe

Until the early 1970s, it was perfectly legal to deny women admission to any school or college, to prohibit their enrollment in any program, and to pay men larger salaries than women for the same jobs in education. In all levels of education—for students and for faculty—sex discrimination was rampant. Although education always has been viewed as the gateway to upward mobility and as a major profession for women, it was systematically and legally restricting their options.

The passage of Title IX, amendments to both Title IV and Title VII of the Civil Rights Act, and extended coverage in the Fair Labor Standards Act changed all that—at least in federal statute. Enactment of these laws was largely the result of efforts by Representative Edith Green (D.,OR), a respected leader in the House of Representatives and chair of an education subcommittee, who introduced sweeping legislative changes in 1970 and saw the last of them enacted in 1972, before she retired.

These landmark laws defined and prohibited sex discrimination and thus provided the legal means to fight it in education. As with all civil rights legislation, these statutes required compliance by educational institutions and provided for enforcement by the federal government. Although the responsibility for compliance lies with educational institutions, the Congress has long accepted a Federal role in providing technical assistance to institutions. Through the activities funded under Title IV of the Civil Rights Act of 1964, for example, such technical assistance on race desegregation has been offered to school districts throughout the country for several years.

Although the civil rights laws prevented schools and classrooms from closing their doors to women and girls, they could not provide funds for the counseling services needed to encourage women to enter fields of study long denied them. Nor were funds available to develop curricula to change existing classroom texts that showed girls in limited roles or claimed, "You can't do this; you're a girl." Funds were also not available to inform people about the meaning and purpose of these civil rights laws for women; nor were funds provided to help schools to implement them. Thus, when Title IX was enacted, the Congress expanded the federal technical assistance role (under Title IV) to include sex desegregation. Then, two years after Title IX was passed, Congress decided that the federal government had a greater responsibility to help institutions both to comply with Title IX and to go beyond mere compliance to attack sexism in education. In 1974, therefore, Congress passed the Women's Educational Equity Act.

An analysis of how this law was passed and later reauthorized by Congress and then administered by the U.S. Office (Department) of Education shows how efforts undertaken by women inside and outside the halls of Congress and the Administration succeeded in putting a feminist perspective into law and practice.

THE PASSAGE OF THE WOMEN'S EDUCATIONAL EQUITY ACT[1]

In 1971, the Women's Educational Equity Act (WEEA) was a gleam in Arlene Horowitz' eye. Horowitz, a college graduate working in a clerical role in Congress, had seen numerous education bills aimed at narrow fields, such as drug abuse education and environmental education. She had also begun to think about the sex role stereotyping that still consigned women, including herself, to positions beneath their experience and training. After attending various seminars and meetings, she started thinking about a legislative proposal that would provide funds to address such issues. She contacted Bernice Sandler, who had recently filed a class action suit on behalf of the Women's Equity Action League (WEAL) charging several colleges and universities with violations of Executive Order 11246, prohibiting sex discrimination in employment by federal contractors. Sandler was initially skeptical about the prospects that such a bill could pass but suggested other women who also might help to develop a legislative proposal.

The women who joined together were experienced and committed to the women's rights movement and had job experience in government and private organizations; but they had never drafted legislation and were naive about the legislative process. In March of 1972, after having spent the winter drafting the bill, the women contacted Representative Patsy Mink's office. Mink had seniority on the Select Education Subcommittee and had been a supporter of women's issues for several years; as early as 1956, she had sponsored Hawaii's Equal Pay Act.

The strategy Mink proposed was a slow and deliberate one, aimed initially at educating Congress to the need for such a bill. She introduced the bill first in 1972 and again in 1973 and held brief hearings in 1973. When it became known that the omnibus Elementary and Secondary Education Act was coming up for reauthorization in 1974, efforts were made to have the bill incorporated into the reauthorization. In the meantime, Ellen Hoffman, then a member of Senator Walter Mondale's staff, had secured Mondale's support and had the bill incorporated into the Senate bill for reauthorization.

Although hearings were held in both the House and Senate with testimony and letters from women's groups and others, the sponsors of the bill kept a low profile to take advantage of the then prevailing "policy vacuum"; there were few established positions on sex equity and no real opposition.[2] They did not want to generate opposition to the bill by making it too public. As Patsy Mink later recalled:[3]

> The idea I had was to get it enacted into law regardless of where it was hidden. If it had to be hidden to get enacted, so be it. So we hid it.

Unfortunately, a number of small programs were all being considered for inclusion in the omnibus reauthorization. When it became apparent that the Women's Educational Equity Act probably would not pass on its own, it was incorporated with the others into a Special Projects Act, an inclusion which would largely determine how the law would be administered by the U.S. Office of Education. Patsy Mink was well aware of the consequences of this:[4]

> It was a retreat, a blow that we had to be lumped in that section. We wanted very desperately to be separately funded as a separate program so that it would have a status of its own, and not be tied with innovative programs that could be junked at one time.

This strategy, however, was successful. On August 21, 1974, the Women's Educational Equity Act became law. Its explicit purpose was to provide educational equity for women in the United States; the act authorized the Office of Education (OE) to fund at all levels of education a diverse set of activities—materials development; training of educational personnel; research and development; guidance and counseling; and educational activities for adult women and women in vocational education, physical education, and educational administration. The Act authorized up to $30 million to be spent on these activities. The law also created a National Advisory Council on Women's Educational Programs whose duties extended beyond making recommendations about the implementation of the Women's Educational Equity Act to include an advisory role to the Commissioner and Assistant Secretary for Education concerning the improvement of educational equity for women.

Implementing the Act became the responsibility of the Office of Education

(OE), which had opposed the bill on the grounds that these issues could be addressed through existing program authorities.[5] It likewise became the responsibility of the women who had helped secure the law's passage to strive to have it implemented as a feminist program, aimed at increasing educational opportunities for women and girls.

IMPLEMENTING THE WOMEN'S EDUCATIONAL EQUITY ACT OF 1974

As soon as the law was passed, the Women's Educational Equity Act (WEEA) was assigned to the Office of Education's existing advocacy office for women— the Women's Program Staff (WPS); this represented the only instance in which an advocacy office in the Office of Education was given responsibility to administer a statutory program. Two days after the law was passed, Assistant Secretary for Education Virginia Trotter transmitted a request for a supplemental budget so that WEEA could be funded in Fiscal Year 1975, a year earlier than the other programs in the Special Projects Act.

The covering memo from Assistant Secretary Trotter was tersely worded, citing "the strong pressure we are under to fund this new authority immediately."[6] She noted that the Title IX regulations had declared a leadership role for the Office of Education in the area of curriculum materials, but that OE would be unable to provide such leadership unless an immediate effort was mounted to develop curriculum materials designed to eliminate sex bias. She also cited the approach of International Women's Year (IWY) in 1975 and mentioned an upcoming White House meeting at which she was expected to discuss education initiatives for IWY with the President. She also explained that women's action groups were already demanding to know what the Administration was planning to do to implement the new authority in Fiscal Year 1975.

The draft justification statement, prepared as an attachment to Assistant Secretary Trotter's request by the Director of the Women's Program Staff, was considerably less forceful and provides one of the first clues that she did not see the WEEA program as an advocacy program.[7]

> OE does not desire a hasty and therefore partially conceived and developed program designed to redress inequity and the attendant discriminatory aftermath. Therefore it seeks to initiate a modest developmental program that will lead to a well-structured approach to be implemented within the next few years.

She later confirmed this impression when asked why she accepted the position of director of the Women's Program Staff and how she viewed its responsibility for WEEA.[8]

I did not see the Women's Program as my golden opportunity to make a contribution to the feminist movement. To me, it was an opportunity to move into a different career area. Once I got there though, I did get a better understanding of the problem. I was very determined that the WEEA program be a "middle of the road" program, not an activist program.

The supplemental request was later turned down by the Undersecretary of the Department of Health, Education and Welfare (DHEW), although funds were transferred to support the comprehensive review of sex discrimination in education mandated by the act and basic research on sex role stereotyping.

After the supplemental request was rejected, OE treated the WEEA program, for the most part, as just another of the Special Projects Act programs, even though WEEA shared little in common with these narrowly focused programs— metric education, programs for gifted and talented children, community schools, career education, consumer education, arts in education and educational television. None of these "special projects" had an explicit equity focus; nor were any concerned with bringing about systemic change in schools. By being administered in conjunction with these programs, WEEA not only had the same time schedule as the others but, more importantly, the same general focus—capacity building. The WPS Director thought "capacity building" essential to WEEA and defined it as follows:[9]

> The focus is on the development of model programs and products which are developed and tested and can be made available for use by other institutions, agencies or individuals. . . . As a result, the program does not fund projects which provide direct services to individuals, or local agencies or organizations.

This general focus on "capacity building" and other requirements were then incorporated into WEEA's program regulations. Regulations are vital to a program, and the regulations development process is central to constituency group involvement. Written by the office administering the program, regulations describe in detail how legislative intent will be carried out. Proposed regulations (NPRM) are first prepared and published in the *Federal Register* for public comment. This is the only opportunity given the public to comment officially on policy implementation. These written comments are than analyzed by the program office; an analysis of the comments received and description of the Program's response then appears in the preamble to the final regulation.

Although public comment is required and encouraged, there is no requirement that the final regulation reflect the concerns raised or changes requested by the public. Comments may be dismissed as irrelevant, illegal, or impossible by the program office; thus, the final regulation can be almost identical to the proposed regulation.

The Women's Program Staff encouraged greater public comment than many federal programs in its original WEEA regulation by raising questions about how best to proceed. Much of the disappointment with WEEA during its initial years rests not with the procedures used to elicit public comment, but rather with the lack of attention paid to the comments received by WPS.

Fundamental conflicts arose between women's organizations and OE about the issues WEEA should address, the strategies it should use, and the manner in which grants and contracts should be awarded. As noted earlier, WPS saw the program as a modest product development effort with tested materials distributed around the country through a publishing contractor. Initial priorities were focused on development of training modules for educational personnel, programs on educational leadership, and programs on career preparation—priorities which reflected the Director's background in education professions development. Initially the program was criticized for relying too heavily on product development and for not helping sustain the momentum generated by parents and community groups already working to change practices in schools. Women's organizations were concerned with WEEA's apparent assumption that schools would automatically change their practices once print materials were available. After first year grants were awarded in Fiscal Year 1976, women's organizations were troubled that many contractors and grantees had poor records in educational equity for women. For each of the first three years of the program, almost half of all grantees were institutions of higher education, a number of which had sex discrimination cases pending against them.

Nonetheless, many worthwhile projects were funded during the first years of the program. Highly regarded materials on Title IX were developed and presented in workshops for state and community educational personnel. At the request of the National Advisory Council on Women's Educational Programs, WPS also funded proposal writing workshops around the country so that people inexperienced in obtaining federal grants could learn the skills of proposal writing.

Pressing local problems were addressed in a number of grants, which then had positive effects beyond the communities in which they were located.[10] Projects ranged from career development programs for rural high school students to academic and social skills programs for women in the penal system to projects giving students active roles in implementing state and federal equal opportunity laws in their schools.

One rural project focused on the disparity between the dreams of high school students to "live happily ever after" and the harsh reality of rural life. Many girls at fifteen years of age were becoming pregnant, marrying, dropping out of school, only to find themselves two years later with two children, no husband, no job, and no skills. No one was preparing them to make more thoughtful decisions or to have the skills needed to find or keep employment. The "Options" project in New Hampshire focused on the needs of these teenagers and operated on the assumption that knowledge of reality, even harsh reality, is better than ignorance and that obtaining information and skills which give young women a measure of control over their destinies is better than relying on chance. The curriculm developed in New Hampshire was then tested in four other rural locations with adjustments made to fit the needs and characteristics of different rural groups.

The Miami-Dade Community College sought to remedy some of the problems faced by female offenders in Florida prisons. With their WEEA grant and funds from the Comprehensive Employment and Training Act, the college offered courses to provide academic information that would help ex-offenders function in society. In this non-threatening atmosphere, they also learned new social skills and worked through conflicts that may have contributed to anti-social behavior. Counseling was offered to inmates and correctional officers as well as potential employers; job training, placement, and follow-up services were provided upon release. The program had profound effects on the inmates, who began to realize that they could improve their lives; it also had considerable impact on correctional staff who then sought the assistance of state legislators to improve state laws on the rights of inmates.

Under a WEEA grant to the Massachusetts State Department of Education, students in Massachusetts were provided the opportunity to assume an active role in implementing state and federal equal opportunity laws in their schools. Massachusetts has a unique mandate to involve students in educational policy making, and in the first two years after Title IX was passed, 300 school systems had contacted the state to ask what the law required. The project focused not only on the content of Title IX and students' right to access to all school courses, but also on attitudes of students.

Although these and many other worthwhile projects were funded in the first three years of the program, women's groups were troubled by what they felt was a "scattershot" approach; they sought to have the program establish priority areas for funding and to focus more resources on implementation of Title IX.

Feminist groups and other constituents had long complained that WPS's failure to set priorities for the WEEA Program resulted in the relative exclusion of various types of projects (less traditional, more feminist ones, for instance), of various population groups (racial and ethnic minority women primarily), of certain levels of education (junior high school), and of particular types of grantees (grass roots feminist and community based nonprofit organizations, for example).

WPS did in fact propose priorities for WEEA again in the second year of operation, but then withdrew all priorities when they saw public comment so divided. Divided public comment was to be expected and women's organizations felt WPS had reneged on its obligations by leaving the WEEA grants competition completely unfocused. Thus, constituents came to believe that a statutory requirement was the only way to force the WPS to make the difficult but necessary decision to focus WEEA's limited resources on certain areas of great need. Although this obviously would exclude many areas, all constituent groups naturally expected their own priorities to be the Program's.

When it became clear that WPS was not going to set priorities or alter WEEA's product development focus, women's groups turned their attention to the reauthorization of the Women's Educational Equity Act. As with virtually all federal education legislation, WEEA was established with a fixed time schedule: The Act was to expire at the end of September 1978. WPS sought to have the Act extended but saw a need for only a minor technical amendment, to increase the ceiling on small grants from $15,000 to $25,000. The Office of Education was not interested in expanding WEEA beyond a modest product development effort; during the first three years of the Program, OE had not requested funds much beyond its initial request of $6.25 million. The Program's appropriation had been increased by approximately one million dollars per year, but not through the efforts of the Administration. These modest increases were the result of extensive lobbying of the Congress, particularly the Senate, by feminist organizations.

The National Advisory Council on Women's Educational Programs and the Coalition for Women and Girls in Education, whose members include almost 50 education associations and women's organizations, sought a number of changes in the Act during the reauthorization debates in Congress; these efforts produced the "new" WEEA.

THE REAUTHORIZATION OF THE WOMEN'S EDUCATIONAL EQUITY ACT

Because the Women's Educational Equity Act was included in the omnibus Elementary and Secondary Education Act, the timing for its reauthorization coincided with the reauthorization of the entire act. Much of the focus in the reauthorization was not on WEEA or other special projects, but rather on the larger or more controversial programs, including the $3 billion Title I compensatory education program and the bilingual education program.

Congress had earlier mandated a $15 million evaluation of Title I and was impatiently awaiting the Administration's bill incorporating those findings into new language. The Administration, however, was months behind in its schedule for submitting the bill to Congress. Finally, Representative Carl Perkins, Chair of the House Education and Labor Committee, submitted a straight extension of the omnibus act in January of 1977 so that Congress could begin debating the merits of the programs included within the Act.

Aware of the pending time schedule on reauthorization, the National Advisory Council on Women's Educational Programs and the Coalition for Women and Girls in Education sought to influence the Administration's bill through other channels than the WPS; they succeeded in persuading officials of DHEW to include major changes in the bill which the Department submitted to OMB and the White House. They then approached staff of several members of the House Education and Labor Committee, focusing on Representative John Buchanan (R., Alabama) who had been a supporter of Title IX and other women's issues.

Buchanan's staff agreed with the concerns raised by the women's groups and asked Meredith Larson, one of the minority staff members on the Education and Labor Committee, to work with them on draft language. Larson met with Coalition members and National Advisory Council staff; she also talked with WPS staff members. Larson came away genuinely impressed with some aspects of the Program, although she did not believe it was managed well. As she later recalled:[11]

> I was put out by the biggest programs, such as Title I. They seemed too tangled up in themselves and suffered from galloping institutionalization. WEEA struck me as not so tangled up in itself. It was giving booster shots at the local level. It had a real local ethic and was doing common sense things about sex equity.

She also agreed with the changes that the Coalition and the National Advisory Council proposed for the WEEA.

While Larson, the Coalition, and the National Advisory Council were drafting the language for these changes, Perkins decided to rush the reauthorization of the entire Elementary and Secondary Education Act through committee; he had become thoroughly annoyed with the Administration's delays. As a result, Larson and the representatives from the women's organizations frantically drafted the new language, and literally ran it to Buchanan while the Elementary and Secondary Education subcommittee was meeting on the bill. It was unanimously incorporated into the bill, and later went through the full committee, the House, and the Senate without change.

The specific content of the new WEEA was less an issue than how to present the program so that it differed from the other titles in the Elementary and Secondary Education Act, titles which were being criticized for their large budgets and apparently perpetual funding.

Representative Buchanan took on this task when he championed the bill on the House floor. As Buchanan noted:[12]

> If half of the nation's population is to participate in and contribute to our country's growth, many large and small changes must be made in our schools. For the most part, these are changes that schools are ready and willing, often eager, to make. But too many schools—from kindergartens to

colleges—lack the *few extra dollars* that would make these changes possible.

The Women's Educational Equity Act truly represents a matured understanding of how to help education. It is not designed for enforcement, it imposes *no quotas*, it prescribes no specific mandates and it does not attempt to buy cooperation with perpetual subsidies. Instead it makes small amounts of money available so that local schools, districts and states can make ther own plans, and then make these plans a reality. Its modest investment will reap a wealth of benefits in the equity and vigor of our schools. I am truly proud to have been able to represent this initiative, which was passed unanimously by the Committee.

The "new" WEEA became law on November 1, 1978, with the changes in its purpose and focus scheduled to take effect in Fiscal Year 1980, beginning in October of 1979.

Essentially, the reauthorization added an additional purpose to the Women's Educational Equity Act, "to provide financial assistance to enable educational agencies and institutions to meet the requirements of Title IX." To implement this purpose, the reauthorized Act established a second tier of funding, which would move WEEA beyond the modest product development focus of its first four years and into support for programs of local significance; these projects would assist school districts and other institutions to ensure educational equity and compliance with Title IX at the local level. So that these local initiatives could be funded at a reasonable level, the authorization level for WEEA was markedly increased—from $30 million per year to $80 million; any appropriations above $15 million were to be earmarked for this new program.

The reauthorization also made other important changes in the WEEA—largely in response to criticisms voiced by feminist organizations and their Congressional allies regarding the implementation of the original program by the Office of Education. For example, the "new" WEEA required the Department to establish priorities for funding under the Act "to insure that available funds are used for programs that most effectively will achieve the purposes of the Act."

The new WEEA also specifically stated that student and community groups are eligible for funding, thus emphasizing the importance of involving these groups in efforts to ensure educational equity.

Because no funds were appropriated to initiate the second tier of funding, the focus of attention for implementation of the new WEEA was on the establishment of funding priorities for the revised demonstration program. As was the case when WEEA was initially passed in 1974, it again became the responsibility of the Office of Education to administer this law, a responsibility which remained with the Women's Program Staff.

IMPLEMENTING THE NEW WOMEN'S EDUCATIONAL EQUITY ACT OF 1978

The Department's primary mechanism for implementing Congressional intent and establishing Program policy is the regulations development process. Shortly after passage of the Act in 1978, therefore, the Women's Program Staff developed a proposed regulation for the new WEEA, following consultation with several feminist organizations and the National Advisory Council on Women's Educational Programs; it was published in the Federal Register on May 25, 1979 and comments were requested from the public.

The regulation proposed six priorities for funding, reflecting the Program's continuing emphasis on improving its demonstration and dissemination activities. Three of the six priorities were "process" oriented and were designed to establish "demonstrations of WEEA materials and programs," "dissemination centers," and a "national WEEA program for change." An additional priority focused on specific target populations ("groups to receive special emphasis"); another priority focused on a specific level of education (elementary and secondary) and a third proposed to support a specific set of approaches ("high risk-high potential projects") to educational equity.

Following publication of this proposed regulation, over 100 letters, including more than 400 separate comments on various sections of the regulations, were received. The Office of Education's regional offices also conducted public hearings (one in each of the ten Federal regions) in June of 1979 to receive additional testimony on the proposed rules.

Near the end of the comment period, a change in administration took place in the WEEA Program Office (formerly the WPS).[13] The new director was appointed and the senior staff member responsible for developing the proposed regulation left to take a position in another city. Thus, the comments were analyzed and studied by Program officials who had been only peripherally involved in developing the proposed regulation and thus had a minimal sense of "ownership" and commitment to the proposed priorities.

The development of the final WEEA regulation—particularly the funding priorities—reveals the extent to which program officials and policymakers can be responsive to constituent comments and suggestions. This experience also shows how collaboration and cooperation between thoughtful constituents and Program officials can produce regulations which effectively implement Congressional mandates.

The new WEEA Program (WEEAP) Director and staff consulted extensively with the staff and members of the National Advisory Council on Women's Educational Programs and representatives of the member organizations of the National Coalition for Women and Girls in Education—both of whom had submitted extremely detailed comments on every section of the proposed regulations. These meetings produced various suggestions for changes to make the final regulations more responsive to the diverse concerns raised by constituents, educators, and other commenters.

The proposed regulation was revised to reflect policy changes requested by the public; every change was strongly supported by majority public comment. In addition, the preamble to the final regulation stated a strong WEEA Program commitment to involving Program constituents in program policy development and implementation:[14]

> The Commissioner believes that, by making many changes suggested by public commenters, the WEEA Program expresses its commitment to public involvement in determining the Program's policy and programmatic strategies for achieving the purposes of the Act. The knowledge and experience of educators, students, the members of the National Advisory Council on Women's Educational Programs, feminist organizations, and other constituents are valuable resources for the WEEA Program.

The most significant changes from the proposed to the final regulation were in the definition of funding priorities. An analysis of the Program's response to public comments and the resulting changes in priorities reveals how this collaborative approach can be conducted within the framework of the existing regulatory process.

Each of the six priorities described in the proposed regulation generated extensive and often impassioned public comment. Three of these priorities—for "demonstrations of WEEA materials and programs," "dissemination centers," and "a national WEEA program for change"—were seriously criticized as unworkable, unnecessary, and confusing.

Most of the commenters on the proposed priority for "demonstrations of WEEA materials and programs" believed that projects funded under the priority would not meet its purpose—to promote more widespread use of WEEA materials—and would, in fact, simply duplicate ongoing WEEA-funded activities. Although WPS officials had considered several of these concerns prior to publishing the proposed regulation, public comment was so overwhelming and convincing that the WEEA Program decided to eliminate the priority completely.

WEEA constituents also expressed confusion and dismay about the proposed priority for "dissemination centers," asserting that the description of these proposed centers was "garbled" and that their proposed activities would simply duplicate those of the ten regional Sex Desegregation Assistance Centers and the WEEA Publishing Center. Many constituents, however, wanted WEEA to know that they still believed its dissemination activities were of great importance and should be improved, though not through a grant priority. In response to the comments, the Program eliminated the priority for dissemination centers.

Further, in a somewhat unusual response, the Program went beyond the requirements of the regulations development process by offering constituents an additional opportunity to share their views on WEEA's dissemination activities in general; the preamble to the final regulation requested further comments. It also expressed official support for the commenters' belief that dissemination of products and materials is one of the WEEA Program's most significant and essential activities. The WEEA Program therefore made a public promise in the preamble to reassess and improve its dissemination policy and practices during the following year. The Program then convened a small conference on its dissemination activities and, as a result, made significant changes in the operations of its Publishing Center.

A third priority also was eliminated in response to strong public concern about its purpose and possible implementation. Although the Program and many commenters agreed on the importance of developing future leaders in educational equity for women, most also believed that the proposed "national WEEA program for change," which would have established training centers at the postgraduate level, was unworkable. Commenters particularly feared that this priority would lead to the development of a "ghetto" of educational equity workers who would not find long term employment in the field and would be consistently underemployed within their school districts.

The WEEA Program responded to these concerns by eliminating this priority and declaring its intention to pursue a somewhat different strategy for change. Under another priority, the Program focused resources on projects designed to influence leaders in educational policy and administration and encourage them to make educational equity a top priority for their institutions.

The remaining three priorities were significantly changed in the final regulation. Because the real purpose of the proposed priority for "model projects on sex discrimination and sex bias in elementary and secondary education" was to develop materials which would be useful to school districts and others attempting to ensure compliance with Title IX, the priority was redefined and entitled "priority for model projects on Title IX compliance." Many commenters had objected to the proposed priority's exclusive focus on elementary and secondary education; the Program agreed that higher education and preschool education activities should be included. Further, several commenters suggested directing the focus to a few critical issues that most urgently need attention rather than using the "scattershot" approach characteristic of earlier WEEA funding. In response to both of these concerns, the Program expanded the priority to address all levels of education and narrowed the focus to Title IX compliance and compliance-related issues.

The priority established by the final regulation for "model projects to eliminate persistent barriers to educational equity for women" responds to serious concerns raised in public comments on the proposed priority for "high risk-high potential" projects. Because all commenters supported its emphasis on difficult and unyielding problems, the revised priority maintains that focus and defines the concept of "persistent barriers." In order to provide for flexibility on the part of applicants and to enable them to define the barriers and "prove" their persistence, the Program does not provide rigid guidelines or lists of those barriers which projects should address. Thus, as requested by commenters, various intractable attitudinal and institutional barriers can be attacked and new strategies for solving old, apparently insoluble, problems can be encouraged under this priority.

Finally, the proposed regulation included a single priority for "groups to receive special emphasis". This priority had two parts; the first focused on "neediest girls and women" and the second on "leaders in educational policy and programs." More comments were received on this priority than on any of the other five; these comments generally reflected a strong concern about the Program's approach to Third World women and its attitude toward "double jeopardy" issues. Several commenters expressed anger and dismay, for example, that the proposed priority's combination of poverty and current or past discrimination as criteria for "neediest" implied that minority women must be poverty-stricken in order to receive any attention from the WEEA Program. Commenters also felt insulted by the terminology used—"neediest" and "special"—to describe racial/ethnic minority women. These terms implied to many constituents that the WEEA Program's approach to the complex issues of institutional racism and sexism was itself built on sex/race and class stereotypes.

However, all commenters enthusiastically supported the Program's effort to establish a priority for projects addressing the educational equity needs of minority, low income, and disabled women. Most comments suggested that a separate priority be established to address the educational needs of minority women, so that WEEA could clearly convey its commitment to combatting both racism and sexism. Commenters also pointed out that combining the two subsections of the priority ("neediest girls and women" and "leaders in educational policy and programs") was a serious mistake because these are very different groups with different needs. Commenters believed that this combination of "apples and oranges" would be detrimental to the interests of minority women. These constituents feared that the power differential between educational leaders and underserved groups represented by "neediest" girls and women would lead to a shortchanging of the latter.

All of these comments crystallized the concerns of the WEEA Program and suggested appropriate ways to revise the priority to fully reflect the Program's actual intention—to focus important resources on addressing the self-defined educational needs of Third World women and the causes and effects of institutional sexism and racism. Thus, three separate priorities were created; one focused exclusively on educational equity for racial and ethnic minority women. Another focused on educational equity for disabled women, thus enabling the

WEEA Program for the first time to address the previously ignored issues of double discrimination, bias, and stereotyping based on sex and disability.

The last priority focused explicitly on "projects to influence leaders in educational policy and administration," to ensure that resources would be available for activities designed to increase the commitment to equity and Title IX compliance among individuals and organizations who manage educational institutions. The preamble to the final regulation clearly states the Program's belief, supported by public comment, that:[15]

> . . . true institutional change can occur only when commitment to it comes from the institution's leaders and is conveyed effectively as a priority for the institution.

Thus, the WEEA Program set a priority on providing to educational leaders the encouragement and assistance which many need to develop and implement mechanisms for ensuring educational equity.

These changes enabled the WEEA Program to clarify its own policy and the purposes of its priorities. Thus, the final regulation defines WEEA Program policy as one which emphasizes the importance of compliance with both the "spirit" and the "letter" of Title IX and of efforts to remove all barriers—even the most recalcitrant—to full equity for women. The Program's policy also emphasizes the necessity for commitment to equity which is both expressed and implemented by top management. And finally, the WEEA regulation clearly states the Program's policy that all activities should devote particular attention to the severe and destructive impact of combined sex, race, and handicap bias.

During the first year of funding under the new priorities (Fiscal Year 1980), the WEEA Program received far more applications than ever before in its history (900 as compared to 650 in the preceding year). Projects funded in each priority concretely reflect the policies set by the new regulations.

Nine grants were awarded under the priority for projects on Title IX compliance. These addressed important Title IX compliance issues—including physical education and sports, in-classroom sex segregation, health services on campus, and legal training in Title IX for attorneys and law students. In addition, other projects addressed compliance-related areas including development of new curricula, teacher and parent training programs, and community support networks for educational equity.

Under the priority for projects on educational equity for racial and ethnic minority women, twelve grants were awarded, addressing a wide range of educational equity issues for Black, Hispanic, Native American, and Asian and Pacific American women and girls. Several projects developed much-needed curriculum materials, including, for example, media and print materials focused on career awareness for Asian and Pacific American girls and women and high school curricula in social studies and the arts focusing on the cultural experience of Mexican American women in the United States.

Other projects developed multi-purpose networks and resources. The OHOYO Resource and Information Center for Native American Women, for instance, conducted regional equity awareness conferences, compiling a bibliography of culture-based curriculum materials developed by American Indian and Alaska Native women, and updating the "Resource Guide for American Indian-Alaska Native Women." The Chinese American Women Educational Equity Program held a national conference and several training and awareness seminars for Chinese American women, and is publishing a monthly newsletter on sex and race stereotyping and educational equity for Chinese American women. The Black Women's Educational Policy and Research Network developed an active network of policymakers and researchers concerned with educational equity for Black women and girls, conducted research seminars nationwide, and published a newsletter.

Other projects focused on teacher training, including one which sought to reshape negative teacher expectations for racial and ethnic minority girls and young women. Finally, several projects focused on skills and leadership development, including a Summer Institute for Hispanic women and girls, a project to improve the status of transitional Black women in the Southeast, and another to provide leadership training and career education for limited and non-English speaking rural Hispanic women farmworkers. An Indian community college conducted a WEEA project to serve the educational needs of reservation and campus women, and an urban university created an Educational Development Institute for Black women and girls.

The priority for projects on educational equity for disabled women and girls represents the first time that a Federal education program has provided funds for the explicit purpose of addressing combined sex and disability bias and stereotyping. Four projects were funded under this priority, including a major national research and demonstration project which developed counseling and teaching materials on the educational needs of disabled women and girls and trained practitioners in their use; the project also developed model curricula and approaches to training disabled teenage girls and young women in their civil rights and educational and career opportunities. In addition, three projects developed curriculum materials, including career educational materials for young (K-3) handicapped and minority girls and boys, preschool and elementary curriculum resources (including classroom materials such as puzzles, games, early reading books, and photo posters) showing disabled children and adults interacting with their nondisabled peers, and a half-hour film showing disabled women in nontraditional careers.

Four grants also were awarded for projects to influence leaders in educational policy and administration, addressing every level of education. One project trained women student leaders while another focused on developing a procedural model to sensitize higher education administrators to the psychological mechanisms which cause unconscious, unintentional discrimination against women in the university. A large urban school district established a Commission for Sex Equity which assisted school board members and top management of the district to improve policies and practices which limit women's educational and employment opportunities. Finally, *Colloquia,* a journal focused on scholarly research on Black women, served as a catalyst for various research and advocacy activities by and for Black women.

Ten projects were funded under the priority for projects to eliminate persistent barriers to educational equity for women. These projects implemented a variety of new strategies to eliminate major barriers to educational equity for women in educational administration, vocational education, physical education, teacher training, curriculum reform, math and science, and in the transition from prison back to society.[17]

LOOKING AHEAD: THE FUTURE OF THE WOMEN'S EDUCATIONAL EQUITY ACT

The projects funded by WEEAP in Fiscal Years 1980 and 1981 supported activities more closely tied to community needs and also expanded networking activities among community groups; the WEEA Program itself was administered with an eye to more direct involvement of women's organizations in program policy development and implementation. In short, the WEEA program sought to instill a feminist perspective throughout its activities.

New developmental efforts always suffer growing pains over the early years; the WEEA Program has done so throughout the process of sorting out priorities, setting program emphases, and addressing the needs of diverse populations at every level of education. It has been a massive task, which has been undertaken with a modest budget. Beginning initially with $6.25 million in Fiscal Year 1976, WEEA's budget has grown by only $1 million each year, reaching a high of $10 million in Fiscal Year 1980. Although WEEA's authorization was for $30 million in its initial years, increased to $80 million in the 1978 reauthorization, the Program has never received more than $10 million in a single year.

While WEEA continues to face the problems of limited funds, the overall Federal role in education is being questioned in both the Congress and the Administration. In response to charges that Federal support for education has produced an unwieldy bureaucracy, a proliferation of small, categorical programs—each with its own purpose and regulations—and Federal "intrusion" into State and local matters, the Reagan Administration has proposed major changes in federal education laws. These changes will affect all Federal programs, including the Women's Educational Equity Act Program.

The focus of these efforts is twofold; the Administration's goal is to reduce Federal spending in education and to give to the States and localities responsibility for activities which traditionally have been defined as part of the Federal role. Thus, for example, virtually every federal education program was affected by a budget reduction in Fiscal Year 1981; WEEA's budget was cut by 18 percent from the $10 million proposed earlier (which would not have provided an increase over the FY 1980 level) to $8.125 million; thus, funds were not available for more than half of the new projects which the program had planned to support; only 16 projects could be funded (of 813 applications submitted).

The proposed grants consolidation effort is an attempt to provide funds directly to the States and localities; existing elementary and secondary education programs would be merged into broad multi-purpose block grants. At this writing (1981), both the House of Representatives and the Senate have agreed to a substantially reduced federal education budget in future years as well as a version of program consolidation, but with some important variations. In the Senate bill, WEEA is incorporated into the consolidation; in the House version, WEEA is one of five separate programs under the Secretary's Discretionary Fund, with the potential for funding apparently close to the present $8.125 million level. While the outcome of consolidation is yet to be determined in Congress, it is clear that all federal education programs will be markedly influenced by a long term budget reduction and by continuing efforts to redefine the Federal role in education.

The implications for WEEA are serious, even if WEEA remains a separate program. With a maximum funding level of no more than $8.125 million per year, WEEA will not be able to initiate the second tier of funding established in the 1978 reauthorization; thus the planned support for projects of local significance cannot be funded under a new "Tier II" program, as originally intended. WEEA thus must reassess its priorities and program directions.

As in the past two years, this reassessment will take place in the public eye. The WEEA Program will continue to seek active involvement of its constituents in determining how the existing priorities can be focused even more sharply on areas of greatest need. These might include, for example, an expansion of networking activities, a movement towards increased development of products only in areas where almost no materials exist, or an emphasis on smaller, more locally significant projects throughout the country.

Once again, the WEEA regulation provides a mechanism for public debate on these issues.[16] The regulation establishes a program policy which is unique in the Department; rather than simply publishing an application notice each year announcing priorities to be funded and the date applications are due, the WEEA Program first requests public comment on which priorities (of the five established in the regulation) should be selected for funding, what percentage of funds should be allocated to each priority, and how each priority should be focused. Before any decisions are made about the future, then, the WEEA Program will have the benefit of the advice and recommendations from its constituents which have proved so important in the past.[18]

NOTES

1. For a more expanded discussion of the passage of the Women's Educational Equity Act, see "Sex Discrimination and the Legislative Process: The Enactment of the Women's Educational Equity Act" by Andrew Fishel and Janice Pottker in *National Politics and Sex Discrimination in Education*. Lexington (MA): Lexington Books, 1977.

2. Jo Freeman discusses the concept of "policy vacuum" more fully in her chapter in this book.

3. Interview with Patsy Mink, May 28, 1981.

4. Interview with Patsy Mink, May 28, 1981.

5. While the Office of Eduction opposed the bill, the Commissioner of Education had established a task force on sex discrimination in OE programs, which found sex discrimination rampant. See "Sex Discrimination and Bureaucratic Politics: The U.S. Office of Education Task Force on Women's Education" by Holly Knox and Mary Ann Millsap in *National Politics and Sex Discrimination in Education*. Lexington (MA): Lexington Books, 1977.

6. Memorandum from Virginia Trotter to the Undersecretary of Health, Education, and Welfare, August 23, 1974.

7. Draft memorandum from Joan Duval to T.H. Bell, Commissioner of Education, August 23, 1974.

8. Interview with Joan Duval, May 26, 1981.

9. Statement by Joan Duval before the Subcommittee on Elementary, Secondary and Vocational Education in the U.S. House of Representatives, July 14, 1977.

10. These examples are all taken from "What's WEEA?", written by Kathleen Maurer for the National Advisory Council on Women's Educational Programs, May 1979. Expanded discussion of these and other projects are found in this useful and highly readable pamphlet. Information on published products from these and other WEEA grants is available from the WEEA Publishing Center (Educational Development Center, 55 Chapel Street, Newton, Massachusetts 02160; toll free: 800-225-3088). A complete catalog of publications is available at no cost.

11. Interview with Meredith Larson, May 8, 1981.

12. House floor statement of Representative John Buchnanan, 1977.

13. At this time, the name of the Office was officially changed from "Women's Program Staff" to "Women's Educational Equity Act Program" to reflect the fact the administration of WEEA is the Office's sole responsibility. A separate Office of Women's Concerns also was established to serve as the Department's advocacy office for women.

14. Final Rule, Women's Educational Equity Act Program, Federal Register, Vol. 45, No. 66, April 3, 1980, 22731.

15. Final Rule, 22731.

16. Final Rule, 22731.

17. Complete descriptions of all funded projects are included in the Fiscal Year 1980 *WEEA Program Annual Report*. Individual copies are available without charge from the WEEA Program (1100 Donohoe, 400 Maryland Avenue, S.W., Washington, D.C. 20202)

18. The Women's Educational Equity Act was revised and reauthorized for five years by the Education Amendments of 1984. For an analysis of the new law, and of the history of the WEEA Program from 1981 to 1984, contact: PEER, 1413 K Street, 9th Floor, Washington, D.C. 20005; 202-332-7337.

WOMEN'S EDUCATION AND WOMEN'S VALUES

Annette K. Baxter

Perhaps the most obvious, as well as the most critical, contrast between higher education and the rest of education is that women faculty are largely absent from the one and in large numbers populate the other. Higher education is the domain of men. While it is true that positions of academic and administrative importance in primary and secondary school are most often held by men, the significant presence of women modifies the male grip on power and colors the environment of the pre-college years with more than a few contrasting shades of female influence. Such cannot be said of the college and post-graduate years.

The reasons for this are familiar to us. The servicing of children's educational needs has always allowed for female teachers, even in the eighteenth and early nineteenth centuries when the male schoolmaster was the more customary figure on the American scene. The developing years of a child's climb to maturity have seemed to require more than the transmission of knowledge and the acquisition of skills. They have called for powers of persuasion, interpersonal sensitivities, contextual responsiveness and, above all, a functioning system of humane values.[1] A negative reflection of this can be seen in the deterioration of the public school system since World War II: the absence of a societal consensus on values has had more visible effects on institutions of lower learning, where values have some role, than on institutions of higher learning, only because the latter are not committed in the same way to the transmission of values.

What are they committed to, and what is the significance for society of this difference in goals? Higher education is preeminently wedded to the search for knowledge. In the course of that search its high priests, the faculty, spend an agreed upon portion of their time sharing that knowledge with a body of acolytes, the students. Their pursuit is the pursuit of truth, untainted by opinion. Opinion may itself be the subject of study, or be used as a vehicle for correcting past error;

145

in either case its use is professedly to enlarge understanding of the truth. The American college and university, therefore, proclaims itself as value-free.

This was not always the case. Throughout the seventeenth, eighteenth and mid-nineteenth centuries, colleges and universities were intimately bound by religious imperatives. The struggle that ensued when modern notions of scientific method came into conflict with those imperatives occupies a central place in the history of American higher education in the last half of the nineteenth century.[2] As a result of the triumph of the value-free university, the mission of higher education underwent subtle redefinition on every level of academic life. The goals towards which even religiously affiliated institutions aspired came more and more to replicate those of the great universities.

In fact, of course, a new complex of values operated in this atmosphere, and we are just beginning to identify them and to penetrate their significance.[3] What is important for our purposes is to recognize that the appearance of women on the horizons of higher education coincided with the growing emphasis on knowledge as value-free. It is in this setting that women first entered upon their intellectual novitiate as college students.

In contrast to the academic environment into which they bravely plunged, the first generation of college women were the inheritors of a value-laden universe. They came out of a tradition of training for domestic virtues, a tradition infused with convictions and loyalties that dictated the scope of the curriculum for girls and young women in the grade schools and dame schools and in the seminaries and academies of colonial times and the early republic. Its goals were family-oriented, whether with the intention of producing mothers who could serve as examplars of true womanhood in the home[4] or creators of a new generation of noble republican citizens in the larger society.[5] The belief that the home was the natural habitat of woman and the breeding ground of her virtues permeated the thoughts and actions of young women in every class, every region, and every occupational stratum in the United States. Even when its desirability as a philosophy of women's place was challenged, it could not be denied or ignored as a reality of women's existence. It helped to shape the lives and thoughts not only of its disciples but of the women who reacted most vehemently against it. Volumes were written in praise of it, and throughout much of the nineteenth century serious attempts were made by Catharine Beecher and others to elevate it into a science.[6]

Indeed, the point of their education prior to women's appearance in colleges seemed to be to produce ever more refined—in both senses—instrumentalities of family life. Family life itself was designed to bolster morality in both the personal and economic spheres, a morality to which men paid lip service but often violated in practice. Thus women's education was a means of shoring up the official values of society by securing them against the dangers posed by mobility, commerce, and the steady dilution of religious orthodoxy. But as women sought to scale the barricades of higher education, they discovered how little these values counted in the context of serious academic life.

The eventual scuttling of two early institutional features—domestic work and the preparatory department—was mandated by the desire for academic legitimacy. When Mount Holyoke Seminary was first established by Mary Lyon in 1837, she built into its fabric a domestic work component intended to bring physical and moral discipline into the lives of the Seminary's students, as well as to help lower the costs of running the institution. Only Wellesley among the leading women's colleges had followed such practice, and before the turn of the century Wellesley had abandoned it altogether. A measure of Mount Holyoke's entrance into the ranks of first-quality liberal arts colleges was its dropping in 1913 of that holdover from an earlier era.

Founded in 1865 with a preparatory department that confessed to women's inadequate preparation for scholarly work, Vassar invited accusations of lesser quality until it did away with its embarrassing appendage in 1888. Wellesley, starting out ten years after Vassar with a similar arrangement, hastened within five years to relocate its preparatory department elsewhere to escape such intimations of inferiority. Smith College, opening the same year as Wellesley, went resolutely further. It had no preparatory department and instituted entrance requirements based on Harvard's. Its founders were determined that neither access nor curriculum be thought less rigorous than that of leading men's colleges. The move away from female models—the domestic work requirement and the preparatory department—and toward male models helped insure the scholarly reputations of these colleges.[7] We might ask retrospectively whether a negligible amount of time spent clearing dishes or the presence of a lower school attached to a college in themselves would have seemed to compromise the quality of mental activity taking place within the walls of a male institution.

Just as the formal structures of women's colleges were adapted to those of men, the attitudes of their students followed suit. The rejection of female institutional patterns of the immediate past was symptomatic of the rejection of the larger female past. Indeed, one could best demonstrate intellectual rigor by discarding the familiar bag of pieties and principles that were the inheritance of women over generations. Inadequate and inferior educational opportunities and experiences in the past, which misrepresented the potential of women, were the rationale for efforts to outdo men at their own game. The predictable consequence of this mood of the last quarter of the nineteenth century was the appearance of M. Carey Thomas and the Bryn Mawr Woman.

The person with whom Bryn Mawr is permanently associated was an exceptional human being. Coming from Quaker roots and from a cultivated background, she was equipped with the confidence in her public self that Quakerism bestows upon its women and an ease with matters intellectual that she owed to her family's professionalism. Rejecting the idea of Vassar because of the preparatory department that seemed to lower the prestige of its degree, she chose Cornell, putting herself to the test of competing directly with men. Five years after winning her A.B. in 1877 she had obtained a Ph.D. *summa cum laude* from the University of Zurich.

Soon after her return to the United States she found the perfect vehicle for her energies and intelligence in the newly opened Bryn Mawr College, which she ultimately served as president for twenty-eight years. In the course of that career she shaped an institution that acquired a reputation for academic excellence second to none; indeed, it was Carey Thomas's wish to exceed, if possible, the leading men's colleges in the demands of Bryn Mawr's academic program. The school flourished and its graduates became noted for their dedication to pure intellectual pursuits and their disdain for lowly vocationalism.

The founding and early decades of Bryn Mawr represent the pinnacle of the effort by women to replicate male models. Carey Thomas's suspicion of marriage as a serious distraction for scholarly women and her own lifelong singlehood, though complicated by intense friendships with women, suggest that in her mind loving and learning were somehow incompatible, particularly when loving entailed the responsibilities of raising children and running a home. "Only our failures marry," she said, and the aphorism neatly expressed the philosophy she inculcated in generations of Bryn Mawr women. The fact is that, while many Bryn Mawr women did marry, they and like-minded women graduates of other leading colleges, both single-sex and co-educational, found that a life of scholarship was indeed often incompatible with marriage.

Two leading women's college heads, Emily James Smith Putnam of Barnard and Alice Freeman Palmer of Wellesley, illustrate this dilemma. A talented Greek scholar and successful administrator, Emily Putnam forsook her deanship at Barnard in 1900 when she discovered she was pregnant. The trustees could barely tolerate a married dean and made it clear that motherhood would be the fatal step beyond the pale. Alice Freeman Palmer in 1887 allowed herself to be persuaded that the presidency of Wellesley and the duties of marriage to Professor George Palmer of Harvard were essentially at odds. These two intellectually brilliant and politically skillful women retired to domesticity, became trustees of their institutions and in both cases took on an impressive variety of civic and educational tasks in the larger world. But in doing so they surrendered the professional momentum they had achieved and the satisfaction of bringing their lives full circle. Their careers were fatalities of the belief that domesticity and the life of the mind are incompatible, and the practical circumstances of their time that largely validated that belief.

What ensued in the early decades of the twentieth century and afterward helps to explain a central paradox that marks the history of women's higher education and ultimately returns us to the contemplation of women in a value-free university. Clearly new and challenging opportunities had been opened up for intellectually aspiring young women by female leaders like M. Carey Thomas, Emily James Smith Putnam, and Alice Freeman Palmer, as well as by forward-looking males like President Andrew D. White of Cornell, who had welcomed women in 1872, only four years after the university was founded. Throughout the teens and twenties women were disproving the male conceit that physical and psychological damage of a possibly irreversible nature would follow upon their undertaking intense mental application. In fact their discovery of a life's work rejuvenated them, as in the cases of Edith Wharton, Jane Addams, and Charlotte Perkins Gilman, some of the noted career women who had suffered psychosomatic symptoms and had consulted the noted Dr. S. Weir Mitchell prior to their recuperation through intellectual activity.

Throughout the academic doldrums of the 1930s and the succeeding "Feminine Mystique" years, there continued to be growing educational opportunities for women even in the face of a discouraging job market in the 1930s and a decline in personal incentive in the 1940s and 1950s. By the 1960s the student revolts and the women's movement together helped create so-called full equality by persuading formerly male Ivy League institutions to become co-educational. Few doubted that it was only a matter of time before women would match men in the number as well as the range of their accomplishments. What better support for such belief than the contributions in the past half-century of women like Alice Hamilton in medicine, Margaret Mead in anthropology, Vida Scudder in literary criticism and social and religious thought, Helen Gardner in art history, and many more.

The reformist spirit of the 1960s and early 1970s seemed to insure triumph after a long history of struggle. Legislation mandating affirmative action in educational institutions was embodied in Title IX of the Education Amendments Act of 1972. Institutions and individuals might resist, but all right-minded people knew that in time women would more fully experience the opportunities for equal education that their predecessors had made possible, and would achieve equally in pure thought and the professions.

Somehow, though, it may not be happening. A recent Brown University Committee on the Status of Women study indicated that college women are now more reluctant to leave home during the early years of child-rearing. Although *The New York Times* is said by the *Brown Alumni Monthly* to have seriously exaggerated the committee's findings, those findings do suggest that women are, if not right back where they were before Andrew D. White and M. Carey Thomas first gave them new options in the 1870s and 1890s, at least facing some familiar dilemmas—dilemmas with which all their education has not helped them cope.[8] Understanding them calls for more than the simplistic thinking with which women are bombarded on all sides by self-proclaimed experts on the woman question. It requires an appreciation of history beyond the mere recital of women's educational progress from past put-downs to present-day affirmative action plans. A reassessment of that history as it was written and presented to us in the past is needed, as well as an awareness of how contemporary historians of women's higher education are revising our views of what happened. By coming to grips with the myths and realities of higher education for women, we can begin to confront the context in which it has all been happening—the value-free university itself.

In documenting the increasing acceptance of women as participants in higher education and its professional schools, historians have traditionally traced an ascending line from the early finishing schools with their lightweight curricula to Catharine Beecher and her predecessors, who, in their absorption with the scientizing of domesticity, had little sympathy for education as we know it, to those intrepid pioneers of the first co-educational universities and early women's colleges who were ready to plunge into the icy waters of Germanic scholarship and take on the most demanding and abstruse studies. These last were feminine exemplars of the post-Darwinian faith in empirical learning, and they have traditionally been applauded as selfless in intention, dedicated in action, and always in command. Thanks to their efforts women are at Yale, female graduate students are performing complex experiments in research laboratories, and some women even teach in universities as tenured professors.

But recent historians of women's higher education are giving us a far more searching and in some ways more disturbing analysis. In *Collegiate Women*, a study of the early history of Bryn Mawr and of Wellesley by Roberta Frankfort, the Bryn Mawr myth has been re-examined with interesting results.[9] Frankfort demonstrates that in the early decades of the college's history the ideal of the pure scholar corresponded in good part to the realities of institutional life and student behavior. In other institutions too, whether co-educational or single-sex, the determination required to be a female pioneer exacted single-mindedness and inner discipline. Charlotte Conable, in *Women at Cornell*, points out that it even took physical stamina, as in the case of the first Cornell co-ed, who dropped out in her freshman year because the absence of a female dormitory required her to live in town and climb the treacherous Ithaca slopes in winter.[10] But soon traditional social pressures transformed these institutions and the young women attending them. Men were for the most part their mentors, and subtle suggestion in women's colleges as well as outright discriminatory practices in co-educational institutions were returning the college woman to her former academic half-way house, uncertain about her own direction except insofar as it involved the acquisition of a husband and family.

In M. Carey Thomas's letter of 1883 to the vice-president of the board of trustees of the newly founded Bryn Mawr College, she offered her services as president to the new institution. Her vision of the college reflected her own immersion abroad in the most advanced scholarship. She put it this way:

> My conviction of the value of a liberal arts education could not be made
> deeper, and my conception of what a college might become, clearer, by

gradual training under German scholars who in a certain sense aid in making the science which they teach; and I began to doubt whether it would not be a more justifiable way of life, to aid in procuring this liberal education for other women, then merely to pursue my studies quietly at home.[11]

She then projected the outlines of such an institution on a Johns Hopkins model, suggesting that the presence of graduate students among undergraduates in an undergraduate college would "raise the standard of undergraduate work, aid in college discipline, incite the professors under whom they study to original research and, as at the Johns Hopkins, draw other postgraduates to the college. . . ."[12]

It was this spirit that prevailed in the first decades of Carey Thomas's leadership, and scholars of women's education have assumed that it persisted with the same intensity throughout Bryn Mawr's history. But Frankfort demonstrates that the scholarly monasticism cultivated at Bryn Mawr was eventually diluted by the ideals of domesticity that still functioned to draw students into conventional life patterns. The weakening of Carey Thomas's hold over the college after 1915 reflected this change.

President Alice Freeman Palmer, the most influential spokesman of Wellesley's early history, was from the beginning more ambivalent in her projections of Wellesley ideal, which, as Frankfort points out, incorporated concrete elements of traditional domesticity and gentility, along with a demanding curriculum. But even with its more rounded approach to the education of women, Wellesley stood for incontestably high academic standards. Mary Barnet Gilson, recalling her student years there in the 1890s, affirmed the presence of those standards:

> Most of the faculty were so absorbed with the great adventure of getting a college for girls on sound and dignified footing that would command the respect of men that they were self-consciously proud of a curriculum almost slavishly imitative of men's colleges. It was still said in certain quarters that because women's brains were smaller than men's they were not so mentally capable.[13]

But as the novelty of Wellesley's arrival on the scene of American higher education diminished, the tone of the college reflected students' return to domestic yearnings. Although the college's academic rigor remained and was even somewhat intensified, Frankfort finds that "by 1910 more Wellesley graduates were marrying and having children than ever before."[14] Indeed, she concludes that "while colleges for women may have offered more of a sophisticated academic training, they did not permanently challenge the domesticity cult. . . ."[15] The documentation Frankfort provides suggests that the inner-directed solidarity and self-consciousness of the women pioneers were displaced by conventional other-directed ambitions in their successors.

The story of women at Cornell reflects much the same pattern. Cornell's founders were a noble pair—Ezra Cornell was an enlightened businessman who had made a fortune in developing the telegraph and Andrew D. White an idealistic scholar who dreamed of founding a nonsectarian university open to all classes. In part because both had wives who inspired their interest in women's education, they sought to welcome women to their newly founded land-grant university. With the establishment on the campus of Sage College, a residence for women, several years after Cornell opened its doors in 1868, women were theoretically free to enjoy all of the rights and privileges of Cornell men. And for a brief period they did. It should be recalled that it was during these early years of Cornell's history that M. Carey Thomas earned her A.B. there. But before long, social fears and traditional constraints imposed severe limits on the activities and ambitions of women undergraduates. Their disproportionately low numbers compared to undergraduate men encouraged competition for their favors among men and thus heightened their dependence on sexuality as a source of self-worth.

Like Frankfort, who paints a picture of early intellectual commitment and drive modified by the return to conventional patterns, Charlotte Conable in her book on Cornell women explains with the assistance of new research the shift from the confident dedication of early female Cornellians to the acquiescence of later coeds in widespread institutional discrimination. The earliest forms of "anticoedism" following the golden age of Cornell and White were dictated by economic considerations. Female undergraduate enrollment had become sluggish. The falling off was attributed to parental fears that, without supervision in a dormitory constructed to meet their needs, daughters would be in jeopardy. The introduction of a requirement of dormitory residence was the solution, but since no such requirement applied to men, it marked a critical shift in the treatment of men and women at Cornell.[16]

Conable details the results, among which were female admissions quotas in the Liberal Arts College set by the number of beds available, the steering of women students away from male-linked fields of professionalization, and the growth of all-powerful fraternities which could go so far as to charge their members extra fees if they brought Cornell women to house parties. Conable concludes that "Cornell University had become by 1960 a place where women had the least possibility for equal opportunity. This condition contrasts sharply with the era of its founding when it surpassed most other colleges and universities in providing similar opportunity for both sexes."[17]

Frankfort and Conable's work persuades us that women's educational history by no means follows the simple forward motion suggested by previous students of the higher education of women. Traditions and mores stubbornly resistant to change were at work at Bryn Mawr and Wellesley. At Cornell economic pressures were added to the usual social ones, and the combination produced an atmosphere that, according to Conable, "reinforced the most conservative social and occupational roles for women."[18]

But what does this tell us, beyond the fact that sex discrimination is built into our social structure, that it attacks even those who are the beneficiaries of efforts to combat it, and that economic forces are often strong enough to resist liberal reforms indefinitely? It may tell us a good deal more. Research and insights coming out of the great contemporary surge of women's history offer us further clues.

A twin biography published by Anna Mary Wells in 1978 and entitled *Miss Marks and Miss Woolley* portrays the symbiotic relationship of two strong-minded academic women, one the president of Mount Holyoke College from 1900 to 1937 and the other a professor of English there. Our knowledge of Miss Woolley has until now been of a generally "official" sort, except for the "informal and personal" *Life and Letters*, so described by Miss Marks, who published it in 1955.[19] Miss Woolley was a strong, able and much loved president who brought Mount Holyoke into the modern era. She was a leader not only in education but in religious, labor, civil libertarian and peace movements.

In Wells's book we understand for the first time the degree of Miss Woolley's dependence on Miss Marks. We can see the emotional isolation within which an intellectually gifted leader would have lived and worked without friendship she came to rely on. Like the author, we can speculate, from our modern liberated perspective, on the possibly sexual nature of that relationship, although perhaps disguised even from its principals as being that. We discern the need for a domesticity that, with all their academic intensity, her own Mount Holyoke students, like their sisters at Bryn Mawr and Wellesley, also sought.

When upon Miss Woolley's retirement the Presidency of Mount Holyoke was given over by the trustees for the first time in the college's history to a man, Miss Woolley vowed never again to set foot on the campus, and she kept her word.[20] She recognized that the gesture might seem anachronistic, but her reasons for it were symbolic in the largest sense. If Mount Holyoke, with its great tradition of preparing women for participation in every activity of consequence in the world, should have failed to produce a woman capable of leading it, and if, furthermore, every other institution, single sex or co-educational, had similarly failed, was that not a circumstance deserving of protest? Miss Woolley's conviction that sex discrimination was at the bottom of the trustees' decision was expressed in the following excerpt from a letter she wrote in 1942, which is quoted in Wells' book:

The policy that I am following in not going back to Mount Holyoke is my protest against what was done. You know me well enough to realize that I never say a word against the present administration. The question is something bigger than the personal. . . . Two or three days ago the *New York Times* listed eight new appointments at Mount Holyoke College, four men and four women. The posts given to the women were of instructors rank . . . I could say much more; perhaps, however, it is sufficient to convince you that I cannot give up my protest.[21]

Both this protest and the gesture that it continued to inspire seem to us today the honest response of a woman ahead of her time to the simple demands of equity.

Two of the myths that were entertained about Miss Woolley—that she was a woman of great self-sufficiency and that she became a fanatic on the woman issue late in life—have been seriously descredited by the research in this book. As with the revisionist institutional histories of Frankfort and Conable, this revisionist biography brings us up against the surprising power of domesticity and the persistence of discrimination in educated women's lives.

One is bound to wonder if there is a connection between the two, and to wonder too about the role men play in creating that connection. Why has the need for domesticity always rendered women suspect? Why do men equate it with inferior intellect, when they fail to so denigrate their own desires for a stable personal life, for a partner, a companion or a family? Could there by any grounds for thinking that qualities required for effective domesticity in any form—tolerance of others, flexibility, compassion and understanding—are qualities which threaten in some way the world of pure intellect that men have always appropriated as their own?

If so, one can understand why women faculty are more in evidence in the pre-college years, when purposive human interaction between teacher and student is seen as more urgent than in the college years, and progressively less in evidence as the stages of higher education become more rarified. One can also understand why today's female inheritors of a more "liberated" mentality who aspire to participation in the life of the college and university will encounter old problems in new form as they attempt to reconcile what they see as their burgeoning opportunities with the demands of personal life. For their own values will inevitably conflict with an ambience that celebrates the absense of values.

There is no reason to believe that either our society as a whole, which is unable to settle upon a priority of values for itself, or the university, which is without values outside the purely instrumental pursuit of knowledge, will assist women with this dilemma. For to do so would require the recognition of the very emotional impulses and psychological traits associated with women as equally necessary and relevant to themselves. The call for androgyny in the largest sense, that is, by the honoring of sexuality in men and women but the sharing of human traits by all, has barely been heard and certainly the realization of its message is as yet far off.[22]

In that glorious last quarter of the ninteenth century when women collectively first felt the special excitement of intellectual yearning and fulfillment, they placed all their allegiance in the purity and authority of the value-free university. They were able to do so because they were still sustained by lingering traditions of morality, civility and, yes, domesticity, which offered a healthy human context in which the search for knowledge took place. They could even withstand the regular discrimination they encountered as female oddities, secure in the faith that a new era was before them and that they were its pioneers.

Today, as we read the accounts of the Skocpol case at Harvard, where a negative tenure decision on a female sociologist has been challenged as unfair, and especially as we read between the lines, we ought to bear in mind that discrimination against women anywhere is not easily eradicated. It goes against the grain of the culture. But discrimination in higher education is even harder to eradicate because the presence of women threatens to prove that humane values can co-exist with the disinterested pursuit of knowledge. And that is a very serious threat indeed.

NOTES

1. It is hard to conceive of a book on higher education carrying an equivalent of the title *Knowledge Without Goodness is Dangerous: Moral Education in Boarding Schools*. This is a volume edited by Charles L. Terry and published in 1981 by the Phillips Exeter Academy Press in Exeter, N. H.

2. A recent study exploring the impact of this conflict on a variety of academic disciplines is Louise Stevenson, *Scholarly Means to Evangelical Ends: The New Haven Scholars, 1840—1890,* Boston University doctoral dissertation in American Studies, 1981.

3. For one clue see Jessie Bernard, *Academic Women* (1964; rpt. Cleveland and New York: World Publishing Co., 1966), p. 141 for discussion of the "fighter" mentality cultivated in graduate schools.

4. For the classic statement of this ideal, see Barbara Welter, "The Cult of True Womanhood, 1820–1860," 1966; rpt. in *Dimity Convictions,* Athens, Ohio: Ohio University Press, 1976.

5. Linda Kerber has explored this function of women in *Women of the Republic: Intellect and Ideology in Revolutionary America*, Chapel Hill, N. C.: The University of North Carolina Press, 1980.

6. Two important assessments of Catharine Beecher are Barbara M. Cross' introduction to *The Educated Woman in America, Selected Writings of Catharine Beecher, Margaret Fuller and M. Carey Thomas,* New York: Teachers College Press, 1956, and Kathryn Kish Sklar's full-length *Catharine Beecher, A Study in America Domesticity,* New Haven and London: Yale University Press, 1973.

7. While it is true that many of the lesser men's colleges had preparatory departments too, the women's colleges, according to Mabel Newcomer, "were more often overshadowed by these appendages than the men's colleges, since they were more able to recruit even fewer adequately prepared students." In *Century of Higher Education for American Women,* New York: Harper and Brothers, 1959, p. 21.

8. Susan Heitman in *On Stage,* in *Brown Alumni Monthly,* March 1981,pp. 14-15, concedes that, despite her criticism of the *Times'* emphasis on the "retreat to the home" motif, most of the young women in the study "felt that it was better for

children to have a mother at home when they were young, and were to varying degrees nervous about how they (the women) were going to accomplish all this."

9. Roberta Frankfort, *Collegiate Women,* New York: New York University Press, 1977.

10. Charlotte Williams Conable, *Women at Cornell, The Myth of Equal Education,* Ithaca, New York: Cornell University Press, 1977, pp. 65–66.

11. Marjorie Housepian Dobkin, ed., *The Making of a Feminist, Early Journals and Letters of M. Carey Thomas,* Kent, Ohio: The Kent State University Press, 1979, pp. 277–278.

12. *Ibid.,* p. 280

13. Mary Barnett Gilson, *What's Past Is Prologue,* 1940; rpt. New York Arno Press, 1980, pp. 11–12.

14. Frankfort, *Collegiate Women,* p. 83

15. *Ibid.*

16. I am grateful to Professor Frederic Kershner of Teachers College, Columbia University for pointing out on the basis of his own research that a similar backlash occurred in midwestern colleges and universities. Women are welcomed in the late 1860s and 1870s but by the mid-1890s overt anti-feminism had taken hold. The earlier liberal attitudes of a less affluent and more egalitarian student body gave way as the children of the upper classes began to dominate these campuses in the late 1880s. By early 1900s there were efforts to abolish co-education in institutions that had previously welcomed women.

17. Conable, *Women at Cornell,* p. 132.

18. *Ibid.*

19. Jeannette Marks, *Life and Letters of Mary Emma Woolley,* Washington, D. C.: Public Affairs Press, 1955.

20. Wells suggests that male chauvinism may have played a role in the decision to replace Miss Woolley with a man. She cites the accession to the chairmanship of the board in 1933 of Alva Morrison, former chairman of the finance committee, who had been "all but openly impatient with Miss Woolley's handling of the financial affairs of the college." And she quotes the Boston *Globe* in 1937 as noting this attitude: " 'In degrees varying with their temperaments, these men of affairs had experienced masculine impatience with the ways of spinster management.' " See *Miss Marks and Miss Woolley,* p. 228.

21. Quoted in *Miss Marks and Miss Woolley,* p. 253.

22. For and exploration of this idea through literature, see Carolyn G. Heilbrun, *Toward a Recognition of Androgyny,* New York: Harper and Row, 1973.

TITLE IX COMPLIANCE AND SEX EQUITY: DEFINITIONS, DISTINCTIONS, COSTS, AND BENEFITS

Rita Bornstein

I. INTRODUCTION

The Title IX Legislation Prohibiting sex discrimination in Federally assisted education institutions was a congressional response to patterns of institutionally perpetuated inequities based on sex. Full compliance with the law does not of itself provide educational equity but is a major vehicle for creating the conditions necessary for equitable schools. Even without the Federal mandate, school personnel are under pressure to confront inequitable treatment of students and employees as inconsistent with the goals of American education and the realities of contemporary American society.

Although significant changes have occurred in schools as a result of the law, many systems have limited their responses to the achievement of minimum legal compliance. The experience of those working in the field clearly indicates that low levels of compliance activity promote neither the equal opportunity goals of Title IX nor the educational goals of the public schools. Minimal compliance efforts fail to alter sex-based disparities in educational and occupational attainments and prove in the long run to be unexpectedly costly and socially inappropriate for schools.

The focus on minimum legal requirements does not necessarily indicate a resistance by school administrators to the achievement of full equity. Instead, it reflects the lack of well-defined equity goals and a rationale for moving beyond minimal legal compliance toward progressively more equitable schools and school systems. Despite the currency of "equity" as a general objective among technical

157

assistance personnel and feminist groups, little serious attention has been given to developing consensus on definition, rationale, and methodology. Rather, attention has been on the promotion of full compliance with Title IX, in itself a major thrust toward equity. School district compliance efforts are strengthened, however, if the goal becomes educational equity instead of the retention of Federal money.

This paper attempts to define and provide a rationale for full equity in terms of outcomes for students and benefits for school districts. It seeks to clarify the relationship of compliance to equity, and to provide a method of analyzing the short- and long-term costs and benefits for students and schools of both minimal and maximal equity responses. In addition, it presents some implications for action based on the goal of full equity.

II. DEFINITION OF EQUAL OPPORTUNITY

Because Title IX was enacted by the United States Congress as, essentially, an extension of Title VI of the 1964 Civil Rights Act, the legislation is commonly understood to be in the spirit of equal opportunity. Yet, experience with Title VI has demonstrated that the elimination of overtly discriminatory practices does not of itself insure equal opportunities for educational and occupational accomplishments.

Equal opportunity, like equity, is a general concept about which there are many common assumptions but a variety of definitions. A provocative article by Onora Nell (1976) attempts to define what we mean when we say that opportunities are equal. Nell delineates an important distinction between *formal* and *substantive* interpretations of the concept of equal opportunity. The formal interpretation, according to Nell, holds that once rules are fair, a society is an equal opportunity society, even if groups have disproportionate success rates. Such disproportion is justified from the formal perspective on the basis of individual variation in capacities and desires, although, as Nell points out, desires and capacities are generally produced or modified by earlier educational and occupational experiences. Thus, it follows that apparently neutral and nondiscriminatory tests and other selection procedures for educational and occupational attainment often result in disproportionate success in some groups and correspondingly disproportionate failure in others.

The substantive interpretation of equality of opportunity, according to Nell, would equalize the rate of educational and occupational attainment of all major groups based on their proportionate representation in society. If prerequisites or qualifications for admissions or positions are established, says Nell, then these requirements must be met with equal frequency by members of all social groups. This view of equal opportunity justifies the use of quotas and other preferential practices because they confer equal (or less unequal) rewards. From this perspective, fair rules are not enough. Rather, equal opportunity for any experience or result means that individuals must be equally likely, as members of particular groups, to achieve that experience or result. This does not mean that all individuals will be equally successful; there will continue to be gaps between the most and least successful people in each group, provided that the same range of differences exists within other groups. Thus, according to Nell, intergroup not intragroup differences would be eliminated.

III. INTERPRETATIONS OF TITLE IX

Formal Interpretation

Title IX, like Title VI, can be given either a formal or a substantive interpretation. Most common is the formal perspective, which views title IX as a mandate to eliminate discriminatory practices in school systems and provide both sexes equal access to all programs and activities. Continuing disproportion in classes, clubs, sports, and employment is not in itself a violation of the law and is thus generally considered to be the result of individual differences and choices. This view prevails, in part, because Congress never addressed such complex issues as guarantees of equal success rates for females and males, indeed never articulated what outcomes it envisioned for students as a result of Title IX.

Substantive Interpretation

Both the Title IX Statute and the implementing Regulation contain language that can also be interpreted from a substantive equal opportunity perspective. They go beyond the prohibition of nondiscrimination and mandate equal benefits from educational programs, i.e., that individuals shall not "on the basis of sex, be excluded from participation in, be denied the benefits of, or be subjected to discrimination under any education program or activity receiving federal financial assistance. . . ."

According to attorney Charles Guerrier in his legal handbook on Title IX (1978), these three protections (participation, benefits, nondiscrimination) are not functionally equivalent. It is possible to provide two of them, participation and nondiscrimination, without the third, provision of equal benefits from educational programs. Guerrier cites *Lau v. Nichols,* in which the Supreme Court had to interpret similar language under Title VI. The Court found that although non-English-speaking students were provided the same facilities, textbooks, teachers, and curriculum as English-speaking students, the fact that they did not understand the language meant that they were receiving fewer educational "benefits . . . which denies them a meaningful opportunity to participate in the educational program" (p. 30). Equal participation did not provide equal benefits for which, the Court ruled, affirmative efforts would be necessary.

The Title IX implementing Regulation goes well beyond the language of Title VI in the specificity of its provisions because it is based on legal and administrative precedents established over the years in the enforcement of Title VI (Fishel and Pottker 1977: p. 107). In Section 86.3, the Regulation requires "remedial steps to eliminate the effects of any discrimination" and permits "affirmative action to overcome the effects of conditions which resulted in limited participation therein by persons of a particular sex."

According to Guerrier, case law suggests that remedial action required by the Federal government to overcome the continuing effects of past discrimination may include utilization of sexual classifications in order to remedy past recognized violations. He indicates that although affirmative action to overcome the effects of limited participation by persons of a particular sex is purely voluntary in the absence of a finding of past discrimination, "in some instances it may be appropriate to actually resort to the 'preference' method, if the goal sought to be achieved is of a compelling nature and can be achieved no other way" (p. 75). It is Guerrier's contention that equal opportunity to participate in and benefit from all programs and activities as mandated by Title IX may require affirmative action in addition to the elimination of discriminatory practices (p. 113).

IV. LONG-RANGE OUTCOMES

Interpretation of the Title IX mandate—formal or substantive—depends largely on the outcomes desired. The formal approach seeks elimination of sex discriminatory policies and practices, while the substantive view promotes equal success rates among males and females. School district focus on minimum compliance activities designed to eliminate overt discriminatory practices and provide access to school opportunities has not significantly altered disproportionate participation and achievement rates for males and females. Diesel mechanics, calculus, and baseball still attract few girls; child care, fine arts, and cheerleading, few boys. Girls continue to lag behind boys in achievement tests, career preparation, and physical prowess. Boys, on the other hand, exhibit higher levels of underachievement, maladjustment, and greater behavior and truancy problems than do girls.

The formal interpretation of equal opportunity implies that continued disproportion in participation and achievement reflects individual ability and preference. However, students may not have the information, experience, and skill to make informed choices. Ability is limited by prior experiences, and preference colored by the subtle influence of sex bias and sex role stereotyping. Thus, neither ability nor preference may be adequate criteria for important educational and occupational choices.

The substantive view of equal opportunity requires that to insure equal success rates among females and males, quotas and preferences are appropriate short-term measures. Language in the Title IX Regulation and pertinent case law suggests that such measures can be justified. These might involve equal assignment of female and male students to all activities and programs and even disproportionate assignments to nontraditional areas until historical imbalances are altered. However, the highly controversial nature of such actions makes them difficult to promote as methods to achieve equity in the public schools. Events, however, may ultimately force a reconsideration of quotas as the only guarantor of equity.

For the purpose of this discussion, the substantive equal opportunity goal of equal success rates for females as a group and males as a group is accepted, but not the use of quotas to achieve it. Short of quotas, well-planned affirmative efforts are needed to insure that females and males are empowered to gain maximum benefit from their educational experiences. Such efforts must focus on the equalization of participation rates, which is a precursor to equalized rates of success.

Specific long-range outcomes of this equal opportunity goal would reflect equalized overall participation and success rates between females and males (without eliminating differences among individuals within these groups). Such outcomes would include

- equal rates of performance by females and males on standardized achievement tests
- equal rates of success in classroom performance
- equal rates of improvement by females and males in physical fitness and development
- equal participation rates of females and males in athletics
- equal rates of participation in all academic and vocational courses
- equal rates of participation in school jobs, clubs, activities
- equal rates of participation in student governance
- equal rates of nurturance and assertiveness responses by females and males as situationally appropriate
- equal representation of females and males in all school employment categories

V. DEFINITION OF EQUITY

The outcomes listed above may appear utopian, but the notion of equal success rates can serve as a focal point for dialogue about appropriate long-term goals for the equity enterprise. Clearly defined goals, in turn, permit the development of strategies for their achievement.

The definition of *educational sex equity* proposed in this paper combines the formal equal opportunity goal of equal access with the substantive equal opportunity goal of equal success rates.

Educational Sex Equity can be defined as the elimination of sex discrimination, bias, and stereotyping in all school structures, policies, and practices and the promotion of proportionately equal educational and occupational attainments between female and males.

VI. STAGES OF EQUITY

The Equity Continuum

The two approaches (formal and substantive) to equal opportunity delineated by Nell (1976) have different goals, but the substantive equal opportunity goal of equal success rates has as a precondition the formal equal opportunity goal of equal access. The clear directionality of these equal opportunity perspectives suggests a continuum which begins with discrimination (or the lack of equity), moves through the provision of equal access, and culminates in equal success rates (full equity). Both the formal and substantive equal opportunity phases of the equity continuum incorporate Nell's descriptors but are divided into specific well-defined stages, as illustrated in Figure 1.

Figure 1.
EQUITY CONTINUUM

	Formal Equal Opportunity				*Substantive Equal Opportunity*		
	Discrimi-nation (No Equity)	Elimina-tion of Discrimi-natory Policies	Elimina-tion of Discrimi-natory Practices	Fair Rules Equal Access	Affirma-tive Pro-grams	Equal Participa-tion Rates	Equal Success Rates (Full Equity)
STAGES	1	2	3	4	5	6	7

The formal equal opportunity phase begins with a move from the initial stage of discrimination to the elimination of discriminatory policies (stage two). This action is fundamental to change, since official policies represent a codification of the philosophy of a school district. Such a change signifies a recognition of the need for fairness in education for all students and employees. Stage three is the elimination of discriminatory practices. Practices change only after policies provide official sanction for fairness in education-related programs. Nondiscriminatory policies and practices arising from stages two and three lead to fair rules and equal access, which represent the final stage of formal equal opportunity. This fourth stage also represents full legal compliance.

Fair rules and equal access, while overcoming discriminatory barriers, provide only limited equity, however, since, as Nell points out, fair procedures may have a disproportionate result when people from some groups have had a history of discrimination. Stage four (equal access) can be considered the first stage of substantive equal opportunity as well as the last stage of formal equal opportunity. It is the basis for stage five, affirmative programs, designed to promote increased levels of participation in all areas by underrepresented groups. Such programs might include recruitment, compensatory training, and extra support services.

Affirmative action is a weaker mechanism to insure equal participation and success rates than are quotas and preferences which, according to Nell, are vital to the goal of substantive equal opportunity. The modification of quotas to affirmative action places what may seem undue confidence in the good will of educational systems. However, a real commitment to affirmative programs can promote higher levels of equity, albeit without the insurance of specified quotas based on representation in the population.

Affirmative programs should lead to equal participation rates (stage six) in all categories (courses of study, athletics, employment, extracurricular activities, etc.). Equal participation rates tend to produce equal success rates (stage seven), which provide an equal range of benefits and rewards such as money, status, and power for all social groups. This is the final stage of substantive equal opportunity and reflects the achievement of full equity.

The Compliance Continuum

While the term *equity* is generally used to represent the spirit of Title IX, compliance connotes the letter of the law. A series of sequential stages in compliance have been identified by Shirley McCune: No Action, Paper Compliance, Pocket Compliance, Systemwide Compliance, and Commitment and Operational Programs (Kaser et al. 1980: pp. iv, 16-17, and subsequent personal communication). These five stages of compliance can be shown on a continuum as illustrated in Figure 2.

Figure 2.
COMPLIANCE CONTINUUM

	No Action	Paper Compliance	Pocket Compliance	Systemwide Compliance	Commitment/ Operational Programs
Stages	1	2	3	4	5

A system first moves from no action at all into paper compliance, stage two. Paper compliance means completion of the procedural requirements of the

Regulation—minimal training and information within the district—but continuation of violations. Pocket compliance is stage three; although it represents movement beyond paper compliance, responses to legal requirements are fragmented and only minimum levels of staff and financial resources are allocated to the effort. There are isolated individual efforts toward equity while some legal violations remain. Systemwide compliance, the fourth stage, proposed by Mc-Cune in a personal conversation with the author, indicates that a system has fulfilled its legal requirements. The goals of compliance, according to McCune, are access to programs, the elimination of within-class segregation, the establishment of a sex-fair curriculum, and role models of both sexes. Compliance with the law leads to "the development of affirmative programs which can stabilize these changes and result in full educational equity" (Kaser et al. 1980 pp. iv-15). This is the fifth stage, characterized by commitment and operational programs.

The Equity/Compliance Continuum Relationship

McCune's compliance continuum, therefore, provides equal access (formal equal opportunity) and culminates with affirmative efforts to promote full equity (substantive equal opportunity). This construct fits nicely into the equity continuum presented in Figure 1. It is important to note that the stages of compliance do not exactly mirror the linear stages of the equity continuum because they reflect uneven systemic adaptations to Federal requirements. In that sense, the compliance continuum is more empirically based than the idealized stages of the equity continuum. Figure 3 portrays the relationship of McCune's stages of compliance to the equity continuum.

Figure 3.
EQUITY/COMPLIANCE CONTINUUM RELATIONSHIPS

Equity Continuum

Formal Equal Opportunity   *Substantive Equal Opportunity*

STAGES	1	2	3	4	5	6	7
	Discrimination (No Equity)	Elimination of Discriminatory Policies	Elimination of Discriminatory Practices	Fair Rules/ Equal Access	Affirmative Programs	Equal Participation Rates	Equal Success Rates (Full Equity)
	No Action	Paper Compliance	Pocket Compliance	Systemwide Compliance	Commitment/ Operational Programs		
STAGES	1	2	3	4	5		

Compliance Continuum (McCune)

Compliance—A Vehicle for Change

Compliance with Title IX must be viewed as one of a variety of vehicles for achieving equity. Other vehicles include pressure from internal and external advocacy groups, commitment from school leadership, changing social values, and workforce patterns. The Federal pressure for civil rights is a major force for change, but equity is an ethical and social value that exists with or without the legal mandate.

School system responses to Title IX can be analyzed along the equity continuum. There can be some degree of equity in a system without full compliance and certainly compliance without full equity, but full equity is undergirded by legal compliance. The continuum can also be used to project goals for school systems beyond legal compliance and the guarantee of fair rules and equal access.

Although responses on the substantive equal oportunity end of the continuum may be more time-consuming, costly, and disruptive in the short run, they are consistent with basic constitutional guarantees and American values, and provide long-term benefits for schools and socially relevant experiences for students.

VII. RESPONSES TO TITLE IX

School district responses to Title IX may be analyzed in functional terms, which involve the assessment of short- and long-term, intended and unintended consequences for system maintenance and growth. There is evidence that the short-term advantages for schools and minimal compliance activities are frequently nullified after a period of time. Unresolved equity issues often result in adverse relationships with internal and external groups, negative publicity, complaints filed with the Federal government, or lawsuits with the court. Conversely, strongly affirmative responses may in the short term seem dysfunctional for a system but in the long run prove cost efficient; they may save the excessive amounts of time, money, and disruption that go into responding to complaints, court suits, community and teacher organization pressures for change, and into the repetition of compliance activities.

Beyond these costs, it is also dysfunctional for school systems to ignore the long-term consequences of failure to provide students with the skills, knowledge, experiences, and motivation to explore nontraditional courses and careers. Although occupational segregation is still a social reality, numerous opportunities now exist, and are expanding, for women and men to engage in hitherto proscribed or delimited vocations. Family structures and roles are also changing. These shifts in both the domestic and occupational spheres require an affirmative response by public schools so that students will be able to respond appropriately.

Two key areas will be reviewed to gain some perspective on the degree to which Title IX implementation efforts have been a response to the letter or the spirit of the law, and on the short- and long-term intended and unintended consequences for school districts of these efforts. The two areas are the procedural and curriculum-related portions of the Regulation, both of which have major implications for change if given maximal equity interpretations. School district responses to other areas of the Regulation can be subjected to similar scrutiny.

Some important research conducted in the past years provides a growing data base for such analysis. The reports of Title IX implementation drawn on here are

—the national study on compliance with procedural requirements conducted by the Rand Corporation for the Office of Education, HEW, hereafter called the Rand report (Hill and Rettig 1980)

—a report for HEW entitled *The Status of Title IX in Region X* (Miller and Associates 1978)

—a review of Michigan school district compliance with Title IX (Michigan Department of Education 1979)

—*Back-to-School Line-Up* (Project on Equal Education Rights/PEER 1979)

—a study entitled *Vocational Education Equity Study* conducted by American Institutes for Research, hereafter called the AIR report (Harrison and Dahl 1979)

—*National Survey on the Impact of Title IX on Public School Systems* (Bornstein 1980)

School District Responses to Procedural Requirements

Title IX procedural requirements were adopted by the government in order to encourage local school districts to monitor and remedy sex discrimination in their systems without Federal interference. These requirements are

—designation of a Title IX coordinator

—development and dissemination of a nondiscrimination policy statement

—development and publication of fair and efficient grievance procedures

—a district-wide self-evaluation to identify and remedy discriminatory policies and procedures

—filing of a formal assurance of compliance with the government

When these requirements are implemented seriously and updated regularly, they become the most effective tools for achieving equity while maintaining local control over educational policy and practice. Voluntary compliance has been minimal, however, according to research findings and observation in the field. In most agencies, "self-evaluations are not comprehensive, sex biased attitudes persist in staff and faculty, and no effort is made to promote Title IX nor examine programs in-depth for sex discrimination" (Miller and Associates, 1978: p. 14).

Generally, Title IX implementation has been treated as an administrative process, handled by mid-level district employees without the involvement of the school board, community, teachers, or students. According to the Rand report (Hill and Rettig 1980),

> . . . .staff members act primarily on their own initiative and according to their own standards. Locally initiated response to Title IX is therefore primarily a function of what LEA employees understand the guaranteed rights to be and of how they are motivated by personal conviction, sense of professional duty, or desire to avoid being the object of a formal complaint. [p. 12]

Many school districts report that they are in compliance with Title IX while, according to in-depth analyses or site visits made to corroborate self-reports, they are actually *not* in compliance. Paper compliance and superficial changes are most characteristic. (In the Michigan Department of Education survey, conducted in 1979, 99 percent of the State's school districts were found to be not in full compliance with all five of the procedural requirements [p. 66].) In most school districts, a Title IX coordinator has been appointed; however, that person ordinarily holds other (often multiple) responsibilities, spends a fraction of her or his time on Title IX matters, lacks a job description, and is torn between conflicting roles—advocate, compliance officer, and defender of the institution (Miller and Associates 1979: p. 21). Thus, role definition is influenced primarily by the top administrator's level of commitment.

Self-evaluation is the procedural mechanism with the greatest potential for achieving and maintaining equity. Many districts completed a superficial self-study several years ago and have never updated or expanded it. Self-evaluation reports rarely contain recommendations for remediation and modification as required by the Regulation. In Michigan, only 14 percent of the school districts surveyed had both of these elements in their self-evaluations (p. 67). The Rand report found that most school districts did not involve teachers, students, or community in the process, and failed to produce a summary report for distribution for a "clear agenda for action" (p. 40).

Internal grievance procedures by which persons can help school district administrators identify and remedy sex discrimination are seldom used. This is, in part, because the procedural mechanisms are generally not well publicized in schools and communities (p. 11). Further, many school district grievance procedures that do not work fairly and expeditiously as required by the Regulation involve a great deal of time and stress for individuals with complaints. "The entire burden of formulating and pressing the complaint is on the grievant" (p. 11).

The minimal compliance activities characterizing public school response to the procedural requirements of the Title IX Regulation are intended in the short run to keep districts out of trouble with Federal bureaucracy and maintain access to Federal financial support. The Rand report asserts

> . . . .it is clear that federal pressure is . . . a real factor in institutional decisionmaking. Institutional officials assume that their practices will come under federal scrutiny, and they make serious efforts to avoid federal government intervention on matters of compliance. Given the very low incidence of punitive action by the federal government, its efforts to put local officials under pressure appear to be highly successful. [Hill and Rettig: 37]

In the short term, such minimal responses have the advantage of requiring little cost, labor, or time to be taken from other school enterprises. Since few teachers, students, or community persons are informed about the law or compliance activities, opposition, advocacy, or lengthy deliberations are avoided.

In the long term, however, what seemed originally a cost-effective approach to compliance, frequently escalates into an expensive nightmare for school administrators. Teacher associations and community organizations publicize the Title IX requirements along with individual rights and Federal complaint procedures. Pressure is applied to administrators to repeat the procedural activities; periodic monitoring is conducted by internal and external groups; and the news media are alerted to Title IX violations.

More serious, complaints are filed with the Federal government and lawsuits are filed in the courts. Federal investigations require considerable staff time to retrieve, analyze, and submit the required documentation and to "host" on-site investigations. Unforeseen results often include negative local publicity, costly remedies, and confrontation with Federal officials and local groups. Often the top administrator and policymakers find that assurances of compliance provided in response to self-evaluation surveys by building-level administrators were inaccurate or inadequate or both, rendering those responsible for compliance personally vulnerable.

These long-term unintended consequences are a reversal of those intended by school administrators. Rather than keeping Federal officials out, noncompliance invites investigation. Instead of being inexpensive, the cost becomes prohibitive. Community activism is not stemmed, it is exacerbated.

Unintended consequences for school districts may also result from studies that explore the low level of compliance with procedural regulations nationally. The Rand report, for example, concludes with a series of recommendations which, if accepted by the Federal government, would tighten up the procedural requirements and reporting mechanisms. The report holds that "local action is the key to the implementation of the civil rights guarantees" (Hill and Rettig 1980:38), and recommends that the Federal government clarify the procedural requirements and inform the public about the existence and use of these mechanisms (p. 39).

Specific recommendations of the Rand report for the government include

—clarification of the purpose, scope, timing of self-evaluations

—participation of students, staff, and interest groups in the self-evaluation process

—periodic renewals of self-evaluations

—written summary % self-evaluation reports disseminated to all employees, students, and local interest groups

—extensive media publicity for grievance procedures (pp. 38-47).

Figure 4 contrasts low compliance/equity responses to the procedural requirements with high compliance/equity responses.

Figure 4. RESPONSES TO PROCEDURAL REQUIREMENTS

LOW COMPLIANCE/EQUITY (LETTER OF TITLE IX)	HIGH COMPLIANCE/EQUITY (SPIRIT OF TITLE IX)
Appointment of Title IX coordinator who lacks interest, experience, or commitment and who has numerous other LEA responsibilities. No job description, mandate for change or authority to initiate or monitor change.	Full-time Title IX coordinator appointed who is committed to equity and secures training and information. Clear job description and mandate from superintendent to whom coordinator reports directly.
Statement of nondiscriminatory policy incomplete and not widely or regularly disseminated.	Annual, broad dissemination of nondiscrimination policy with reference to appropriate legislation and enforcement agency as well as information about local Title IX coordinator and grievance process.
Grievance procedures developed, but not disseminated. Use of procedures results in ridicule, retribution, inaction.	Grievance procedures, which work fairly and expeditiously as determined through resolution of grievances, broadly disseminated to staff, students, community. Persons encouraged to identify problems so they can be remedied.

Self-evaluation conducted once by a central office administrator. Superficial. No monitoring or up-dating.

In-depth self-evaluation conducted by committee composed of administrators, teachers, counselors, students, community. Implementation and monitoring of recommendations designed to eliminate discriminatory practices and promote equity. Periodic site reviews conducted by trained staff.

School District Responses to Curriculum and Instruction Issues

Differences between minimal and maximal compliance and equity actions relating to the curriculum have the most profound and far-reaching consequences for students. From kindergarten through graduate school, women and men are affected academically, psychologically, and vocationally by overt and covert forms of sex discrimination, bias, and stereotyping in the classroom (Sadker and Sadker 1980).

The Title IX Regulation provides that "no person shall, on the basis of sex, be excluded from participation in, be denied the benefits of, or be subjected to discrimination under any academic, extracurricular, research, occupational training or other education program or activity. . . ." (Section 86.31). To date, only one of these three protections—nondiscrimination—has been seriously addressed by most school administrators. Most course offerings are now available to all students regardless of sex, although vestiges such as "powder puff football," "bachelor cooking," and "slimnastics" remain. In Michigan, 39 percent of the school districts responding to a survey conducted in 1979 still offered courses limited to one sex (Michigan Department of Education 1979:68).

Despite a decline in the number of sex-restricted courses and discriminatory prerequisites, participation rates, although changed, are still disproportionate in courses traditionally oriented to one sex or the other. The Title IX Regulation requires an analysis of disproportionate enrollments to determine whether discrimination in counseling materials or techniques is responsible. Such analysis is not undertaken by school districts where the prevailing view is that enrollment figures reflect student choice. Only 40 percent of the Michigan districts surveyed had established procedures to insure that bias in counseling was not responsible for disproportionate enrollments (p. 68).

Curriculum ghettoes persist and should, by their very nature, raise suspicions about the degree to which students have the information, training, experiences, role models, and teacher and counselor support to make informed choices. For example, the large disparity in numbers of boys, as compared to girls, taking advanced mathematics is not solely the result of differences in student interest.

Several studies demonstrate that boys who take advanced mathematics do so because they believe it to be important to their career goals, not because they like the subject better than do girls (Rappaport 1978:196).

While greater numbers of females than males suffer from math anxiety, even the most adept female math students tend not to take advanced courses. Higher mathematics has not been sex designated, but without affirmative efforts to interest girls in the career potential of math, enrollment figures remain the same. Few remedial programs have been established in the public schools for girls deficient in math-related skills such as spatial visualization, while remedial reading programs geared primarily to assist boys are a standard feature of the curriculum from the elementary grades through high school.

In physical education, differential participation patterns are often concealed behind newly adopted coeducational schedules. Physical education is a particularly difficult area of the curriculum to change because of its long history of sex segregation. Title IX technical assistance personnel rate physical education one of the areas most significantly changed as a result of Title IX and also one of the most resistant to change (Bornstein 1980). In the past, female and male teachers ran separate programs, students were separated for instruction, and curriculum and institutions were different for female and male students because of stereotyped assumptions about innate sex differences, abilities, and potential.

Despite nominal desegregation as a result of the Title IX mandate, real integration has been sabotaged in many places by a proliferation of practices that keep the sexes separated. These practices include forced choice scheduling where students are asked to choose between modern dance and football; a soccer unit where students are asked to sign up with the male or the female coach; and ability groupings based on physical fitness norms that keep students at the same level in all sports activities even though an individual student might be mediocre in soccer and outstanding in badminton.

Differential enrollment patterns are most apparent in vocational education. According to a study conducted for the government by American Institutes for Research (AIR) (Harrison and Dahl 1979) on equity in vocational education programs throughout the country, "in 1979 enrollment patterns are overwhelmingly sex segregated and . . . progress in reducing sex segregation since 1972 has been minimal" (p. 3). The report indicates that women comprise 90 percent of the enrollment in traditionally female occupations in business and office, health, and trade and industrial areas, substantially the same percentage as in 1972. An increase was noted in the percentage of men enrolled in traditional female home economics courses from 7 percent to 17 percent. Men continue to predominate in enrollments in traditionally male occupations, although there has been an increase from 3 percent to 8 percent of women enrolled in technical and agricultural programs. Women comprise 6 percent of the enrollments in traditionally male trade and industrial programs; no change since 1972. Overall, the percentage of male students in traditionally female areas (10.9 percent) is greater than the percentage of female students in traditionally male areas (7.8 percent) (p. 3).

Why aren't girls signing up for that diesel mechanics class? Chances are that peers, parents, teachers, and counselors think it unsuitable, that girls do not have information on the nature of the work, amount of pay, kind of hours and benefits involved, and that they have no experience in repairing mechanical objects. Deprived of encouragement, information, skill, and experience, girls are not making real choices; they are conforming to stereotyped expectations no longer relevant to the job market.

The AIR study also found that "no more than one-third [of local school districts] are sponsoring or conducting specific activities aimed at fostering greater sex equity" (p. 18). Further, "there is clear evidence that those schools putting the most effort into various kinds of activities to further equity are also those experiencing the greatest amount of nontraditional enrollment" (p. 20).

Without a significant effort on the part of school personnel to equalize participation rates, there is no likelihood that the goal of roughly equivalent success rates for females and males can be achieved. No innate sex differences have been identified to account clearly for the grossly differential participation and achievement rates of females and males in education and work. This places a good deal of responsibility on the socialization and training students receive as they go through school.

Yet, as noted earlier in this paper, even full participation and nondiscrimination will not necessarily provide equity.

The third Federal mandate—that students shall not "be denied the benefits of" education programs—has the greatest implications for equity. The key question is: In what ways might students of one sex be receiving fewer benefits from instruction than students of the other sex? Are male students in a sewing class discouraged by the teacher from threading the machines because "boys are so careless and clumsy"? Are females in physical education class prevented from trying to compete against the male or combined male/female presidential physical fitness norms "because the boys will be embarrassed if girls outperform them"? Are female students deprived of role models in a history class that highlights only male explorers, scientists, writers, and educators? Are male students denied support for development of child-rearing skills by seeing males portrayed in textbooks almost exclusively in occupational roles?

The Title IX Regulation does not provide guidelines for determining whether benefits derived from education programs are unequal for females and males. It acknowledges that bias in curricular materials is a serious matter but does not address the issue. Sex bias and stereotyping in curriculum content, curricular materials, and instruction are not specifically prohibited. Staff training and information to change biased practices and provide nonsexist educational experiences for students are not required. Without the elimination of bias and stereotyping based on sex, however, both female and male students are unfairly limited to a narrow range of behaviors, roles, and career options. This, in turn, represents a real denial of the full benefits to be derived from education programs that impinge on future educational and occupational choices.

As demonstrated earlier, each action of the school district in response to Title IX bears long- and short-term, intended and unintended, consequences. When school district compliance in the area of curriculum is minimal, there are the short-term advantages of only minor adjustments and costs necessary to purge a system of single-sex courses. But the longterm unintended negative consequences are so dysfunctional for schools that they bear serious scrutiny. Most significantly, failure to prepare all students to make informed choices relevant to current social realities in the domestic, leisure, and vocational spheres of life is a failure of the schools themselves.

School districts must, therefore, evaluate each response carefully in terms of consequences. Consider, for example, the implementation of a truly coeducational physical education program, kindergarten through twelfth grade, after an intensive training and information program for staff, students, and parents. The short-term intended consequence of such a program is obedience to the law and revision of the physical education curriculum around fitness and lifetime sports. Other short-term consequences involve the spending of time and money to conduct training, establish new procedures, and overcome resistance. The long-term intended result is to provide quality education equally for male and female students and to remedy the disparities in student ability that are based on prior inequities in experience and training.

Unplanned positive consequences of such program implementation include (as reported by professionals) improved staff communication, better teaching practices, increased girls' skills in competitive sports and boys' in individual sports, and better attitudes toward physical education among both girls and boys who are not athletically gifted. Further, such a program is appropriate to the current societal emphasis on health, fitness, and physical strength. It also prepares young women for new opportunities available in athletics, which may ultimately provide college opportunities through scholarships.

On the other hand, dysfunctional long-term unintended consequences, such as resegregative practices within classes, may also result. Other negative unanticipated consequences of a combined program may be the loss of female physical education staff through the establishment of apparently neutral job criteria that more men than women can fulfill. Thus, all actions, even those ostensibly affirmative, should be evaluated with a view toward long-term effect on the system.

Dysfunctional consequences can be avoided with more long-range planning for equity, planning that includes careful assessment of sex equity needs, design of a series of activities based on those needs, consideration of possible consequences of proposed activities, continuous evaluation of activities to determine if goals are being met, and redesign of activities and strategies as necessary. Figure 5 contrasts low compliance/equity responses to curriculum and instruction issues with high compliance/equity responses.

Figure 5.
RESPONSES TO CURRICULUM & INSTRUCTION ISSUES

LOW COMPLIANCE/EQUITY (LETTER OF TITLE IX)	HIGH COMPLIANCE/EQUITY (SPIRIT OF TITLE IX)
All courses open to students of both sexes without prerequisites or requirements that have an adverse impact on one sex.	Students and parents regularly informed about the accessibility and desirability of nontraditional courses. Compensatory courses to remedy previous discrimination.
Annual tally of numbers of females and males enrolled in course offerings. Notation regarding disproportion sent to Counseling Department.	Disproportionate enrollments monitored for bias in counseling and teaching practices and materials. Teachers and counselors actively recruit students for nontraditional courses.
Since gender-specific language not mentioned in Regulation, no attempt to change it. Those who propose the use of non-sexist language may be ridiculed.	Course descriptions free of gender-specific language or references.
Since no requirement in Regulation to evaluate course content for bias and stereotyping, no such process initiated.	Course syllabi, content, format, assignments, related media analyzed to eliminate sex bias and stereotyping.
Textbooks specifically omitted from Regulation. Despite referral by HEW to local school districts to remediate, no action undertaken since not required.	Textbooks and other curriculum materials examined to assess degree of bias and stereotyping. Supplemental plans and materials ordered or developed.

Teacher training and information not required, so not undertaken. Concern may exist that teachers will take time away from regular curriculum for equity activities.

Teachers trained on regular basis to identify and remedy bias in classroom management and curriculum materials. Information on equity issues, materials, and techniques regularly disseminated to teachers.

Teachers may receive negative feedback from initiating equity activities, since these are not required and no climate of support exists.

Teachers supported and rewarded for equity activities woven into regular curriculum.

School District Responses to Other Title IX Areas

Responses to other activities and practices covered by Title IX can also be analyzed in terms of their consequences for schools and students. Short-term advantages of minimal compliance responses in counseling, athletics, extracurricular activities, and employment may be latently dysfunctional in the long term. For example, the assumption that inequities in staffing patterns and employment procedures are not covered by Title IX, and therefore require no remediation, is hazardous. Despite a number of court rulings that Title IX regulations covering employment are invalid (most significantly, *Romeo Community Schools v. United States Department of Health, Education and Welfare*), remedies to employment discrimination can be pursued under Title VII of the 1964 Civil Rights Act, the 1963 Equal Pay Act, Executive Order 11246, and a variety of local and State statutes.

Beyond the cost and disruption involved in responding to Federal investigation, there is a price to be paid for failure to institute employment policies and practices that promote equal rates of participation, particularly in school administration. This price ultimately is a loss of confidence in schools for failure to tap their best resources regardless of sex, provide children with role models of both sexes, and promote respect and good working relationships between persons of both sexes.

Affirmative steps that bring women into school administration include

—identification of women who are qualified or qualifiable and interested in administration
—development of nondiscriminatory job criteria
—wide publicity for available administrative positions
—active recruitment of women with good potential for specific job openings
—training and internship experiences as appropriate
—nondiscriminatory interview procedures

—objective selection procedures
—administrative support for newly selected female administrators
—provision of relevant information to new female administrators
—standardized evaluation criteria and procedures for all administrators
—development of an affirmative action plan with clear goals and timetables
   for increasing female participation in administration
—effective monitoring process for plan

The long-term impact of minimum compliance actions is hazardous for athletics, also. Although there has been a dramatic increase of over 600 percent in the number of females participating in interscholastic sports between 1971 and 1977 (U.S. Department of HEW 1979: Appendix A), women still comprise only 33 percent of all athletes (PEER 1979). Title IX technical assistance personnel rate athletics, like physical education, both most significantly changed due to Title IX and most resistant to change (Bornstein 1980).

Despite greatly increased participation in sports competition, failure by the schools to provide affirmative opportunities in all structures and practices prevents female athletes from receiving full benefits from these programs. Such inequitable practices include

—limited access to practice and training facilities
—lack of opportunities to play before prime-time audiences
—denial of the best quality coaching and officiating
—limited school support such as cheerleading, pep rallies, and publicity

A serious long-term result of limited support for and interest in girls' sports may be the lack of real improvement in the quality of competition. This, in turn, reduces the number of girls who might potentially win college athletic scholarships, which is the only access many poor and minority students have to a postsecondary education and credential. In sum, to achieve the objective of equalized participation and success rates, short-term practices in all education-related areas must be evaluated carefully for long-term implications.

VIII. IMPLICATIONS FOR ACTION

Since the passage of Title IX by Congress in 1972, many new possibilities for growth, participation, and success have become available to both females and males in the nation's schools. In many school districts, however, responses to Title IX have been more cosmetic than fundamental. Overall participation and success rates of females and males, while changing, are still only minimally altered.

It is the central thesis of this paper that failure to establish full equity as a goal is in the long run severely dysfunctional for students and schools; it is costly in both financial and human terms and creates disjuncture between the schools and society. While maximal equity responses to Title IX may appear radical now, they are essentially practical and cost-effective when viewed from a long-range perspective.

Investigations of factors related to the level of compliance indicate that although urban school districts report a higher priority for Title IX than do rural school districts (Miller and Associates 1978:15), no systematic differences have been found in Title IX compliance among regions of the country or among districts with different levels of previous civil rights activity (Hill and Rettig 1978:7). Further, no consistency exists among regions or States when ranked according to percentage of female participation in high school interscholastic athletics, school administration, and traditionally male vocational courses (PEER 1979).

The single factor cited as most related to the level of compliance activity is the degree of commitment, leadership, and support from school superintendents. Of Title IX coordinates surveyed in Region X, 85 percent indicated that administrative support is an important factor in successful implementation of Title IX while 70 percent reported that they do not have such support (Miller and Associates 1978: 16). This report makes a useful distinction between administrative support and leadership.

> . . . Leadership implies an active, personal commitment in the initiation or execution of all activity. Administrative support does not require leadership; it only requires a willingness to take positive action which may range from acquiescence to enthusiastic commitment. [p. 39]

Site studies conducted by Miller and Associates (1978) reveal that leadership can come not only from the top administrator, but also from an athletic director, a school board member, a Title IX advisory committee, or a Title IX coordinator (p. 39).

The Rand report (Hill and Rettig 1980) indicates that while leadership from the chief administrator is important, other conditions are necessary for successful implementation of Title IX. One of these conditions is pressure for change "from both the federal government and interested parties within the institutions or in the communities served by them" (p. 36). To Title IX professionals, it has long been apparent that while administrative support is important for change to occur, leadership can indeed emanate from a variety of sources. In some school districts the impetus for change has come from community groups and in others from teacher organizations. Occasionally, a lone parent or teacher is responsible for significant change in one or several parts of the school system, often in the area of athletics.

Leadership for school district responsiveness to Title IX can also come from the State department of education. For example, the survey conducted by the Michigan Department of Education (1979) and quoted extensively in this paper will be used by the staff to plan future assistance to local school districts. The report states that "to support the State Board of Education policy and expressed goal of eliminating and preventing sex discrimination in Michigan school districts, this report contains specific recommendations which identify areas for future involvement and assistance from the Michigan Department of Education" (pp. v-vi).

Impetus for change in school districts also comes from Federally funded Title IV projects focusing on sex desegregation, such as local school board grants that generally support a compliance officer and some training activities, training institutes that conduct in-depth staff development activities in school districts, and regional centers that provide, upon request, technical assistance and training related to Title IX and sex equity without charge to school districts.

The major Federal impetus for change, of course, is the Office for Civil Rights (OCR), which is the agency responsible for enforcement of Title IX. However, the extreme sensitivity of OCR to political pressure has resulted in unclear and inconsistent enforcement and interpretation of the regulations. ". . . A sense of impermanence and an air of confusion surrounds the regulations, which reduces their credibility" (Miller and Associates 198:27). School personnel doubt that OCR uses data that they are required to submit, and "do not believe that the federal government will enforce compliance" (p. 26).

A leading advocate for sex equity in education, Holly Knox, Director of the Project on Equal Education Rights (PEER), asserts that "cutting off funds is the only way to get school districts and colleges to stop discriminating against women. . . . There's no evidence that they will act for any other reason except under court order, under massive monetary damages, or under the threat of losing federal money" ("An Interview . . ." 1979:519).

The Rand report (Hill and Rettig 1980), on the other hand, indicates that "federal pressure is . . . a real factor in institutional decisionmaking" (p. 37). Cynthia Brown, former Assistant Secretary for Civil Rights, admits that OCR is not initiating enforcement proceedings or terminating Federal funds with anything like the frequency it did in the sixties, but indicates that the agency has been successful in negotiating compliance in most Title IX areas ("An Interview . . ." 1979:518).

Momentum for Title IX compliance and equity can come from a variety of sources. No matter what the source, action will be more or less functional for students and schools if long-range outcomes are clearly defined and strategies for change geared to those outcomes. Desirable outcomes proffered in this paper have to do with equalizing participation and success rates for males and females.

IX. STRATEGIES FOR CHANGE

Integration of Civil Rights Activities

The most efficient and least alienating way of fulfilling school district civil rights responsibilities is to combine activities while assuring attention to the unique problems in each area. This is particularly appropriate since the Office for Civil Rights is conducting combined reviews. Some of the areas that lend themselves to coordination are

—compliance coordinator responsibilities
—self-evaluations
—board policies
—affirmative action plans
—employment practices
—treatment of students
—school-community relations
—staff training

A major factor in achieving successful implementation instead of minimal compliance of Title IX, according to the Miller and Associates report (1978), is the philosophy "equal educational opportunity is good education" (p. 35). From this perspective, equity is not viewed as an "enrichment" activity but rather as a fundamental element of quality education, which seeks to help each child develop her or his full potential.

Although this paper focuses on sex equity, its major points are applicable to all equity areas, including those dealing with race, national origin, and the handicapped.

Self-Assessment for Long-Range Planning

School district self-assessment should become a periodic, planned activity. Statistical, observational, and anecdotal data should be collected and used as a basis for identifying and investigating differential treatment, participation, and success rates based on sex. Reporting should include recommendations for modification of discriminatory policies, practices, and structures, as well as procedures for remedying the effects of previous discrimination. A summary of the annual report should be disseminated widely in schools and the community.

Long-range planning is essential to institutionalize change and insure that individual behavior and school norms are reflective of equity principles. Such planning should grow out of the self-assessment report and be accompanied by a system for monitoring progress.

Informing and Training Staff

The achievement of equity outcomes depends largely on staff agreement about the value of striving for such goals. Thus, it is incumbent upon those committed to equity principles to present clearly and effectively the rationale for equity along with strategies for achieving it.

To carry out Federal mandates, staff must not only understand equity goals and requirements, but have the skills and resources necessary for change. This involves regular dissemination of information about discrimination, bias, and sterotyping in education and their cost to students in terms of academic, psychological, career, and family development.

Staff training must move beyond awareness of these issues to the development of skills required to overcome such practices. As Shirley McCune has indicated, some of the needed skills and competencies are in "interpersonal relationships with students; curriculum modification and supplementation; educational management; and multi-cultural group processes" (1976:22).

A number of excellent materials are available for school district use to facilitate equity training and revision of curriculum and instruction. One major source of sex equity materials is the Women's Educational Equity Act Program. Among the best materials available are the training modules for administrators, teachers, counselors, vocational educators, physical activity specialists, and community produced for the Title IX Equity Workshops Project by the Resource Center on Sex Equity (McCune 1978). These modules include needs assessment, cognitive information, skill building activities, and action planning. Regular information should be disseminated to staff on the resources, programs, techniques and materials that promote equity. Pressure must also be applied to schools of education to assume responsibility for providing equity information, resources, and skills to the teachers, counselors, and administrators they train.

Support and rewards for teachers, counselors, principals, and others who initiate affirmative programs are vital. These include visibility for exemplary projects and for individuals with good programs and materials. In this way, a climate can be created in which the goal of full equity is the norm and not the exception and in which that goal permeates the entire system and not just some of its parts.

Community Involvement

Most parents and community members are not aware of the requirements and protections of civil rights legislation. School systems should assume responsibility for providing such information and involving the community in its equity activities, including self-evaluation, compliance activities, and affirmative programs. Local grievance procedures should be publicized as ways of identifying and remedying discriminatory practices and, thus, avoiding investigation by the Federal government. Time and attention must be given to developing strategies that build community support for equity goals. Initial negative reactions to coeducational physical education can be reduced by building enthusiasm for a program based on physical fitness and lifetime sports. The support of booster clubs for particular sports can often be broadened to include a commitment to the development of the total sports program.

X. TOWARD FULL EQUITY

Actions oriented toward full equity may be more costly, time-consuming, and disruptive in the short run than activities designed solely to meet minimal Title IX obligations. Often, however, such maximal responses have short-term as well as long-term advantages. They may, for example, result in positive media coverage; garner State or national attention; promote a spirit of cohesiveness in a system; and generate student, staff, and community involvement in school issues.

Long-term benefits to be derived by students and schools from promoting full equity are significant. Student achievement will be predicated on individual differences and not on sex-based sterotypes, and school systems will fulfill their essential function of preparing students with the knowledge and skills they need to assume adult responsibilities as defined by a twenty-first century society.

REFERENCES

"An Interview on Title IX with Shirley Chisholm, Holly Knox, Leslie R. Wolfe, Cynthia G. Brown, and Mary Karen Jolly."
1979 *Harvard Educational Review* 49(4):504-526.
Bornstein, Rita
1980 *National Survey on the Impact of Title IX on Public School Systems.* Southeast Sex Desegregation Center, University of Miami.
Fishel, Andrew, and Janice Pottker.
1977 *National Politics and Sex Discrimination in Education.* Lexington, Mass.: Lexington Books.
Guerrier, Charles.
1978 *Title IX and the Achievement of Equal Educational Opportunity: A Legal Handbook.* Washington, D.C.: Resource Center on Sex Roles in Education, Council of Chief State School Officers. HEW Contract No. 300-78-0493.
Harrison, Laurie R., and Peter R. Dahl.
1979 *Vocational Education Equity Study.* Palo Alto: American Institutes for Research, U.S. O.E. Contract No. 300-77-0318.
Hill, Paul T., and Richard Rettig.
1980 *Mechanisms for the Implementation of Civil Rights Guarantees by*

Educational Institutions. Santa Monica: Rand Corporation. 65p. (ERIC Document Reproduction Service No. ED 190 719).

Kaser, Joyce, et al. (Comps.)
1980   *Training and Legal Resources Notebook: Regional Conference on Compliance and Training for Title IV Grantees*. Washington, D.C.: Department of Education, Office of Equal Educational Programs. (Not available for distribution.)

McCune, Shirley.
1976   *Title IX and Title VI: We Must Live Together or Perish*. Address given at National General Assistance Center Conference, Kansas City, Missouri, May.

McCune, Shirley, and Martha Matthews.
1978   *Implementing Title IX and Attaining Sex Equity: A Workshop Package for Elementary-Secondary Educators*. Washington, D.C.: Resource Center on Sex Roles in Education, Council of Chief State School Officers. HEW Contract No. 300-76-0456. 168p. (ERIC Document Reproduction Service Nos. ED 185 469 through 185 472).

Michigan Department of Education, Office for Sex Equity in Education.
1979   *The Report on a Review of Michigan School District Compliance with Title IX*.

Miller and Associates, Inc.
1978   *The Status of Title IX in Region X: An Evaluation of Models and Barriers to Implementation of Title IX of the Education Amendments of 1972, for Region X of the U.S. Department of Health, Education and Welfare*. Olympia, Washington. HEW Contract No. 101-77-0003. 178p. (ERIC Document Reproduction Service No. 177 250).

Nell, Onora.
1976   "How Do We Know When Opportunities Are Equal?" In Carol C. Gould and Marx W. Wartofsky (Eds.), *Women and Philosophy: Toward a Theory of Liberation*. New York: G. P. Putnam's Sons. Pp. 334-346.

Project on Equal Education Rights.
1979   *Back-to-School Line-up: Where Girls and Women Stand in Education Today*. Washington, D.C.

Rappaport, Karen D.
1978   "Sexual Roles and Mathematical Expectations." *The Math Journal* 12(3):195-198.

Sadker, Myra, and David Sadker.
1980   *The Report Card: The Cost of Sex Bias in Schools*. Washington, D.C.: The Mid-Atlantic Center for Sex Equity, The American University.

U.S. Department of Health, Education and Welfare, Office of the Secretary.
1975   "Prohibiting Sex Discrimination in Education." *Federal Register* 40(108)Part II:24128-24145.
1979   "Intercollegiate Athletics: Sex Discrimination." *Federal Register* 40(239):71413-71423.

III.
NATIONAL ORIGIN DESEGREGATION

BILINGUAL EDUCATION IN
THE UNITED STATES:
A VIEW FROM 1980

Charles C. Harrington

INTRODUCTION

In the fall of 1969, I visited an elementary school in Manhattan with a friend who had just been appointed its principal. We toured the school, which neither of us had seen before. It had once had a good reputation under a strong principal famous for his reading program, but because of failing academic achievement, had recently been regarded as a problem school. It didn't take us long to identify the problem or discover why my friend, a bilingual Puerto Rican, had been appointed principal. Sixty percent of the school's 1,600 students were Spanish-speaking, but only one teacher spoke Spanish. We made our first priority the hiring of staff fluent in both Spanish and English. We had two goals: (1) to provide the children instruction in their native language until they could function in English, and (2) to teach them English. To facilitate these processes, we applied for a new kind of funding—a grant under what the Bilingual Education Act of 1968 had added as Title VII to the Elementary and Secondary Education Act of 1965 (hereafter Title VII)—to support the new programs that would be required.

Five years later, in 1974, the Supreme Court of the United States, at the prodding of a parent named Lau, unanimously came to the same conclusion we had reached that day in New York. They went even further. What we had seen as a good for the child, they defined as the child's *right*. The court argued:

> . . . there is no equality of treatment merely by providing students with the same facilities, textbooks, teachers, and curriculum, for students who do

not understand English are effectively foreclosed from any meaningful education. [*Lau* v. *Nichols*, 414 U.S. at 566]

Since that time, our nation's efforts to serve non-English-speaking populations have assumed greater visibility. The purposes of this paper are to review the history of Federal policy regarding bilingual education, to discuss the sociopolitical context, to discuss the evaluations of bilingual programming done to date, and to examine the implications of these factors for schools and classrooms at the local level. We will focus our review on what has happened since the Supreme Court's decision on *Lau* v. *Nichols*, and the degree to which efforts have actually improved the quality of education received by non-English-dominant children.

HISTORY OF FEDERAL INVOLVEMENT IN BILINGUAL EDUCATION

Despite the migration of large numbers of non-English-speaking people to this country in the nineteenth and twentieth centuries, prior to 1968 little attention was paid by the Federal government to bilingual education or to the problems of non-English-dominant minority students. The factors that led to a change in this also provide answers to the often-asked question: Why do these groups need special treatment? My group (Italian, East European, German, Belgian, etc.) didn't get it, why should they? (This question is sometimes linked to a philosophy of education that says children will learn faster if they are taught only in English, and that bilingual education is actually doing them a disservice.)

Today's linguistic minorities are different from those of past years, and the generation of 1968 is different from previous ones. The most obvious difference is the size of the non-English-speaking population. In many parts of the country (e.g. Southern California, parts of Texas, New York City, and Miami) the concentration of Spanish-speaking peoples had become so great by 1968 that it was virtually without precedent in the United States. All current indications point to a continued growth of these populations. While those labeled "Hispanic" are not necessarily assumed to be Spanish-speaking, Pifer (1980) estimates that today Hispanics comprise 30 percent of the school population in New York City, 45 percent in Los Angeles, 52 percent in San Antonio, 32 percent in Miami, 31 percent in Denver, and 35 percent in Hartford. (It should be noted that because of the Hispanic impetus for Federal involvement in bilingual education, the literature that we are discussing is most often about Hispanics, even though other groups are in need of and currently being served by bilingual programming.)

Another factor leading to changes in Federal policies for bilingual students was the recognition, by some, that equal educational opportunity was a myth for large numbers of the students not able to learn in English. Whether the real reason was educational/linguistic or more directly a reflection of discrimination against Hispanic groups in the larger society, Hispanic students were seriously disadvantaged educationally, compared to their classmates. They had joined, with Black and Native Americans, a level of American society from which it was difficult to emerge. Merely changing languages, or in some cases surnames as well, was not enough for many of these people to escape what Ogbu (1974, 1978) was to call the caste-like status into which they were placed by the larger society. Further, the civil rights movement had taken place, and the consciousness of the nation about discrimination against Blacks was rising; this concern was transferred to and sought by Hispanic leaders. Indeed, as we will see in the next pages, the Civil Rights Act of 1964 was itself to become the chief impetus for bilingual education in the United States. This was clearly a situation different from the one that characterized previous migrations to the United States.

Federal attention to the non-English-minority students received further impetus from the desire on the part of certain ethnic groups not to give up their culture. (This led to a general confusion of language and culture which still persists.) Two fundamentally different arguments were in fact offered for bilingual education, and the contradiction between those arguments is worth examining. It was argued, on the one hand, that teaching children in English only was not only ineffective, but destructive of the child's culture, which could only be preserved by teaching and learning in Spanish—an argument for maintenance models of bilingual education. On the other hand, it was argued that transitional (to English) bilingual education was necessary because without it, Hispanic children would not learn enough to gain employment and resources in the English-speaking world. Maintenance (of Spanish) bilingual programming would be protective of the child's identity and cultural heritage, but not designed to help the child learn English (transitional), which was important to guarantee economic equity over the long haul. Failure to do so would perpetuate a caste-like dependent group.

In response to these sometimes conflicting trends, the Bilingual Education Act of 1968 emerged. The act stated that:

> . . . in recognition of the special education needs of the large number of children of limited English-speaking ability in the United States, Congress hereby declares it to be the policy of the United States to provide financial assistance to local educational agencies to develop and carry out *new and imaginative* elementary and secondary school programs designed to meet those special educational needs. [PL 90-247, 1/2/68, Stat 816 Sec. 702]

The act made its first priority the learning of English.

> Bilingual education was to accomplish three purposes: (1) *increase* English language skills, (2) maintain and *perhaps* increase mother tongue skills, and (3) support the cultural heritage of the student. [Leibowitz 1980:24]

While it is, therefore, supportive of the transitional view, the act gained the support of the proponents of the maintenance view as well. Although the act gave home language and culture lower priorities, it was clearly an improvement over the status quo of English-only instruction.

Congress has continued to strengthen the emphasis on English language purpose in the Bilingual Education Amendments of 1974:

> The goal of the program in the Committee Bill is to permit a limited English-speaking child to develop proficiency in English that permits the child to learn as effectively in English as in the child's native language—a vital requirement to compete effectively in society. [Senate Report 93-763, Education Amendments of 1974:45]

In 1978, they declared that the policy was

> . . . to demonstrate effective ways of providing, for children of limited English proficiency, instruction designed to enable them, while using their native language, to achieve competence in the English language. [Bilingual Education Act, as amended, Sec. 702(a) (7) B]

In 1970, the Civil Rights Act of 1964 became, for the first time directly, an instrument for bilingual education in the United States. The Office for Civil Rights (OCR) of the Department of Health, Education, and Welfare, mailed a memorandum to all school districts in the United States listing the following areas of concern related to the enforcement of the Civil Rights Act in educational practice:

> 1. Where inability to speak and understand the English language excludes national origin-minority group children from effective participation in the educational program offered by a school district, the district must take affirmative steps to rectify the language deficiency in order to open its instructional program to these students.
> 2. School districts must not assign national origin-minority group students to classes for the mentally retarded on the basis of criteria which essentially measure or evaluate English language skills; nor may school districts deny national origin-minority group children access to college preparatory courses on a basis directly related to the failure of the school system to inculcate English language skills.
> 3. Any ability grouping or tracking system employed by the school system to deal with the special language skill needs of national origin-minority group children must be designed to meet such language skill needs as soon as possible and must not operate as an educational dead-end or permanent track.

4. School districts have the responsibility to adequately notify national origin-minority group parents of school activities which are called to the attention of other parents. Such notice in order to be adequate may have to be provided in a language other than English.

School districts should examine current practices which exist in their districts in order to assess compliance with the matters set forth in this memorandum. A school district which determines that compliance problems currently exist in that district should immediately communicate in writing with the Office for Civil Rights and indicate what steps are being taken to remedy the situation. Where compliance questions arise as to the sufficiency of programs designed to meet the language skill needs of national origin-minority group children already operating in a particular area, full information regarding such programs should be provided. In the area of special language assistance, the scope of the program and the process for identifying need and the extent to which the need is fulfilled should be set forth. [Office for Civil Rights, Memorandum of May 25, 1970]

While the memorandum was largely ignored, it was used as the basis of a lawsuit in San Francisco in which a parent named Lau in effect brought suit against the city of San Francisco (in the person of school superintendent Nichols) for depriving his child of equal educational opportunity because of her national origin. The city maintained, among other things, that it was not discriminating on the basis of national origin, but simply carrying out its traditional function of providing schooling in English. While this might have the same effect of denying non-English-speaking children equal education, they were being given the same opportunity to learn in English as everyone else—if they couldn't, it was their problem, not the district's. The district's responsibility was to provide the opportunity, and that would be in English. The district maintained that nothing in the Civil Rights Act of 1964 mandated different treatment for non-English-dominant children, and that OCR had exceeded its authority by interpreting the law as it had. Although Lau's attorneys also claimed protection under the 14th Amendment to the Constitution, the Supreme Court in its *Lau* v. *Nichols* decision did not reach that argument, and ruled simply that the OCR had correctly interpreted the 1964 act, and that the rules it had promulgated in the May memorandum had to be followed.

SOCIOPOLITICAL CONTEXT

Lau v. *Nichols* had the effect of putting virtually every school district of the United States with more than five percent non-English-dominant students on notice that it was violating Federal law if it had not complied with the May 1970 memorandum. Few such districts were able to show that they had. Over ensuing years these districts faced two choices: get into compliance with that memo or be found out of compliance with that memorandum by subsequent OCR investigation and be forced to comply. This latter step would require the district to create a "compliance plan" that would convince the Federal government that past discrimination against these national origin groups would cease since, under contract, the district would now take affirmative steps to guarantee educational equity. These plans were heavily influenced by a document known as the "Lau remedies." Written by a committee composed more of academics than practitioners, it specified steps that would ensure a district's compliance with Lau. While it acknowledged that other solutions might also work, a plan following the Lau remedies was assured of successful review by OCR. The remedies, since they apply to districts found to be doing something illegal, however inadvertently, are intended to assure relief to the students. The Lau decision and its results, therefore, are linked to a larger issue of the loss of local autonomy over education, which some saw begun by the Civil Rights Act of 1964. We may think of this as the first of what we will describe as five larger political problems with which bilingual education has become enmeshed: loss of local autonomy.

The record of compliance with Lau since 1974 has been uneven. It should be remembered that Lau does not require or even mandate bilingual education, but states that a bilingual program is one appropriate way to get into compliance with the law. This may seem hairsplitting to some, but it is nevertheless widely assumed that Lau mandates bilingual education; it does not. It mandates that a child not be disadvantaged, compared to other children, because of his or her language. The Lau decision has crystallized Federal policy toward bilingual education, however, and has served as a lightning rod for political opponents of bilingualism. The Supreme Court was clearly ahead of the legislative branch in saying that a child had a *right* to instruction in his or her native language under the Civil Rights Act of 1964. However, since Lau could be undone only by modifying the Civil Rights Act itself, which would open the whole act to review, there is great reluctance to change Lau, even by some of its strongest critics, for fear of what might happen if other parts of the law were also changed. In any event, part of the controversy attaching to Lau is really a conflict between legislative prerogatives on the one hand, and the executive's use of regulations, on the other—in this case backed by the judiciary—to construct policy. And this has become the second political problem with which Lau is enmeshed.

Beside Title VII funds, the Office of Education took a number of steps to help local school districts get into compliance with the 1970 memorandum—but only *after* the 1974 decision, not before it. This delay did not help the implementation process from 1970 to 1974 or later. An apparent inconsistency, therefore, was the third political reality that school districts had to face.

In 1975, USOE established nine "Lau Centers" across the country in regions with large numbers of non-English-dominant students. These centers were located for the most part at universities and were designed to assist local school districts by providing technical assistance to enable them to develop Lau-sensitive programming. While USOE had previously made funds available under Title VII to such districts, they now withheld or threatened to withhold all ESEA (Elementary and Secondary Education Act) funds if districts were out of compliance and had no compliance plan approved. Lau Centers were to help them. The amounts of money for Title VII and Lau Center programs are small, however, in comparison to the needs of the populations to be served, and funds have been eroded by inflation over the years. The bulk of the money for implementing Lau has had to come, and must continue to come, for local funds (themselves scarce) over which extreme competition exists. Funding, then, becomes the fourth, and perhaps crucial, political problem faced by bilingual education since Lau.

A further difficulty is that, in implementing Lau, school districts have not only relied on Title VII funds for help, but have often imitated Title VII programs. However, ESEA was designed and continues to be a compensatory program, that is, a program designed to remediate a perceived deficit. The language of compensatory programming is absent from the Lau decision. Indeed, the whole trust of Lau is that the mismatch between the home language and the language of instruction is the district's responsibility, not the child's fault. Further, the 1968 legislation implicitly mandated transitional bilingual education. This means that children should learn English as quickly as possible. Lau mandates instead that children be instructed in their native language until they can learn in English, and that instruction in English not be at the expense of their learning required subjects in their native tongue. In the past, children were taken out of regular programming and given nothing but ESL (English as Second Language) until they functioned in English and could be put into regular programming, even if this put them years behind in school. Under Lau this could be illegal. Under the compensatory models, teachers and administrators often saw children as not only linguistically disadvantaged, but unmotivated and underachieving as well. The programs mandated under Title VII had more than linguistic goals; they were also designed to get children functioning better in school environments. Lau makes no other assumption than that teaching in a language children do not understand is the problem. But because of the link between bilingual education and ESEA Title VII, new programming earns the enmity of those opposed to the paternalistic assumptions of compensatory models, thus creating the fifth political problem with which bilingual programming since Lau has become enmeshed.

In addition to these five political hornets' nests, problems of a more practical nature also characterize bilingual programming today. Teachers are not trained to deal with the heterogeneous language skills of children in bilingual educational programs; nor do we have very good ways for even measuring the diversity.

Then too, the home languages of linguistic minority groups such as Hispanics have lower status than English in the reward system of the larger society (Ogbu

1978). This social problem invades the classroom itself, providing an advantage to White Anglo students and disadvantaging Hispanics. As we shall see in the next section, Troike (1978) concluded that the relative social and cultural status of groups in the community may be a fundamental variable that affects the outcome of bilingual programming:

> It is significant that children who succeed so notably . . . are for the most part middle-class children from supportive homes whose language and culture are in no way threatened or demeaned by their being taught in another language. [Troike 1978: 18-19]

There also continues to be a shortage of well-trained teachers to staff bilingual classrooms. Gray (1980) reports that less than 14 percent of such teachers have even one course in bilingual education.

Add to this disturbing picture the fact that, for the political reasons just reviewed, implementation has been actively resisted, both overtly and covertly, and the picture becomes even more confusing. In New York City, for example, it is now six years since the Aspira consent decree, under which the city accepted a legally binding requirement that it implement bilingual programming for children whose English language "deficiency" prevents their effective participation in the learning process, and the implementation is far from complete (see Santiago-Santiago 1978). Districts that genuinely wished to move also found their efforts thwarted by a lack of basic knowledge of language assessment, preventing a rational placement of children in programs. Add to this the lack of adequately trained staff and other factors just described, and it is questionable whether any reasonable assessment of bilingual education could take place in even twenty-five percent of the schools claiming to have such programs. Finally, a well-planned program, even one exemplary in every respect, is still subject to all the normal hazards of educational programming.

EVALUATION OF BILINGUAL EDUCATION

The Problems

While research concerning bilingual programming is important, it receives very little funding from the Federal government. Consequently, there has been little critical research and virtually no longitudinal research (but see Cohen et al. 1975, Lambert and Tucker 1972) to evaluate the potential or actual effectiveness of bilingual programming. In fact, by one estimate, less than half of one percent of Federal funds allocated to bilingual education are actually devoted to research. (Other countries offering bilingual education, notably Canada and Scandinavia, have spent much higher porportions of funds on research, sometimes as much as

50 percent.) Fundamental or basic research studies that may lead to programs are particularly sparse. The existing research base is dominated by after-the-fact evaluations of existing projects. [The National Diffusion Networks are currently disseminating information about successful programs. For information write: Educational Diffusion, Materials Support Center, 1855 Folsom Street, San Francisco, California 94013.] But these studies reveal important flaws in the design of evaluation research more often than they illuminate anything about the strengths or failings of the bilingual programs themselves (see e.g. Rodriguez-Brown 1978, Cardenas 1977, Zappert and Cruz 1977). When the Center for Applied Linguistics surveyed over 150 evaluations reports to develop a master plan that would enable San Francisco to get into compliance with the requirements laid down by the Supreme Court in *Lau* v. *Nichols,* they found that only seven met minimal criteria for research design that could produce useful information (Troike 1978). A survey of 108 evaluations by the Northwest Regional Laboratory rejected all but three. The problems included: no control for socioeconomic status, inadequate or improper sampling techniques, absence of baseline or control data, absence of measure of initial language dominance, the presence of significant confounding variables (teacher qualification, e.g.), and insufficient or imporper statistical manipulations (Zappert and Cruz 1977). In the studies that did meet their criteria, Zappert and Cruz found that only one percent of the comparisons showed negative outcomes for bilingual programs, while 58 percent of the comparisons were positive, and 41 percent showed no differences. For the last statistic they note:

> . . . a non-significant effect is not a negative finding with respect to bilingual education. A non-significant effect, that students in bilingual education classes are learning at the same rate as students in monolingual classes, demonstrates the fact that learning in two languages does not interfere with a student's academic and cognitive performance. [Zappert and Cruz 1977:39]

In addition, such students have the advantage of learning a second language.

The well-designed studies that have been done have shown that bilingual education fosters cognitive development, achievement in school, positive attitudes toward schooling, and positive attitudes toward other ethnic groups. Other studies have shown improved second language acquisition, readiness for schooling, and improved self concept. It must also be noted that other studies have contradicted each of these findings. But since these studies were done on different programs, and there is no one definition of what constitutes a bilingual program, we may be comparing apples and pears. It is simply not possible, given the current research, to explore precisely what characteristics or programs produce which simple successful outcomes in order to compare them with programs producing negative outcomes, as obvious as that need may seem.

Particular Studies

The Purpose of this section is to examine what we have learned to date from overall evaluations of bilingual education, and to focus on critical issues common to all such evaluation efforts. We first review a study said by Leibowitz (1980) to have had considerable influence on the 1978 educational amendments, then review other studies perhaps more worthy of attention.

The American Institute for Research Study. The American Institute for Research (AIR) published the results of a three-year, 1.3 million dollar study conducted under contract with the United States Office of Education to examine thirty-eight Title VII projects with a total of 12,000 students. Given the influence this study seems to have had, a few observations about this massive undertaking are pertinent:

1. The research design called for the compiling of data from many separate projects, each having different purposes, staffs, and programming. Such differences may have obscured the design, rendering the results uninterpretable.
2. Such designs evaluate programs that have received Federal funds without checking independently to see if the funds have been spent as they were intended. (This results in an evaluation of the performance of districts receiving Federal funds, which is not the same thing at all as an evaluation of the Federally funded programs.)
3. AIR evaluated performance by pretesting children at the beginning of the year and posttesting at the end of the year for each grade studied, thus limiting the main effects to what could be observed over a period of *six months,* without considering cumulative (year after year) effects. As Pifer (1980) has observed, it takes a longer time for bilingual programming to have its effect than we initially believed.
4. AIR took little time to investigate the previous experience of the students. We know that the average number of years previously spent in bilingual education is three years for the sixth grade group. Why were these children switched into Title VII programs late in their careers? What was the effect of the switch? Were these in fact children who were failing and were placed in what was seen as a remedial program? This would have the effect of biasing the evaluation of Title VII programs by over-representing two unpromising groups: those children who hadn't made it in regular programming and those who hadn't learned English in Title VII programs and had remained there.

5. No attempt was made to follow up students who succeeded in Title VII programs and returned to regular programs.
6. AIR chose to lump results across all programs, making no attempt to isolate successful programs from unsuccessful programs. This makes it difficult, if not impossible, to ascertain what constitutes successful programs: the whole Federal effort rides or falls on the group norms. It can be seen as a device to minimize both *positive* results (by those politically opposed to bilingual programming) and *negative* results (by proponents of bilingual programming). See Cardenas (1977) and Gray (1980).
7. Since the goals of Title VII are both linguistic and the improvement of school performance, evaluation instruments measure both variables. It is unrealistic to expect, particularly in a six-month period, any program to show improvement in both goals. Yet a failure in either is considered a program failure. Further, since it is technically difficult to measure language usage, most weight falls on the school performance variables. When this is understood in the context of the points made earlier (4) about the previous program experiences over-representing under-achievers in the higher grades, the methodological limitations become acute.

The St. Lambert Studies. We now turn to a discussion of a very different style of evaluation research—the studies of Lambert and Tucker (1972) on evaluations of bilingual programming in St. Lambert, Quebec. To be sure, the sociopolitical context of bilingual programming in Quebec is different from that in the United States, but the political controversy is similar. The St. Lambert study is of one program designed to make truly bilingual (in French/English) children currently functioning in English only. The programming was basically immersion—programming in the second language (hereafter L2) only—except for two half-hour daily periods in English. Children were volunteered for the program by parents, and this meant a high degree of home support could be expected. Parents were heavily consulted and became part of the overall program design. English-only control classes were also given, and children in the treatment group and the control group were carefully matched for intelligence, social class, and parental attitudes toward the French-Canadian people and culture. Moreover, the control parents were as motivated as the experimental parents in wanting their children to learn French!

Children were tested annually and followed through the program until fourth grade, in contrast to the six-month follow-up period for the AIR study. The evaluation was limited to language learning, langue proficiency attitudes, and cognitive flexibility—not performance in school, as was true of the AIR-studied Title VII programming. Children were carefully matched on intelligence and social class variables with controls, unlike the AIR study. Finally, in assessing linguistic competence, Lambert and his colleagues assessed both English and French, whereas such dual assessments are rare in other research. Indeed, testing in or reporting results for L2 only is very much a trait of American studies.

Results from Canada indicate that:

1. The bilingual/experimental group was doing just as well as the monolingual/English control group at the end of Grade IV in reading ability, reading comprehension, and knowledge of English concepts. The bilingual group, as well as the controls, was above the 80th percentile of national norms in English word knowledge, word discrimination, and language use.

2. The bilingual group also compared extremely well with children from French-speaking homes who were following a French program. The competency in French increased the longer they were in the program. Although they were not as fluent as French speakers, their vocabulary and comprehension was as good.

These results show the importance of the research design in determining the outcome of the evaluation. Careful matching of students on school performance characteristics as well as socioeconomic and home characteristics is essential to an evaluation of a program concerning language. Gain of competency in L2 in the Canadian study came over time—not in six months. Longitudinal evaluation is essential for adequate treatment of bilingual programming. Competency in L2 did not come at the expense of L1 learning competence. This is an important point in the political debate in the United States.

Ramifications of Lambert's Study. Lambert distinguishes betwen additive bilingualism and subtractive bilingualism. In subtractive bilingualism the learning of the second language is at the expense of the learning of the first language. In additive bilingualism, there is no supposed loss. I think it important to distinguish additive bilingualism from enrichment models of bilingual education. In enrichment programming, as described by Fishman and others, the child is enriched by L2, but there is no presumed penalty to be paid if the child fails to learn. In additive programming, linguistic competence is clearly the goal, and certain penalties can be expected to be paid in the larger society by a child living in French Canada who does not learn French, akin to the penalty a child living in New York City without English might have to pay.

Lambert maintains that negative results in bilingual education tend to be associated with programs fostering subtractive bilingualism. These would be the kind of programs funded by Title VII in which the goal is often English at the expense of L1 (Spanish). Therefore, we might argue that even if a reasonable evaluation of Title VII programming were accomplished, such *programming* would unlikely achieve a record of sustained growth in L1 and L2. Studies of

Finnish migrants to Sweden show that programs that neglect L1 impair learning of both L1 and L2! Skutnabb-Kangas and Toukomaa (1976, 1977) found that when children immigrated to Sweden at preschool or primary school ages, they did more poorly than children who immigrated after five or six years of education in their native (Finnish) language. Troike (1978) argues a similar pattern exists in the U.S. Southwest for Mexican Americans. My students and I have also observed that when young Caribbean migrant children in New York are immersed in L2 programming, they can fail to develop competence in either language.

This suggests that younger subordinated minority children should be in L1 until they function adequately, but that for older minority children immersion approaches in L2, which do not ignore L1, might succeed. If programs that provide for continued development in L1 improve acquisition of L2, this is an important point. It argues that for younger children the traditional distinction between maintenance and transitional programming is inappropriate. The best transitional program is one which provides a maintenance of learning in L1! These programs are therefore developmental: L2 is added to a continuing base of L1. Programs that erode the base of L1 can impair the learning of L2.

This clarifies some of the findings of the studies reviewed for this paper. It supports our own experience in the implementation of Lau. Prior to Lau and the Lau remedies, a non-English-speaking child was removed from regular programming and given intensive training in an ESL kind of programming. From the point of view of the courts, this deprived the child of continuing development in those subjects—math, science, social studies, etc.—required of all children in the school. In a similar sense, a program that tries to inculcate L2 at the expense of L1 deprives children of continuing development of communication skills that are important to them in non-school areas of life. Many programs, like those studied by Cohen and Laosa (1976) and by Legarreta (1977) are conducted primarily in English, whatever the readiness of the child, perhaps leading to a negative perception of Spanish, and certainly raising questions about the adequacy of L1 development. Since much language learning goes on outside of school, the child under these conditions is disadvantaged in comparison to children whose home language development is reinforced by the school. In our evaluations we must never lose sight of the fact that we are examining what is happening to children in only one part of their lives. We must be attentive to the interaction between school, home, and peer effects in understanding our evaluation data. This means that we must have reasonably clear data about the treatment of L1 and L2 not only in the school, but in the community as well.

Trying to learn to read simultaneously in two languages can be confusing. One well-constructed longitudinal study was done of a bilingual program in Redwood City, California, in which reading in both L1 and L2 is introduced at the same time. (Cohen and Laosa 1976). Their findings show that reading competency in both languages is retarded by such an approach. Strangely, children scored below control classrooms in reading English as well as in Spanish, even though the control classrooms had no instruction in reading Spanish! This finding is interesting in regard to the AIR studies, because fifty-two percent of Title VII programs in 1969-1970 were of this type (Troike 1978).

Lambert's work also supports the notion that slow, steady growth of programs with strong community support is preferable to instant solutions. We will raise this point in our discussion of exemplary bilingual programs, to which we now turn, but it is important to emphasize that few of the American programs to be evaluted—and by definition, none of the studies evaluated by AIR—met this criterion.

EXAMPLARY BILINGUAL PROGRAMMING

Recognizing the inadequacies of the data base, we can review what we know and artifically construct an examplary program by examining characteristics related to positive outcomes in research reviewed in evaluation studies approved by Troike, and Zappert and Cruz, and in our own experience at the Lau Center in New York during the past five years. Our composite exemplary bilingual program seeks to achieve two goals: acquisition of another language and protection of equal educational opportunity.

District Level Criteria

In our experience, crucial to the success of bilingual programming is the commitment of district level staff to bilingual education—from district superintendent (or surrogate) level all the way down to the building principal level. The allocation of district resources to bilingual programming is an indication of staff commitment. For example, successful programs often have their teachers on tax levy or regular funding rather than special Federal funding or at least in addition to special Federal funding. Through the allocation of local resources, the bilingual program is given a greater likelihood of continuity and stability, which improves the opportunity for planning on a more than year by year basis—and which makes a more attractive job opportunity for staff. Invetment of local funds is also a tip-off to the attitude of district staff toward bilingual programming. Finally, the investment of time and energy in planning is improved when the staff is stable enough to see the fruits of such planning over time.

Another criterion at the district level is the community support for bilingual programming. The importance of such efforts have been argued by Brisk (1977), Inclan (1976), Andersson (1970), and Botana (1975); their studies indicate that things go better when community support initiates a bilingual program in the district. (This does not mean unanimity, but rather that some local initiative takes place.) There is also evidence that it is useful for local ethnic groups to be represented at the district level, either on the school board or at the administrative level (see Bouton 1975, Gottlieb 1965, Shiraishi 1975, and Ogbu 1978).

School Level Criteria

At the school level, coordination between the bilingual program and the rest of the school is important. This can be measured in a number of ways. Does the school administration accept the responsibility of coordinating the bilingual and monolingual components? Is there an administrative policy of orienting the staff of the school to the purpose and process of bilingual education? Do ESL and bilingual staff meet jointly? Is the bilingual program integrated with the rest of the school? Are similar support services available to non-English-dominant students and monolingual English-speaking students—e.g., counselors, reading specialists, etc.? Do the majority of teachers in the school accept the bilingual teachers and the bilingual program? Are the attitudes of the school principal and other school administrators in line authority over the program accepting and supportive? Attitudes of school staff toward bilingual programming are crucial to the success or failure of a bilingual program (see Fishman 1974). Sometimes bilingual programming is perceived as a threat by existing staff—especially when local tax dollars will support the program.

The degree to which administrative and teaching staff are sensitive to the goals (educational and occupational) of the cultural groups in the district is another important criterion at the school level. Brice-Heath and others (Brice-Heath 1978, Philips 1972) have argued that programs whose options reflect the goals of the community groups are more successful. There are several ways to assess this. Do parents have options for their children? Can parents with different goals for their children find programming suitable to their goals? Such options might include

1. a transitional bilingual sequence where parents can choose to have students use Spanish as a bridge to an all-English curriculum
2. an all-English curriculum—immersion in English
3. a program of continuing support for Spanish in addition to option 1
4. different teaching styles (traditional vs. open) from which parents may choose the one they are most familiar with or value most

These options are also important because children not performing well in one program may be moved to another more suitable one.

Respect for the cultural values of the community groups is evident when school-community relations are given priority by the administrative staff, notices are sent home in the parents' native languages, and parents are involved in school activities other than in program activities.

Program Level Criteria

In an exemplary bilingual program, students are not assigned to a program, they (or their parents) influence the choice of program. Free choice of program can provide parents with a powerful lever against the segregation of their children: if parents find a program to be stigmatized, they can take their children out and choose another.

One of the dangers of bilingual education programs is that the can become ghettoized. They can become sti‚matized as remedial. This is not the case in an exemplary bilingual program. The advantages of an integrated education over a segregated one are well documented. Nothing concerned with linguistic ability changes that fact. While it may be necessary at certain points of the day to isolate children into groups on the basis of their linguistic ability, this need not justify the creation of linguistically segregated classrooms. Indeed, research strongly suggests that there are positive advantages to linguistically integrated classrooms. In a two-way program, English-dominant students learn and develop skills in Spanish at the same time that Spanish-dominant students learn English. Since these are voluntary assignments, English-speaking students are here because they want to be. (See Gardner 1967, for the one-way/two-way distinction) A two-way reciprocal program provides the opportunity for peer learning—for informal learning of the second language from peers who speak that language as natives. John et al. (1969) and Cazden and Leggett (1976) stress the importance of peer learning as one of the most effective methods of learning a second language.

What is it exactly that exemplary bilingual programs do differently in terms of curriculum, teaching, and outcomes? As we have seen, one of the most vexing problems facing planners of bilingual programming is the question of language learning, particularly in the area of reading. In an exemplary program for older children, a child already reading in L1 would not have his or her development in L1 reading stopped. It would continue along with the learning of L2.

Should a younger child learn to read first in L1 or L2? Research surveyed by Engle (1975) suggests that learning to read in L1 is the best approach, and this is supported for lower status languages by the literature reviewed earlier. Modiano (1968) also addresses this issue. The issue is complex, however. Consider the following three situations:

1. A child enters reading not at all, and is entirely Spanish monolingual.
2. A child enters with some reading ability in Spanish, and is Spanish monolingual.
3. A child enters with some reading ability in Spanish and English and is bilingual.

For elementary school children, particularly before age 10, the literature *suggests* Spanish reading instruction as the most effective for child 1. The same would be true for child 2. The decision for child 3 is more problematic: We don't have an answer firmly grounded in research.

While mastery of reading in Spanish by elementary students facilitates later transfer of reading skills to English and premature transfer can impede reading in both languages, there is also evidence that oral ESL development should precede learning to read in English (Robinett 1965).

Content learning in social studies, math, and science proceeds in L1 in the exemplary bilingual programs until a child has reached sufficient competence in English to opt into English-only instruction programming. Teachers also structure their classrooms to accommodate a range of learning styles. Particularly significant is the work of Ramirez and Castenada (1974) on learning styles; that of Cazden and Leggett (1976) is also important.

One of the curricular benefits of having children from different cultural backgrounds in one program is that in interacting with other students, they learn about cultures different from their own (Gibson 1976). Involved parents can benefit from this, too. In addition, students bring to the classroom different school histories and experiences in other schools as well as different competencies and skills that can often benefit from a heterogeneous grade grouping.

The issue of linguistic assessment is an especially troubling one, as is the problem of training teachers to deal with the linguistic diversity they will actually encounter in classrooms. Low staff turnover is characteristic of successful bilingual programming. The rate should be comparable to the other programs of the school. As to staff capabilities, in addition to meeting the same certification requirements as regular programming staff, they should

1. have communicative competence in both languages (Hymes 1967)
2. be sensitive to cultural differences
3. have a graduate degree geared to teaching in bilingual programs
4. reflect the ethnicity of the students in the community (as a group, not individually by teacher) and live in the community
5. attend periodic in-service and conference activities in bilingual education

With the exception of the first, these are simply criteria associated with good staff in any program.

What, ultimately, should a successful bilingual program achieve? First, the range of achievement in L1 instruction in required subjects should be no different from the average for English-only students. Second, for older children, the range of achievement in reading and functioning in English should over time—say several years—be comparable to the range of achievement among English monolingual students. For younger and older children, oral English should show improvement. Cazden and Leggett (1976) have also suggested a high percentage of students participating in class as a desirable output characteristic. But, in essence, successful bilingual programs are those that meet the two criteria we set out at the beginning; they achieve language acquisition without setting the child back in his or her skill development.

In summary, we have reviewed the history of Federal involvement in bilingual education, the present sociopolitical context, the research and evaluation research base upon which we must build, and concluded with a brief review of all these factors in examining the components of an exemplary program. That bilingual programs to date have been able to demonstrate any success whatsoever is testament to the need for such programs, and the urgent need for critical research that would allow us to construct programs to implement what Lau was intended to implement: equal educational opportunity for America's linguistic minorities.

REFERENCES

Andersson, T., and M. Boyer.
   1970 *Bilingual Schooling in the United States.* 2 Vols. Austin, Texas: Southwest Educational Development Laboratory. 589pp. ED 039 527.
Botana, J.
   1975 "Community Involvement in Bilingual Programs." *Illinois Career Education Journal* 33 (1): 17–18.
Bouton, L.
   1975 "Meeting the Needs of Children with Diverse Linguistic and Ethnic Backgrounds." *Foreign Language Annals* 8 (4): 306–16.
Brice-Heath, S.
   1978 *AIR Evaluation of Bilingual Education.* San Antonio, Texas: Intercultural Development Research Association.
Brisk, M.E.
   1977 *The Role of the Bilingual Community in Mandated Bilingual Education. CAL/ERIC/CLL Series on Languages and Linguistics, No. 49.* Arlington, VA: ERIC Clearinghouse on Languages and Linguistics, 21pp. ED 138 086.
Cazden, C.B., and E.L. Leggett.
   1976 *Culturally Responsive Education: A Response to Lau Remedies II.* Paper prepared for Conference on Research and Policy Implications of the Task Force Report of the U.S. Office of Civil Rights: Lau Remedies. Austin, Texas: Southwest Educational Development Laboratory. 52pp. ED 135 241.
Cohen, A.D., A. Fathman, and B. Merino.
   1976 *The Redwood City Bilingual Education Project, 1971-1974: Spanish and English Proficiency, Mathematics and Language Use Overtime. Working Papers on Bilingualism No. 8.* Pp. 1–29. Toronto: Ontario Institute for Studies in Education. ED 125 248.

Cohen, A.D., and M. Laosa.
1976 "Second Language Instruction: Some Research Considerations." *Curriculum Studies* 8(2): 149–165.

Danoff, M.N., et al.
1977 *Impact of ESEA Title VII Spanish/English Bilingual Education Programs:* Vols. I and II. Palo Alto, California: American Institute for Research in Behavioral Science.

Engle, P.L.
1975 *The Use of Vernacular Language in Education: Language Medium in Early School Years for Minority Language Groups.* Arlington, Va.: Center for Applied Linguistics.

Fishman, J.A.
1974 *A Sociology of Bilingual Education.* Final Report of Research under Contract OECO–73–0538, Division of Foreign Studies, Department of HEW USOE.

Gardner, B.A.
1967 "Organization of the Bilingual School." *Journal of Social Issues* 23: 110–120.

Gibson, M.
1976 "Approaches to Multicultural Education in the United States: Some Concepts and Assumptions." *Anthropology and Education Quarterly* 7(4): 7–18.

Gottlieb, D.
1964 "Teaching and Students: The Views of Negro and White Teachers." *Sociology of Education* 37: 345–353.

Gray, T.
1980 *Research in Bilingual Education: Implications for Lau Compliance.* Paper presented at the National Conference for Title IV Directors of State Educational Agencies and Desegregation Assistance Centers, Washington, D.C., January 29.

Hymes, D.
1967 "Models on Interaction of Language and Social Setting." *The Journal of Social Issues* 23: 8–23.

Inclan, R.G.
1976 "School-Community Relations." *Journal of the National Association for Bilingual Education* 1(2): 73–77.

Intercultural Development Research Association.
1977 *The AIR Evaluation of the Impact of ESEA Title VII Spanish/English Bilingual Education Programs: An IDRA Response with a Summary by Dr. Jose Cardenas.* 27pp. ED 151 435.

John, V., et al.
1969 "American Voices." *The Center Forum, No. 7.* New York, New York: Center for Urban Education.

Lambert, W.E., and G.R. Tucker.

1972   *Bilingual Education of Children: The St. Lambert Experiment*. Rowley, Mass.: Newbury House Publishers, Inc.

Legarreta, D.

1977   "Language Choice in Bilingual Classrooms." *TESOL Quarterly* 11(1): 9–16.

Leibowitz, A.H.

1980   *The Bilingual Education Act: A Legislative Analysis*. Arlington, Va.: National Clearinghouse for Bilingual Education. (Reprinted in this volume).

Modiano, N.

1968   "Bilingual Education for Children of Linguistic Minorities." *American Indigena* 28: 405–415.

Ogbu, J.

1974   *The Next Generation: An Ethnography of Education in an Urban Neighborhood*. New York: Academic Press.

1978   *Minority Education and Caste: The American System in Cross-Cultural Perspective*. New York: Academic Press.

Pifer, A.

1980   *Bilingual Education and the Hispanic Challenge*. 1979 Annual Report. New York: Carnegie Corporation.

Philips, S.

1972   "Participant Structures and Communicative Competence: Warm Springs Children in Community and Classroom." In *Functions of Language in the Classroom*. C. Cazden, et al., eds. New York: Teachers College Press.

Ramirez, M. III, and A. Castenada.

1974   *Cultural Democracy, Bicognitive Development and Education*. New York: Academic Press.

Robinett, R.A.

1965   *A "Linguistic" Approach to Beginning Reading for Bilingual Children*. *Perspectives in Reading, No. 5*. First Grade Reading Programs, International Reading Association. 21pp. ED 001 694.

Rodriquez-Brown, F.

1978   *The Do's and Don'ts in Regard to the Evaluation of Bilingual Programs*. Paper presented at the Seventh Annual Meeting of the National Association for Bilingual Education in San Juan, Puerto Rico, April. 18pp. ED 156 717.

Santiago-Santiago, I.

1978   *A Community's Struggle for Equal Educational Opportunity: Aspira v. Board of Education. OME Monograph Number Two*. Princeton, N.J.: Office of Minority Education, Educational Testing Service. 126pp. ED 162 034.

Shiraishi, R.R.

1975   *Effects of A Bilingual/Bicultural Career Guidance Project on the Occupational Aspirations of Puerto Rican Adolescents*. Unpublished dissertation. Boston: Boston University School of Education.

Skutnabb-Kangas, T., and P. Toukomaa.

1976 *Teaching Migrant Children's Mother Tongue and Learning the Language of the Host Country in the Context of the Socio-Cultural Situation of the Migrant Family.* Helsinki: Finnish National Commission for UNESCO.

Toukomaa, P., and T. Skutnabb-Kangas.

1977 *The Intensive Teaching of the Mother Tongue to Migrant Children of Pre-School Age. Research Report No. 26.* Tampere: Department of Sociology and Social Psychology, University of Tampere, Finland.

Troike, R.C.

1978 *Research Evidence for the Effectiveness of Bilingual Education.* Arlington, Va.: National Clearinghouse for Bilingual Education. 23pp. ED 159 900.

Zappert, L.T., and B.R. Cruz.

1977 *Bilingual Education: An Appraisal of Empirical Research.* Berkeley, Ca.: Bay Area Bilingual Education League/Lau Center. 106pp. ED 153 758.

HISPANICS, SCHOOL DESEGRETATION, AND EDUCATIONAL OPPORTUNITY: CONCEPTUAL ISSUES

M. Beatriz Arias

INTRODUCTION

Thirty years ago, with the *Brown* v. *Board of Education* decision, the U.S. Supreme Court interpreted the Constitution to ban segregation in public schools. Discrimination against blacks in schools had been manifested in the de jure separation of the white and black races, and the legal remedy was integration.[1]

Just prior to the Brown decision, the Supreme Court also ruled on the constitutional rights of another minority group, the Mexican Americans. The court found that the constitutional guarantee of equal protection of the laws was not directed solely against discrimination between whites and negroes.[2] The evidence in this case supported the fact that persons of Mexican descent constituted a separate class distinct from "whites."

Despite the fact that the constitutional entitlements due to both blacks and Mexican Americans have been established by the courts since 1954, little scholarly attention has focused on the segregative practices imposed on Mexican Americans, Hispanics, and other language minority students in U.S. schools. Because of the ignorance of the nature and consequences of the racial and linguistic isolation experienced by these groups, Remedies to achieve equal educational opportunity have been poorly defined because the racial and linguistic isolation suffered by these groups has not been fully understood.

While the evidence shows that historically both blacks and Mexican Americans have suffered the ills of segregated schools, the bulk of data and litigation has stemmed from black and white contexts. Consequently little has been compiled regarding the implementation of remedies for racial isolation in tri-ethnic or multi-ethnic settings.

This paper will address the issue of equal educational opportunity within the context of desegregation cases where Mexican-Americans, Hispanics, and/or national origin minorities[3] have been a significant part of the school population. It will elaborate on the history of Hispanic involvement in desegregation cases, explore the ramifications of racial and linguistic isolation, and review approaches used for attaining equal educational opportunity in tri-ethnic school districts under court-ordered desegregation.

DEFINITION OF HISPANIC

Hispanics in the U.S. today constitute a group that is experiencing phenomenal growth. In the last ten years, the Hispanic population has grown over sixty-one percent, from nine million to over fourteen-and-a-half million in 1980. This dramatic demographic change has been felt primarily in five states: California, New York, Florida, Texas, and New Mexico. Hispanic students comprise the second largest minority population enrolled in public schools, and the school age population is projected to outnumber blacks by the year 2000.[4]

Of this group, Mexican-Americans comprise the largest subgroup, 59% or approximately 7 million. Puerto Ricans number around 2 million, Central and South Americans 1 million, Cubans .7 million and "other Spanish" 1.5 million.[5] Undocumented Hispanics are estimated to be between 2 and 4 million.

Geographically, it is important to remember, that while every state has Hispanics, seventy-five percent of all Hispanics are found in five states: California, Florida, New Mexico, New York, and Texas.[6] Consequently, in reviewing desegregation cases, it will be actions primarily filed in these states that will be of interest.

Further aspects of this geographic picture include the fact that Mexican Americans are concentrated in the Southwestern states. Puerto Ricans are concentrated in the industrial Northeast—particularly in New York and New Jersey—and in Illinois. Cubans reside in large numbers in the South, particularly in Florida. This regional distribution of Hispanic sub-groups is important to keep in mind in understanding the geographical factors that influence the struggle for equal educational opportunity.

While Hispanics share a history of exclusionary practices, low status and political impotence[7], each group's history has varied in the initial contact it has had with Anglo society and includes such diverse experiences as annexation, colonization, and conquest. Historically, as a result of this contact, each sub-group became identified as "inferior," "deprived," or "low status." Hence, emanating from this stigmatized "low status" Hispanic students have been characterized as "at risk" due to the prevalence of a high drop out rate and poor academic performance. Hispanic, then, can be seen as a generic term which encompasses all these sub-groups with different histories, regional distributions, and patterns of accomodation to the dominant culture. The term is useful ONLY for identifying national origin minority students who share the linguistic heritage of Spanish, different levels of acculturation, and great variance in Spanish proficiency.[8]

In fact, not all Hispanics speak Spanish. Spanish monolingualism and Spanish/English bilingualism have been found to vary within Hispanic subgroups.[9] In general the distribution of monolinguals and bilinguals within U.S. Hispanics reveals that about 21% of the group is English monolingual, 54% is bilingual and roughly 14% Spanish monolingual.[11] Data collected in 1976 suggest that within the Mexican-American group there is the largest number of English monolinguals, about 23%, compared to 13% and 3% for Puerto Ricans and Cubans respectively. The degree of bilingualism is high within each of these groups. Puerto Ricans reporting 63%, Cubans 69% and Mexican-Americans 53%. Spanish monolingualism is highest in the Cuban community, 23%, with 14% for Puerto Ricans and 13% for Mexicans.

The distribution of bilingualism has been particularly difficult to measure within the Hispanic school age population.[10] A national survey conducted in 1978 found an estimated 2.4 million children with limited English language proficiency aged 5 to 14. This limited English proficiency was found to be much greater in households where Spanish was spoken and in three major states, California, New York, and Texas.[11] This data underscores the fact that within this group called Hispanic, there is great variation in language proficiency.[12] Consequently, while all Hispanic students are designated as national origin minority (NOM) by virtue of their historical relationship to the Spanish language and its culture, each individual student has different levels of bilingualism and each group has accommodated to the dominant English-speaking society in historically different ways.

Group variation within the Hispanic bilingualism points to the different historical status that Spanish has been accorded. For example, Puerto Ricans enjoy full U.S. citizenship, and Spanish is the language of instruction on the island and one of the two official languages of the commonwealth. Spanish is also the official language of Cuba, and all those political exiles, refugees and immigres upon arrival to the U.S., insured that Spanish would be retained through the implementation of the first bilingual education programs. Mexican-Americans have experienced contact with English since the Southwest was still a part of Mexico. Due to the conflicts and hostilities that characterized this conquest, Spanish became identified as the language of the "conquered" and de-valued despite assurances by the Treaty of Guadalupe Hidalgo.[13]

The complexity of determining equal educational opportunity for Hispanics requires an understanding of the extent to which language and/or ethnic characteristics have limited the attainment of educational equity.[145] Therein lies the complexity: equal educational opportunity for this group must include remedies for both linguistic and racial isolation yet, as we will see, much of the rationale for racial and ethnic exclusion was based on linguistic arguments.[15]

HISTORY OF HISPANICS AND DESEGREGATION

"Brown . . . was not written for Blacks alone . . . The theme of our school desegregation cases extends to all racial minorities treated invidiously by a State or any of its agencies."[16]

For Hispanics, linguistic segregation has often been used as an excuse for pervasive segregation due to race and national origin. Hence, we see the Mexican-Americans in the Southwest after 1848 and after the onset of public education atending schools that were intentionally established to perpetuate the separation of Mexican from Anglo and from black. These schools were legitimized as "language schools." "Mexican Schools" were schools established by local rules for the attendance of colored or Mexican students.[17] Where the majority of the students were Mexican, the curriculum stressed English and assimilation. In some instances, entire school districts were established for the Mexican students.

Hispanic students have suffered the consequences of racial isolation and discriminatory practices based on the groups' appearance, language, and cultural orientation. These types of segregation practices have been documented: classroom assignment because of "language deficiency"; weak enforcement of mandatory attendance laws; early grade retention; state-supported unequal school conditions; the use of linguistically and culturally biased assessment measures.[18]

While these practices appear on the surface similar to the discriminatory practices experienced by black students, the segregation of Hispanic students, especially Mexican-American students, has been different from that of blacks in the South and North. Chicano school segregation was not specifically mandated by state statute as in "southern" black segregation, nor did it only result from administrative decision, as in "northern" black segregation. Uniquely, Chicanos were relegated to Mexican schools by local rules and regulations which required them to attend separate schools.

LEGAL EFFORTS: PRE-BROWN

Since the 1900s, Mexican-American students were segregated in public schools wherever they resided in significant numbers. The English-speaking majority demanded separate schools for Hispanic children. As late as 1930, the California state attorney general, Ulysses S. Webb, argued that since Mexicans were Indians, it was legal to separate them.[19]

The history of the Hispanic struggle against formal school segregative practices began in the 1920s and '30s. At this time Mexican parents in California and Texas were able to get the Mexican government to file official protests regarding the segregation of Mexican children in American schools. When these protests had little effect, the Mexican government commissioned two American scholars, Chavez and Manuel, to report on discrimination against Mexicans in schools.[20]

The first school desegregation case which was filed on behalf of Mexican-Americans was *Del Rio Independent S.D.* v. *Salvatierra* in 1930. The Texas Supreme Court held that school officials "had no power to separate Mexican-Americans because they are Mexican-American." (21) However, the Court found that the language "deficiency" of Mexican students justified separate classrooms, even separate buildings until the 3rd grade.

> On pedagogical grounds a very good argument can be made for segregation in the early grades. In the opinion of the survey staff, it is wise to segregate, if it is done on educational grounds, and results in distinct efforts to provide the non-English speaking pupils with specially trained teachers and the necessary special training resources. This advices is offered with reluctance, as there is danger that it will be misunderstood by some. By others it may be seized upon as a means of justifying the practices now obtaining in some communities. In some instances segregation has been used for the purpose of giving the Mexican children a shorter school year, inferior buildings, inferior equipment, and poorly paid teachers.[22]

Thus the "language handicap" was early established as the rationale for the separation of Mexican-American students from Anglos and blacks. The effect of *Del Rio* was to ligitimate this separation based on language. In reality, few Mexican-American students at this time went beyond the third grade. Retention in the 1st grade for two to three years was not uncommon. Consequently, most Mexican-American students, whether they experienced a "language deficiency" or not, attended segregated schools in Texas.

Similarly in California, while the segregation of Mexican students had been explained on the basis of their "language handicap," their actual language proficiency had never been measured. In *Mendez* v. *Westminster,* (1945) the officials' segregation of Mexican-American students on this basis was formally outlawed. By 1947, the 9th District Court of Appeals upheld this decision, making this the first time that public school segregation had been denounced in a federal court: "Equal protection of the laws pertaining to the public school system in California is not provided by furnishing in separate schools the same technical facilities, textbooks, and courses of instruction to children of Mexican ancestry that are available to other public school children regardless of their ancestry. A paramount requisite in the American system of public education is social equality. It must be open to all children by unified association regardless of lineage."[23] Although this decision was very significant, it only applied to the 9th circuit.

The justification for segregation based on language was almost terminated with

Delgado v. Bastrop in 1948. In this case the U.S. District Court held that segregated schools for Mexicans were unconstitutional in Texas, "language deficiency notwithstanding." However, the court did allow segregation for "educational purposes" only in the first grade.

Most recently, in Arizona, *Gonzalez v. Sheely* (1951) held that the segregation of children of Mexican descent deprived them of their constitutional rights. (24).

These cases which were litigated before *Brown* have in common an attempt to dismantle the segregated school system that was established on the rationale of "linguistic deficiency." It is important to consider that the segregative practices experienced by Hispanics, in this case Mexican-Americans, were rationalized on the basis of their different language background, and not on their racial or ethnic characteristics exclusively. After *Brown*, the desegregation cases that included Hispanics addressed both the racial and linguistic issues as well. As we will see, whether Hispanics were more similar to "blacks," or "whites," became problematic in multiracial districts.

LEGAL EFFORTS: POST-BROWN

The history of the litigation of school desegregation cases after the Brown decision, indicates that the first successful school integration activities affected the Southern states, and later on the Northern states. As the wave for educational equity reform swept the nation it encountered multi-racial communities where segregative practices involved Hispanics as well as blacks. "Texas" style desegregation for a time came to be known as mixing two minority groups, in this case Mexican-Americans and blacks, and excluding Anglo students from the "integration."[25] This type of desegregation was found to contradict the establishment of a unitary system of education. In the integration case of *Cisneros v. Corpus Christi* (1971), the combining Mexicans and blacks was questioned and Mexicans were brought into the suit as a separate class.[26]

The issue of special separate class status for Mexican-American students in a multi-racial school district was established in *Keyes v. Denver.*[27] Here the court found that Mexican-Americans students were a separate class that had also experienced the harms of racial isolation. As much a class they were entitled to a remedy. However, the court rejected bilingual education as the *only* remedy for racial isolation: "Bilingual education is not a substitute for desegregation. Although bilingual instruction may be required to prevent isolation of minority students in a predominately Anglo school system . . . such a plan *must* be subordinate to a plan of school desegregation"[28] [author's emphasis].

The court was giving precedence to the harm of racial isolation over linguistic isolation for the Mexican-American students in the Denver desegregation case. This suggests that as Hispanics argue for equal educational opportunity it is necessary to establish that harm is resulted because of *two* types of isolation and exclusion: racial/ethnic isolation *and* lingistic isolation.

EFFORTS AGAINST LINGUISTIC ISOLATION

In addition to segregation by race, national origin minority students often suffer the discriminatory efects of linguistic exclusion through laws requiring that instruction be in English only, or prescribing punishment for speaking languages rather than English in school.[29] For example, policies that call for teaching substantial numbers of limited English-proficient (LEP) students English while their English-proficient peers are receiving substantive instruction in science and social studies lead to linguistic exclusion, and may be considered by the courts as a denial of equal educational opportunity.[30]

In a landmark decision, *Lau v. Nichols*,[31] (1973) the U.S. Supreme Court found that the San Francisco Unified School District had violated Title VI of the Civil Rights Act of 1964[32] by denying 1,800 Chinese-speaking students an education comprehensible to them. The Court held that children who cannot benefit from an education conducted solely in the English language must be afforded at least the opportunity to learn English, and at public expense. "Basic English skills are at the very core of what these public schools teach. Imposition of a requirement that, before a child can effectively participate in the educational program, he must already have acquired those basic skills is to make a mockery of public education.[33]

The Supreme Court based its decision not on the constitutional equal protection issue (as had been the argument in desegregation cases), but rather on the statutory requirements of HEW guidelines issued in 1970: "Where inability to speak and understand the English language excludes national origin-minority group children from effective participation in the educational program offered by a school district, the district must take affirmative steps to rectify the language deficiency in order to open its instructional program to these students."[34] Similar language was later codified in the Equal Educational Opportunities Act of 1974. However, commentators[35] have noted that the weakness of the Lau decision lies in the fact that it was based on a statutory provision rather than a constitutional principle. Consequently the compliance and enforcement procedures can always be revised or rescinded by Congressional action.

REMEDIES FOR LINGUISTIC ISOLATION

In its holdings on the isolation of language-minority students, the Lau court offered general guidelines that allowed local school districts to design remedies according to their particular situations: "Teaching English to students of Chinese ancestry who do not speak the language is one choice. Giving instruction to this group in Chinese is another. There may be others."[36]

Several specific types of programs to remedy language isolation in schools have been implemented with varying degrees of success. Prior to 1968 most states had provisions in their education codes which prevented the use of any language other than English for purposes of instruction. Consequently, the common approach for "teaching" English to non-English speaking students, prior to the Lau decision, was the "language submersion" method. In itself this did not constitute an affirmative step to rectify the linguistic exclusion of language minority students. Simply put, this "sink or swim" approach allowed students who had no comprehension of English to sit in classes conducted in English. It was the student's responsibility to acquire English skills.

This approach is no longer accepted by the courts. The two most popular methods for teaching English to NOM (national origin minority) students have been ESL (English as a Second Language), and bilingual education. Both of these approaches have the goal of bringing a child's comprehension of English to a level where one may participate effectively in regular English monolingual classrooms. The primary difference between the two approaches is the perspective on the use of the student's native language.

The English as a Second Language approach derived much of its pedagogy from the teaching of English as a foreign language.[37] This leaned heavily on the audio-lingual method that included an emphasis on mechanical drill and practice, repetitive drills, and choral speaking. While these approaches have been useful in the teaching of ESL to persons who have had no exposure to the sound system of English, it may be less appropriate in settings where there already exists a receptive understanding of English, and/or that the status of English is not that of a foreign language. The ESL methodology, therefore, has been very effective in teaching English to adults or adolescents who already have a command of their native language.

Bilingual education in the United States utilizes the student's native language as the bridge to English proficiency. In the United States, bilingual education has had the most success in those settings where the student has not yet acquired literacy skills (reading and writing) but has extensive oral proficiency (speaking and comprehending) in the mother tongue. The asset of the bilingual approach is that the young student's education is not delayed in other areas such as social studies or math.[38] In a program where ESL was the only language program provided, the student would eventually fall behind in content areas. This approach is typified by a "pull-out" methodology in which the students involved are taken out of their regular classrooms for a portion of the school day (not to exceed twenty-five percent) solely to participate in learning languages where the use of the mother tongue is discouraged. Some of the most exemplary bilingual programs combine both the bilingual and ESL approaches.[39] Skilled teachers are critical to the effective implementation of each method, and they are in short supply. Whichever method is selected, it is important to assure that student isolation is minimized and curricular continuity maximized.

Court approved national origin desegregation plans are necessarily as varied as the school districts in which they must be implemented. In order to fashion an appropriate remedy, a court must carefully examine the unique needs of a particular community. In the many suits now pending where language minority students have intervened, the nexus of remedies for linguistic and racial isolation has become most apparent.

While the principles of *Lau* and *Brown* are compatible,[40] both rulings left unanswered questions concerning the implementation of the constitutional or statutory requirements.[41] As the composition of the Supreme Court has changed, the constitutional protections enunciated in *Brown* have taken on a different meaning.[42] Consequently, because of the lack of a precise definition of the nature of equality required in public schools, the scope of an individual student's right to equal educational opportunity remains uncertain.

It becomes very important to keep in mind the words of Justice Warren regarding the contextual nature of equity: "Traditionally, equity has been characterized by a practical flexibility in shaping its remedies and by a facility for adjusting the reconciling public and private needs. These cases call for the exercise of these traditional attributes of equity power."[43]

In meeting the challenges of equity for groups that have experienced differential or similar sources of discriminatory practices, courts have responded in the following ways: 1) requiring assignment of bilingual students before other students to assure clustering of bilingual classes for maintaining the necessary curricular continuity; 2) ruling that bilingual programs must remain intact regardless of the final integration plan; and, 3) ruling that school boards must insure that students in need of language instruction be placed in schools in sufficient numbers ("critical mass") to allow the program to continue.

School districts in turn, have devised approaches for enhancing multi-racial and multi-linguistic contact in magnet schools, magnet centers and learning development centers that attract students of diverse backgrounds. The key to achieving equity is this flexibility in designing the remedy.

CONCLUDING REMARKS

Equal educational opportunity for Hispanics and other language minority students is a critical issue in the educational reform movement of the 1980s. School enrollments in major U.S. cities reflect the large percentages of Hispanics: New York, 30%; Los Angeles, 45%; San Antonio, 52%; Miami, 32%; Denver, 31%; and Hartford, 35%. Coupled with these figures are also those multi-racial school districts that have recently or are currently devising integration remedies where Hispanics outnumber Black students. These districts include Austin, Texas; San Diego, California; and Tucson, Arizona, to name a few.

For Hispanics, access to equal educational opportunity must be implemented at several levels. Impediments to racial and ethnic integration begin at the highest levels of school district administration, trickling down to the rank and file of teachers and support personnel. Extensive documentation exists on the underrepresentation of Hispanics on school boards, district administrators, and teacher training programs.

The fact that remedies for racial isolation and linguistic isolation have been construed to be at loggerheads reflects a misunderstanding of the fundamental pedagogical needs of Hispanic students. This paper has documented the evolution of this misconception as it was historically interpreted by the litigation process.

The remedy for linguistic isolation is equal access to English. The implementation of this access for language minority students is at the crux of the problem. Poor bilingual instruction can be as bad, if not worse than no bilingual instruction[45] and until school district personnel understand the ramifications of thorough English instruction for national origin minority students, equal access for these children will remain an elusive goal.

NOTES

1. *Brown* v. *Board of Education,* 347 U.S. 483 (1954).

2. *Hernandez* v. *Texas,* 347 U.S. 475 (1954).

3. Title VI of the 1964 Civil Rights Act, 42, U.S.C. 2000d, 2000d-1 (1976): "No person in the U.S. shall, in the ground of race, color, or national origin, be excluded from participation in, be denied the benefits of, or subjected to discrimination under any program or activity receiving federal financial assistance."

4. "U.S. Hispanics: The rising tide" *San Francisco Chronicle,* September 4, 1983.

5. *Digest of Educational Statistics,* 1983, National Center for Education Statistics, Washington, D.C. 1982.

6. Brown, Olivas, O., et al. *The Condition of Education for Hispanics,* National Center for Education Statistics, Washington, D.C. 1982.

7. Carter T., Crain, R., et al. "Neither Black Nor White: Public School Desegregation and the Hispanic Student." Office of Education, NIE Law and Public Management Section, Report February 1982.

8. Pifer, A. "Bilingual Education and the Hispanic Challenge." 1979 Annual Report of the Carnegie Corporation of New York.

9. Macias, R., El Mirlo, "Language diversity among U.S. Latinos." UCLA 9, March-April 1982.

10. Spencer, M., "Issues related to estimates of LMP and LEP children," National Center for Bilingual Education, 1982.

11. O'Malley, M., Children's English and Services Study: Language minority children with limited English proficiency in U.S. National Institutes of Education Report, 1980.

12. Dubois, D. "The Children's English and Services Study: A Methodological Review." unpublished manuscript, August 1980.

13. *Treaties and Other International Agreements of the United States of America, 1776-1949,* vol. 9, Washington, D.C. GPO, 1972.

14. Plastino, A. The legal status of bilingual education in America's public schools. Testing ground for a statutory and constitutional interpretation of Equal Protection." *Duquesne Law Review,* 17, 1978-79.

15. Leibowtiz, A., "English Literacy: Legal Sanction for Discrimination." Notre Dame Lawyer, 45, Fall, 1969.

16. Justice Wm. O. Douglas re: San Francisco in 404 U.S. 1214, 1216-17 (1971)

17. Sanchez, G. "Concerning the segregation of Spanish-speaking children in the public schools," in *Education of the Mexican American,* University of Texas at Austin, repr. Arno Press, 1974.

18. Rangel, and Alcala, J., "De Jure segregation of Chicanos in Texas schools," Harvard Civil Rights-Civil Liberties Law Review, 1972.

19. Carter, T., Crain, R., et al. op. cit. Note 7.

20. Ruiz, M. "Mexican-American Legal Heritage in the Southwest." Financial Center Building, Los Angeles, Suite 602.n.d.

21. *Del Rio Independent School District* v. *Salvatierra,* 335 S.W. 2d 790 (Texas Civil Appeal, San Antonio, 1930), cert. denied 284 US 580 1931.

22. Rangel, C., and Alcala, J., op. cit. Note 18.

23. *Mendex* v. *Westminster,* 67 F. Supp. 544 (S.D. Cal 1946), aff'd 161 F. 2d 744 (9th Cir. 1974).

24. *Gonzalez* v. *Sheely* 96 F. Supp. 1004 (D. Ariz. 1951).

25. Birnberg, G. "Constitutional law-desegregation *Brown* v. *Board of Education* applies to Mexican American students and any other readily identifiable ethnic minority or class." *Texas Law Review* 49, 1971.

26. *Cisneros* v. *Corpus Christi* ISD F Supp (S.D. Texas 1970).

27. Kutner, P. "*Keyes* v. *School District #1:* A Constitutional Right to Equal Educational Opportunity?" Journal of Law and Education, 8, January 1979.

28. *Keyes* v. *School District #1,* Denver, 521 F.2d 465, 480 (10th Cir. 1974) cert. denied 423 U.S. 1066 (1976).

29. McFadden, B. "Bilingual Education and the Law." *Journal of Law and Education,* 12 January 1983.

30. Johnson, W. "The Constitutional Right of Bilingual Children to an Equal Educational Opportunity." *Southern California Law Review,* 47, 1974.

31. *Lau* v. *Nichols,* 414 U.S. 563 (1973).

32. Idem at 566.

33. *Lau* v. *Nichols,* op. cit.

34. 20 U.S.C.A. sec. 1703f.

35. "An analysis of the Federal Attempt to Regulate Bilingual Education: Protecting Civil Rights of Controlling Curriculum?" *Journal of Law and Education* 12, January 1983. (no author listed)

36. *Lau* v. *Nichols,* op. cit.

37. Saville, M. and Troike. R. *A Handbook of Bilingual Education,* Revised Edition. Washington, D.C.; Teachers of English to Speakers of Other Languages (TESOL), 1971.

38. Carter, T. and Maestas, L. *Effective bilingual schools serving Mexican American students.* Sacramento, CA.: California State University, School of Education, March 1982.

39. Cazden, C. "Effective Instructional Practices in Bilingual Education." Harvard University, July 1984 (unpublished manuscript.)

40. Carter, T. *Interface Between Bilingual Education and Desegregation: A Study of Arizona and California.* California State University, School of Education, August 1979.

41. Yudorf, M. "Implementation Theories and Desegregation Realities," *Alabama Law Review,* 32, 1981.

42. McCarthy, M. "Is the Equal Protection Clause Still a Viable Tool for Effecting Educational Reform?" *Journal of Law and Education,* 6, April 1977.

43. Chief Justice Earl Warren in stating the majority opinion in *Brown* v. *Board of Education* 349 U.S. 294 (1955).

44. Olivas, M. *The Dilemma of Access.* Washington, D.C.: Howard University Press 1979.

45. Willig, A. "The effectiveness of bilingual education: Review of a report." NABE *Journal,* 1981-82, 6.

THE BILINGUAL EDUCATION ACT:
A LEGISLATIVE ANALYSIS

Arnold H. Leibowitz

HISTORICAL BACKGROUND: TOLERANCE AND RESTRICTION

The United States has from the outset been somewhat ambivalent in its English language attitudes. On one hand, the U.S. Constitution makes no mention of language.[1] This is somewhat unusual since the designation of an official language is quite common in constitutional documents, not only in multilingual countries,[2] but also in countries where only one language is generally used.[3] On the other hand, John Jay in the *Federalist Papers* saw the English language as one tie which bound the federal structure. "Providence has been pleased to give this one connected country to one united people—a people descended from the same ancestors, speaking the same language . . . very similar in their manners and customs."[4]

These different points of view throughout our history have been debated with the government choosing to emphasize one or the other as a function of economic needs and political stresses between the established classes and the different visions of America's strength and weaknesses. This chapter will examine a selected view of the many language groups which have emerged and evolved in the United States and will show how their experiences have shaped the federal role in bilingual education.

The Hispanic Population in the Southwest

The Spanish conquistadores came to Mexico in 1519. Many of them intermarried with the Indians, and the mestizo population expanded and gradually moved northward. By 1790 an estimated 23,000 Spanish-speaking people were living in areas which later became the states of Arizona, California, New Mexico, and Texas.[5]

After the Mexican-American War of 1848, Mexico ceded to the United States a vast territory, including California, Arizona, and New Mexico and also approved the prior annexation of Texas. All citizens of Mexico residing within the ceded domain became United States citizens automatically if they did not leave the territory within one year after treaty ratification. Thus, the Spanish-speaking inhabitants of the Southwest became a minority group in a country different in language and culture.[6]

At the end of 1848, there were approximately 15,000 residents in California, half of Mexican descent. But the Gold Rush quickly changed that. Within a year the population expanded to approximately 95,000 people, almost all Anglo-Americans. The Gold Rush not only initiated a monumental increase in the Anglo population but also resulted in a struggle over land, both of which operated to the political detriment of the Spanish-speaking inhabitants.

At the time of statehood, eighteen percent of all education in the state was private and Catholic.[7] These private schools were composed of pupils mainly of Spanish-speaking descent, and the children were taught in the Spanish language under the direction of the *padres*. Initially, these schools were state-supported.

In 1870 California passed a law requiring that "all schools shall be taught in the English language."[8] This linguistic purism in the state-supported school system went hand in hand with the nativistic sentiments expressed in other fields. For example, in the early 1850s California passed statutes suspending publication of the state laws in Spanish, requiring court proceedings to be in English, and imposing a new tax of five dollars a month for foreign miners and a head tax to discourage the immigration of people ineligible for citizenship.[9]

The two earliest New Mexico school laws, those of 1863 and 1869, contained no language provisions. The conditions in the territory leave no doubt that the public schools provided for in the laws had a predominantly Spanish character. There were practically no Anglos in the state; the laws were in fact first drafted in Spanish and translated only later into English. According to the 1874 annual report of the territorial school authorities, the composition of the New Mexico public schools was five percent English speakers, sixty-nine percent Spanish speakers, and twenty-six percent bilingual.[10]

Gradually, Anglo-Americans from the East who were unsympathetic toward Mexican culture came to dominate the territory.[11] In 1891 a New Mexico statute was passed requiring all schools in New Mexico to teach in English[12] as part of a broader struggle over land which was developing between the Anglo settlers and the Mexican Americans.[13]

The American Indian

In Indian affairs, the evolution was similar. Congress made its first provisions for the expenditure of funds not to exceed $15,000 per year to promote "civilization among the aborigines" in 1802; and in 1819 Congress enacted a provision which "still stands as the legal basis for most of the education work of the Indian Service":[14]

> The President may . . . employ capable persons . . . for teaching [Indian] children in reading, writing, arithmetic . . . for the purpose of . . . introducing among them the habits and art of civilization.[15]

No specific mention is made regarding the use of the English language in either the 1802 or 1819 provisions. Both attempt to promote "civilization." That the English language is the "civilized" tongue and the Indian language "barbaric" is implied in these provisions, but not stated.[16]

However, some Indian-initiated educational programs were quite significant. Thus, by 1852 the Cherokee Indian tribe ran a school system of twenty-one schools and two academics—1,100 pupils. Other tribes—the Choctaws, Creeks, and Seminoles, for example—also had begun to establish, and operate their own schools.[17]

As America expanded, the desire for the land owned and occupied by the Indians became very great. Initially the hope was that the problem would solve itself: that as the Indians became "civilized" their need for land would naturally decrease.[18] Educational policy was seen as a means to "civilize" the Indians and, thus, permit the taking of their land. President Monroe, writing in 1817, stated: "The hunter or savage state requires a greater extent of territory to sustain it than is compatible with the progress and just claim of civilized life . . . and must yield to it."[19]

The discovery of gold on the Pacific Coast and in the Rocky Mountains had an explosive effect on the population. The promoters of the transcontinental railroads sought grants of land along their routes increasing the pressure on Indian land and tribal units.[20]

In response to the demand for more land, the Homestead Act was passed in 1862, which opened up the plains to white settlers. To facilitate the process, "encouragement was given to the slaughter of big buffalo herds, the Indians' principal source of food. With their meat gone, it was believed the tribes would be forced onto the reservations by the promise of rations."[21]

English language in the Indian schools was first mentioned in the report of the Indian Peace Commission, a body appointed under an act of Congress in 1867 to make recommendations for the permanent removal of the causes of Indian hostility. Its report of 1868, motivated by a combination of humanitarianism, militarism, and expansionism, states:

> . . . in the difference of language today lies two-thirds of our trouble. Schools should be established which children should be required to attend; their barbarous dialects would be blotted out and the English language substituted.[22]

After the treaty period came to an end in 1871, government schools conducted exclusively in English began to be established, gradually displacing the mission schools and their bilingual approach; many of the Indian schools which the tribes had begun to establish and run themselves were also eliminated.

The Experiences of the European Emmigrant

During the middle decades of the nineteenth century, there was an extraordinary increase in immigration to the United States. It began soon after the Napoleonic Wars in Europe, gained momentum steadily in the thirties and forties, and reached its crest in 1854. Federal statistics (comprehensively collected for the first time in 1820) document the change. In the decade of the twenties, the number of arrivals was 151,000; in the 1830s a fourfold increase to 500,000; in the 1840s, 1,713,000; and in the decade of the fifties, 2,314,000.

In this pre-Civil War period the only large number of non-English speaking immigrants were the 1.5 million Germans who aroused little hostility. They settled in the relatively unpopulated frontier areas of the country where they were unnoticed and generally were in the majority, giving them a political and social advantage not available to other groups at that time. In these farming districts, the Germans initially had no teachers at their disposal who were familiar with English, and in any event, there was little need for a command of English during those early settlement years.[23] Thus, most of the earliest school laws made no mention of the language to be employed in the public schools.[24]

The German migrants did not want English to be excluded, but they asked that German be taught as well. In response to the German demand, the Ohio legislature passed a law by which the German language could be taught in the public schools in those districts where a large German population resided;[25] and in 1840 German-English public schools were introduced in Ohio.[26]

In this initial state of tolerance, Pennsylvania, a few years earlier, had gone even further than Ohio. In 1837 a Pennsylvania law was passed permitting German schools—in some, all instruction was to be given in German—to be founded on an equal basis with English ones.[27] In Wisconsin it became the norm that whenever a newly created school district contained a large German population, teachers were hired and the schools were conducted either exclusively in German or in both German and English.[28]

After the Civil War, immigration continued to increase sharply; from 1815 to 1860, five million; 1860-1890, ten million; and from 1980 to 1914, fifteen million. The increase was in large part due to the steamship line which had replaced the sailboat in the transatlantic immigrant trade, reducing the hazards of the journey and broadening the geographic origins from which one could embark.[29] It was this later migration that became an increasing issue in the United States. From 1860 to 1890, as in the prewar years, immigrants came mostly from the British Isles, Germany, and Northern Europe; but in the later period (1890-1914), they came from Southern and Eastern Europe, from the non-English speaking countries of Russia, Austria, Hungary, and Italy.[30] Without money and with English language difficulties, they gravitated toward the cities where pay was somewhat higher and where the population density reflected the close contact of village life at home.

As the end of the nineteenth century approached, nineteen of America's largest cities consisted of over half immigrants and their children. While 18.37 percent of all Americans were the children of immigrants in 1890, 86.36 percent of Milwaukee's residents were immigrants and the children of immigrants; 80.12 percent of New York's; 77.79 percent of Chicago's; 56.58 percent of Philadelphia's; 71.04 percent of Brooklyn's; 67.46 percent of St. Louis's; 74.98 percent of Cleveland's; and 77.11 percent of Buffalo's. Their ethnic distinctiveness and religious differences—most were Catholic or Jewish—their concentration, their great visibility, and their initial exercise of political power raised great fears among the American establishment.

Restrictionist sentiment grew, aimed at both limiting immigration and restricting access by the alien to the political and economic institutions in the country. The image of the immigrant as unlettered and easily corrupted focused attention on education and the English language as the unifying and uplifting element. Representative of this view is the characterization of the immigrants by Dorman B. Eaton in his major work, *The Government of Municipalities:*

> What spectacle could be more humiliating to an American patriot . . . than those often presented in grog-shops, low lodging houses, and gambling dens, when party leaders and captains . . . are competing . . . among the degraded and criminal emigrants, as ignorant of our laws and language, perhaps as they were regardless of the laws of the country from which they fled.[31]

Restriction and Tolerance

From 1880-1925 English language requirements expanded rapidly gaining special vigor after World War I. English literarcy requirements as a condition of voting and holding office passed in over three-fourths of the states of the Union and limited access to the political arena. Statutes imposing English language tests for various occupations from lawyers to bankers restricted economic access to the American mainstream.[32] These hurdles were paralleled in education: thirty-seven states required English as the language of instruction in the public schools.[33] In 1879 the off-reservation boarding school was established, separating Indian language customs and dress.

There were some judicial challenges to English language requirements in the twentieth century with mixed results. A ban on German language instruction was overturned,[34] but English literacy tests as a condition of voting were sustained.[35]

By 1968 when the federal government for the first time, by its passage of the Bilingual Education Act, suggested the permissibility—even the desirability—of instruction in the native language, the political context had substantially changed. By 1960 the civil rights movement, gaining strength after World War II, was at flood tide. The executive and legislative branches had both come out rather strongly for civil rights and focused on the deprivations suffered by various minority groups. In addition to civil rights legislation, the Economic Opportunity Act of 1964[36] and the Elementary and Secondary Education Act of 1965[37] had focused on the poor and made education a matter of national policy and priority for all disadvantaged youth.

The result of this legislation was that the needs of Mexican Americans and Puerto Rican groups increasing attention. The wave of ethnic consciousness which accompanied the civil rights movement and social changes in the sixties no longer required Spanish-speaking parents to remain mute or to soften their desire that the Spanish language be given a more meaningful role in their children's education.

The 1960 Census[38] counted the Spanish-surnamed population in the five southwestern states of Arizona, California, Colorado, New Mexico, and Texas, and the figures were indeed significant. The total Spanish-surnamed population had increased more than fifty percent over the 1950 totals: to 3,464,999 from 2,281,710. The 1960 figures from Texas showed that the Spanish-surnamed population was 1,417,810 out of a total population of 9.5 million people, or almost fifteen percent of that total. California had the largest Spanish-surnamed population, 1,426,538—a figure which showed an 87.6 percent increase over 1950.

In the other southwestern states (Arizona, New Mexico, and Colorado), the Spanish-surnamed population was also identified and was, in all cases, approximately ten percent or more.[39] On the East Coast, although not as numerically significant, there was a large number of Puerto Ricans, for whom Spanish was the native tongue; there were over 600,000 Puerto Ricans in New York City in 1960, and by 1966, they represented almost twenty-one percent of the total public school population of that city.[40]

The federal government and the individual states had begun to respond to this increased constituency. For example, in 1965 the federal government established the Interagency Committee on Mexican American Affairs[41] to concern itself with Mexican American issues, and on July 1, 1967, a Mexican Affairs Unit began to function within the United States Office of Education. Within the next few years the Equal Employment Opportunity Commission published its first study of Mexican Americans, *Spanish-Surnamed American Employment in the Southwest;* the U.S. Civil Rights Commission held its first hearings on Mexican Americans and published its first report, *Mexican Americans and the Administration of Justice in the Southwest.* The Congress, in the Voting Rights Act of 1965, suspended English literacy tests as a condition of voting where past performance indicated discriminatory administration of the test[42] and, as a special concession to the educated Puerto Rican voter, banned English literacy tests when the voter had completed the sixth grade in an American school where the language of instruction was *other* than English.[43]

At the local level, the New York City Board of Education in 1958 published its comprehensive *Puerto Rican Study* dealing with the difficulties encountered by these native Spanish-speaking pupils in the New York school system.[44] The Texas Education Agency in 1965 investigated the problems of Spanish-surnamed pupils in the Texas schools, and Colorado published in 1967 a general study of the status of the Spanish-surnamed population in that state.[45]

These studies pointed out that education was in the forefront of the concerns of the Spanish-speaking. The 1960 Census statistics on the educational level of Spanish-surnamed students in the five southwestern states showed that Mexican American children had completed an average of 8.12 years of schooling, four years less than their Anglo counterparts. The high dropout rate that these statistics evidenced caused great concern.

Although the Spanish-speaking were the primary force behind the bilingual education movement, the language issue was present elsewhere as well, most notably in connection with Indian children. Indian policy in 1950 focused upon terminating federal recognition of the Indian tribe, eliminating services and relocating Indians into cities.[46]

In the later years of the Eisenhower administration, the emphasis on termination abated; and when the Kennedy administration entered office, it conveyed to the Indians its desire for reversal of the termination policy. A special task force, appointed to investigate the status of Indian affairs, addressed itself to bilingualism in Indian education but did not provide a very strong case for it.[47] It asked only that the Bureau of Indian Affairs make a special effort to keep abreast of the latest developments in language training and instruction and carry on inservice training programs in conjunction with local universities. Under the federal poverty program, additional monies were provided to the Bureau of Indian Affairs, and special innovation centers were set up to develop new educational methodologies for Indians.

That something new was required was clear. The country's Indian educational policies were reflected in the following statistics. In the 1800s the Cherokees had an educational system which produced a "population 90% literate in its native language and used bilingual materials to such an extent that Oklahoma Cherokees had a higher English literacy level than the white populations of either Texas or Arkansas"; in 1969, "40% of adult Cherokees were functionally illiterate."[48]

The culmination of the new approach was President Lyndon Johnson's Message on Indian Affairs delivered to Congress on March 6, 1968. The statement placed the highest priority on the improvement of education for Indians and the control of Indian schools by Indian school boards. It also stressed language needs and cultural reinforcement.

> These schools will have the finest teachers, familiar with Indian history, culture, and language—feature an enriched curriculum . . . a sound program to teach English as a second language.[49]

Moreover, educational theory had changed. Quite apart from the political developments mentioned, there was an increasing interest in introducing foreign language programs in elementary schools. This activity was assisted by a series of government grants under the National Defense Education Act, passed in 1958 in response to the Russian launching of Sputnik. Title VI and, later, Title XI of that act emphasized the retention and expansion of our foreign language resources, a theme which was to be repeated at the 1967 Bilingual Education Act hearings.

> The most active language maintenance institution in the majority of ethnic communities in the United States is the ethnic group school. Over 2,000 such schools currently function in the United States, of which more than half offer mother tongue instruction even when there are many "non-ethnics" and "other ethnics" among their pupils. On the whole, they succeed in reinforcing or developing moderate comprehension, reading, and speaking facility in their pupils. They are far less successful in implanting retentivist language attitudes which might serve to maintain language facility after their students' programs of study have been completed, approximately at the age of 14. . . . the levels of facility attained usually are sufficient to provide a foundation for cultural bilingualism. This foundation, however, is rarely reinforced after the completion of the study in the ethnic group school.[50]

This renewed interest in foreign language and foreign language teaching enabled new groups such as ACTFL (American Council on the Teaching of Foreign Languages) and TESOL (Teachers of English to Speakers of Other Languages) to assert themselves in educational circles.

There were increasing numbers of experiments in bilingual programs to meet the needs of particular communities. Dade County in Florida (responding to the educational wishes of the Cuban refugees), Rough Rock School in Arizona (run by an all Navajo school board), and a number of cities in Texas and California initiated programs and experimental approaches testing different methods to reinforce the cultural backgrounds of the community and meet their educational needs.[51] The international field as well provided paradigms and suggestions for action as a number of countries initiated and extended bilingual programs.[52]

The National Education Association (NEA) late in 1966 sponsored a conference on the education of Spanish-speaking children in the schools of the Southwest, which led to the publication of NEA's report entitled *The Invisible Minority, Pero No Vencibles*. This report strongly recommended instruction in Spanish for those children who speak Spanish as a native tongue. In April 1967, at a San Antonio, Texas, conference on the Mexican American, demonstrations were given of the work of bilingual and English as-a-second-language programs already established in a few elementary schools in Texas. One of the major conclusions of the conference was the need for bilingual education with a call to the federal government to assume an important part of this responsibility.

Need and experience had conjoined for the establishment of a nationwide bilingual education program.

THE TERMS OF THE BILINGUAL EDUCATION ACT

Breadth of Coverage

All Non-English Proficient Students

At present, the act embraces those "of limited English proficiency." Estimates are that there are 3.5 million students with limited English proficiency, only 250,000 of which are served by Title VII.[53]

The 1967 Senate Bill as introduced by Senator Ralph Yarborough directed itself to the Spanish-speaking only: "In recognition of the special educational needs of the large numbers of students in the United States whose mother tongue is Spanish and to whom English is a foreign language."[54]

The approach was rationalized on the basis of their number and different history from that of other groups.

> We have limited the bill to the Spanish language because there are so many more of them than any other group. If you spread this idea to every language it would fragment and destroy the bill. There is also a basic difference between the Spanish-speaking and the other non-English-speaking groups. If you take the Italians, Polish, French, Germans, Norwegians,

or other non-English-speaking groups, they made a definite decision to leave their old life and culture and come here to a new country and set up a way of life here in accordance with ours, and we assumed they were consenting at that time to give up their language, too.

That decision to come here carried with it a willingness to give up their language, everything.

That wasn't true in the Southwest. We went in and took the people over, took over the land and culture. They had our culture superimposed on them. They did not consent to abandon their homeland and to come here and learn anew. They are not only the far more numerous group, but we recognize the fact that they are entitled to special consideration.[55]

The Yarborough bill defined the Spanish-speaking student by birth: "Elementary and secondary school students born in, or one or both of whose parents were born in, Mexico or Puerto Rico, and, in States for which such information is available, other students with Spanish surnames."[56]

Both the limitation to the Spanish-speaking and the definition were sharply attacked by other members of Congress and educators.

It is most doubtful whether the goals of these measures can be attained if its provisions are limited to one language and one culture alone. Unless all Americans regardless of their national origin are made to feel that the preservation of the various languages and cultures brought here by immigrants is important to the United States, there is little reason to believe that such a program restricted to Spanish alone can be successful.[57]

The most serious side defect of S. 428 is that it recognizes only the problems of the Spanish-speaking population. There are many other groups across the land who have the very same problem who would be ignored by this legislation. There are, for example, French speaking people in Louisiana and the far northeast. There are Indians scattered throughout the country, some on reservations, and others, in fact some twelve thousand or more organized groups in this country with ethnic interests of one kind or another. Each one of these organizations, and the ethnic groups they represent, has a real interest in Federal programs dealing with the special problems of the non-English-speaking citizens of this country. The bill as drawn ignores these interests and denies to these other groups what it gives to the Spanish-speaking. I believe that this is unjust, and may very possibly be unconstitutional. It appears to me that in view of our long history of pluralism, and in view of our continuing efforts to promote mutual respect and tolerance, we would be inviting grave and justly deserved criticism from many ethnic groups if we recognize the problems of only one.

No matter whether the legislation is aimed at one group, which I believe would be wrong, or whether it intends to assist all non-English-speaking citizens, I believe that the definition of terms should not include a national origins test, and should not be restricted to persons born in a designated foreign country, or whose parents were born in such a country.

There are many thousands of people in this land who do not speak English even though their families have been here for many generations.[58]

In the House of Representatives at about the same time a number of similar bills advocating bilingual education were introduced, most notably by Congressmen Augustus Hawkins and Edward Roybal of California and Congressman Jerome Scheuer of New York.[59] The Hawkins-Royal bill expanded on the Yarborough bill to include assistance to the French-speaking as well, and the Scheuer bill authorized bilingual instruction for all children whose native tongues were not English.

The final 1968 law adopted the broadest approach and was directed at "children who come from environments where the dominant language is other than English."[60] Both the Spanish language limitation and the definition which linked the Spanish-speaking to national origin were eliminated. This expansion of the program was in keeping with the Johnson administration's position which supported bilingual programs in principle, although it felt much of the need was being met by existing educational activity.

> The primary beneficiaries of any nationwide bilingual education program would undoubtedly be Spanish-speaking children. But there are also other groups of children needing special programs whose home language is not Spanish. There are French-speaking children in Louisiana and near the Canadian border, children of oriental ancestry, and American Indians in significant numbers in various areas.
>
> We expect that the number of children from other linguistic groups will increase in the next few years as a result of last year's liberalization of the Immigration Act.[61]

The 1974 amendments broadened the definition of those included to children of "limited English-speaking ability," and the 1978 amendments changed the law to direct it at individuals with "limited English proficiency."[62] The 1978 law expanded the act's coverage considerably. The change was also made to eliminate the somewhat pejorative connotation of the previous law and to maintain the focus on English learning while allowing administrative flexibility. The new definition no longer requires children to be removed from bilingual programs prematurely (once they have gained the ability to *speak* English although their *overall* English proficiency is limited). On the other hand, students would not continue receiving bilingual instruction after they have developed English proficiency.[63]

This 1978 definition may be contrasted with the suggestions made by the National Council of La Raze which sought to add a bicultural element to the bilingual description and to broaden the scope and objective of the act beyond a mere improvement of English language abilities by extending it to encompass overall cognitive and affective development. The council recommended changing the statutory direction from 1974's "children of limited English-speaking ability" to "children with linguistically different skills" and changing the goal from "to achieve competence in the English language" to providing "opportunities to expand their conceptual and linguistic abilities and potentials in a successful and positive manner, and enhance cultural and ethnic pride and understanding."[64]

The same thrust was recommended by the National Association for Bilingual Education when it proposed broadening the legislation from an emphasis on improvement and development of English skill to a more comprehensive educational process—which "facilitates the mastery of two or more languages (one of which is English)." The association recommended changing from "limited English-speaking children" to "children with linguistically different skills" and providing eligibility for all children rather than limiting eligibility to children of limited English proficiency.[65]

The 1978 statutory language arose in the Senate embracing some of the ideas which were in the original House bill. In discussing the 1978 amendments, the House Committee broadened the criteria of eligibility to include those "who cannot read, write, or understand English at the level appropriate for their age and grade"; entrance into the program was no longer to be based solely on English speech. Under this broader definition the local school districts would still have the responsibility for making determinations of which individuals would participate in accordance with the other requirements of the act.[66]

Thus, the term "limited English proficiency" refers to individuals (1) not born in the U.S.; (2) whose native language is other than English; (3) who come from environments where languages other than English are dominant; and (4) "who are American Indian and Alaskan Native students and who come from environments where a language other than English has had a significant impact on their level of English language proficiency" and, "by reason thereof, have sufficient difficulty speaking, reading, writing, or understanding the English language to deny such individuals the opportunity to learn successfully in classrooms where the language of instruction is English."[67]

The 1978 definition broadening the act's scope to reach those "of limited English proficiency" was reinforced by the 1978 Senate Report which noted the desire to expand the existing outreach of the program. The act, therefore, charged the Commissioner in the consideration of applications "to give priority to . . . geographical areas and . . . to assist children in need than have historically been underserved by programs in bilingual education."[68] Specifically, it also noted the "potential need for bilingual education programs among Franco-Americans and Portuguese-Americans in New England and Spanish-speaking persons of Caribbean origin throughout the Northeast," and urged "the office of Bilingual Education to give appropriate attention to applications designed to meet this need."[69]

Indian Students

The expansion of the legislation beyond the needs of the Spanish-speaking, although related broadly to a number of ethnic groups—the French, Polish, and Chinese were specifically mentioned in the 1968 House hearings—was particularly related to Indian education. Statistics were presented by tribe on achievement, and considerable testimony, both by HEW and the Department of Interior, in addition to Indian groups, focused on the educational needs of Indian children. To some degree, this was linked to additional control being transferred by the federal government to the Indian with respect to curriculum and school staffing.[70] The official executive position was not very supportive; the educational benefits of bilingual education were desirable, but such a program would be difficult to implement.

> If either bill is favorably considered, we urge that it be amended to permit the bilingual assistance program to be extended to children and teachers in elementary and secondary schools operated by this Department for American Indians. We also recommend that it be amended to permit the program to be extended to the Trust Territory of the Pacific Islands.
>
> The Bureau of Indian Affairs has been aware of the possibilities of bilingual instruction for some time, having developed a few bilingual teaching materials some 25 years ago only to have the movement stopped by the advent of World War II. Since that time such programs have not appeared to be practical due to the difficulty of developing and planning them while at the same time having to operate a full-fledged school system. With the added sophistication that has evolved in the general field of the foreign language teaching and learning, it poses an exciting possibility for the Indian children of America who need the dignity and strength such a program could add to their schools and to their intellectual development.[71]

Prior to 1978 the law provided for carrying out programs to serve "individuals on reservations where the school is approved by the Commissioner."[72] Under these circumstances, the commissioner could make payments to the Secretary of the Interior to carry out the purposes of the act.[73]

The 1978 amendments changed somewhat the provision of bilingual education for Indian children by providing that the commissioner may fund applicants directly to carry out programs of bilingual education for Indian children on reservations rather than, as in the past, to have to make payments to the Secretary of the Interior to serve these educational needs.[74]

Special Puerto Rico Provision

The 1978 amendments, in addition, made a special provision with respect to children in Puerto Rico. The 1974 Act permitted the Commonwealth of Puerto Rico, like local governments in the continental United States, to improve the English proficiency of children residing in Puerto Rico. But the law now also provides that the Commonwealth of Puerto Rico may serve the needs of students with limited English proficiency in *Spanish*. The amendment is designed to serve those children who return to Puerto Rico from the States who are unable to function adequately in Spanish.[75]

Children in Private Schools

The Bilingual Education Act, from the outset, provided for participation by private school children in the programs. Nevertheless, participation by this segment of the school population was very small. The 1978 amendments strengthened the commissioner's power to withhold approval of an application or to reallocate funds to assure that children of nonpublic schools are included in the program.[76]

> The Committee adopted this amendment in response to the serious problems of a lack of participation of private school children in bilingual education programs. It is the clear intent of Congress that there be equitable participation of these children in Title VII programs.[77]

General Purpose

The 1968 Bilingual Education Act was directed at "the special education needs of the large number of children with limited English-speaking ability in the United States."[72] This broad statement of purpose reflected the Congressional concern for and recognition of the special needs of children coming from homes where the dominant language was other than English. Thus, Senator Ralph Yarborough (Democrat, Texas), who introduced the first bilingual education bill in the Senate,[79] stated in his opening address:

> Our educational policies on the teaching of the Spanish-speaking have not been among our more enlightened areas of educational endeavor. For instance, take our children who speak only Spanish, if there were only a handful, a few hundred, you couldn't afford to establish separate methods of instruction, but millions of children from Spanish-speaking homes come to schools speaking only Spanish.
> The tragic results are shown in the dropout rate. Among adults 25 and

over, Mexican-Americans in 1960 had an average of 7.1 years of schooling, as compared to the 12.1 years for Anglos, and nine for non-whites. The gap between Anglos and Mexican-Americans is 5 years, or 41 percent.[80]

The dropout rate was to be repeated again and again throughout the hearings as an indication that matters had gone wrong. But, although there was agreement on the effect on the non-English-speaking child of the present educational system, the reason was unclear.

To some, the issue was psychological.

Imagine the situation that confronts a certain youngster from my part of the country. A youngster spends his formative years in the warm, friendly environment of his family and friends—an environment in which Spanish is spoken. At the age of 5 or 6 he is taken to school. What a profound shock he encounters the first day there, when he is made to know in no uncertain terms that he may speak no Spanish at school. He must speak English, a language which he scarcely knows, both in the classroom and on the playground. If he is caught speaking Spanish, he will be punished.

Expert witnesses who will appear later before this subcommittee will comment on the psychological damage which such practices rendered unto millions of children. Even to a layman the injustice and harm of such practices are obvious. Unfortunately, this practice has all too often been the rule rather than the exception in the education of children from Spanish-speaking backgrounds.[81]

This idea of strengthening one's self-image reflected current educational thinking relating one's image of self to both learning and maturity.[82]

The four-year-old placed in a relaxed atmosphere with an unstructured program learns language effortlessly. Following pursuits which interest him, he has the need, the desire, and the opportunity to communicate in the new language. Our program has stressed the expansion of the child's world. We have been interested in sensitizing him to the sight and sound and feel of experience and in helping him to differentiate it and develop the vocabulary necessary to describe it.

These children, by virtue of their language training and their broadened experience, are now able to start kindergarten on an equal footing with their peers. They start without the frustration and the experience of failure.

They are accustomed to the sweet feeling of success—and the pattern can continue.

This pattern can be extended. It must be expanded to include not only the economically deprived, but those who are deprived by virtue of their language difficulty.[83]

The educational need was linked also to broader issues of economic opportunity. Bilingual education, a new approach to education, represented the hope that the traditional avenue in American society—education—would open the door to the disadvantaged non-English-speaking group.

> There is [sic] still discrimination and inadequate job opportunities for the impoverished, poorly educated Mexican-American. I am convinced that better education is the key that will open the door of equal opportunity to this patient, very worthy ethnic group.[84]
>
> According to a report on poverty just completed at Texas A&M University, families with Spanish surnames are much more likely to be poverty stricken than Anglo-American or Negro families.
>
> The A&M report shows that there is a clear relation between poverty and low education; and the Spanish-Americans are Texas' least educated major group.[85]

Some related the bill to the immigrant tradition in the United States.

> Let me conclude in a more general tone. This bill would contribute to increased cultural and social maturity in our society.
>
> Let us show long-range leadership by making it possible to enjoy our cultural diversity. Let us never forget that our great strength has stemmed from being a land of immigrants. Whether Irish, Jew, Scot, Swede, or Mexican, all races and nationalities have [contributed] in years before, and will contribute more to our unique society. As Americans first, cultural diversity simply benefits all of us.[86]

There was a recognition that what was being asked was novel, somewhat different from the approach of other language groups within the United States. Here were groups requesting assistance to maintain their cultural strength and language, but this was necessary to assist their children's self-image and permit the learning process to take place.

> Our children suffer from a poor self-identity because they speak a foreign language. A bilingual educational program can impart knowledge and pride in their ancestral culture and language.[27]

And the historical experience was different. The Spanish-speaking and Indian groups, the key minority language groups to be served by the legislation, had become part of the United States, it was said, by conquest rather than voluntary migration.

The bilingual approach was also supported by some representatives of other language groups. Thus, the General Secretary of the YIVO Institute for Jewish Research testified:

America has traditionally been a monolingual country. Immigrants have been expected to learn English as quickly as possible and quite frequently were encouraged to abandon their ancestral language and culture with all deliberate speed. The bill, now before the Senate, is important in large measure because it clearly announces to bilingual Americans that not only does the United States Government not expect them to forget their ancestral language and culture, but it is prepared to support their maintenance with funds and other resources."[88]

The multipurpose character of the legislation was reflected in the statue which remained broad and very general on educational purpose and approach.

Declaration of Policy

In recognition of the special educational needs of the large numbers of children of limited English-speaking ability in the United States, Congress hereby declares it to be the policy of the United States to provide financial assistance to local educational agencies to develop and carry out *new and imaginative elementary and secondary school programs* designed to meet these special conditional needs. (emphasis supplied)[89]

The committee reports made clear that the broad, unspecific charges were purposeful.

The purpose of this new title is to provide a solution to the problems of those children who are educationally disadvantaged because of their inability to speak English.

The solution to this problem lies in the ability of our local educational agencies with high concentrations of children of limited English-speaking ability to develop and operate bilingual programs of instruction.[90]

Because of the need for extensive research, pilot projects and demonstrations, the proposed legislation does not intend to prescribe the types of programs or projects that are needed. Such matters are left to the discretion and judgment of the local school districts to encourage both varied approaches to the problem and also special solutions for a particular problem of a given school. The legislation enumerates types of programs as being illustrative of possible solutions.[91]

Specific Purposes

Bilingual education was to accomplish three purposes: (1) increase English language skills, (2) maintain and perhaps increase mother tongue skills, and (3) support the cultural heritage of the student.

The threefold purpose and the interrelationship was set forth by the Puerto Rican Resident Commissioner in his testimony urging the passage of the Bilingual Education Act of 1968.

> The solution, however, is not so easy, for at the same time we must produce fluency in the English language. I wish to stress that I realize the importance of learning English by Puerto Ricans and other minority groups living in the States. I concur fully in Senator Yarborough's statement that "it is essential in a pluralistic land such as ours that we have a common language and means of communication in order to live and work together." But I do not feel that our educational abilities are so limited and our educational vision so shortsighted that we must teach one language at the expense of another, that we must sacrifice the academic potential of thousands of youngsters in order to promote the learning of English, that we must jettison and reject ways of life that are not our own.
>
> The essense of my legislative proposal is simple in concept and structure: I propose the establishment of programs which (a) will utilize two languages, English and the non-English mother tongue, in the teaching of the various school subjects, (b) will concentrate on teaching *both* English and the non-English mother tongue, and (c) will endeavor to preserve and enrich the culture and heritage of the non-English-speaking student.[92]

The multipurpose role of bilingual education was reiterated during the passage of the 1974 Bilingual Education Amendments.

> . . . bilingual education involves the use of two languages, one of which is English, as mediums of instruction to assist children of limited English-speaking ability. Both languages are used for the same student population— not as an isolated effort, but as a key component of a program embracing the total curriculum.
>
> Rather than an objective in itself, bilingual education is part of a much larger goal: encouraging a child of limited English-speaking ability to develop fully his individual skills and talents. It is the use of the child's native language and respect for his cultural background that best distinguished bilingual education from programs more narrowly focused, such as ESL and remedial reading.[93]

The act tread carefully between the issues of language maintenance v. transition, cultural pluralism v. utilization of the mother tongue solely to assist in learning English. The manual for project applicants and grantees which was issued by HEW shortly after the act's passage reaffirmed both approaches.

It is intended that children participating in this program will develop greater competence in English, become more proficient in their dominant language, and profit from increased educational opportunity. Though the Title VII, ESEA program affirms the primary importance of English, it also recognizes that the use of the children's mother tongue in school can have a beneficial effect upon their education. Instructional use of the mother tongue can help to prevent retardation in school performance until sufficient command of English is attained. Moreover, the development of literacy in the mother tongue as well as in English should result in more broadly educated adults.[94]

To Increase English Language Skills

Increasingly, Congress has emphasized the English language purpose. Thus, in passing the 1974 law, Congress stated:

The goal of the program in the Committee bill is to permit a limited English-speaking child to develop the proficiency in English that permits the child to learn as effectively in English as in the child's native language— a vital requirement to compete effectively in society.[95]

The primary importance of English is underscored also in the 1978 declaration of policy which is to "demonstrate effective ways of providing for children of limited English proficiency, instruction designed to enable them, while using their native language to achieve competence in the English language."[96] The 1978 law requires the commissioner to develop models to evaluate bilingual education programs to determine the "progress made by participants therein attaining English language skills."[97] This latter requirement and the changed definition of the population to be served assured a response to the American Institutes for Research's evalution study which found that Title VII students were doing no better than non-Title VII students in English learning.

In general, across grades, when total Title VII and Non-Title VII comparisons were made, the Title VII students in the Study were performing in English worse than the Non-Title VII students. In Mathematics, across grades, they were performing at about the same level as Non-Title VII students.

Generally, less than a third of the students in the Title VII classrooms were there because of their need for English instruction (limited proficiency in English) as judged by the classroom teacher.

As part of the date collection efforts, each project director was asked, "After the Spanish-dominant child is able to function in school in English, what happens to the child?" Eighty-six percent reported that the student remains in the bilingual project.

These findings reflect Title VII project activities which run counter to the "transition" approach strongly implied by the ESEA Title VII legislation. (Transition in this sense implies that the native language of the student with limited English-speaking ability is used temporarily as a bridge to help the student gain competence in English. Under this approach, when a student is able to function in a regular English instruction classroom, he or she is transferred out of the bilingual project classroom.) In fact, project goals were more consistent with a maintenance approach to bilingual education.[98]

The changed definition of the population to be served to those of limited English proficiency also reflected in part the concern of the Congress that a segregated minority group was being created. A number of witnesses noted this during the hearings.

There is nothing in the research to suggest that children can effectively learn English without continuous interaction with children who are native English speakers, yet the Federal money has supported programs with only about one-tenth Anglos in the average class. In a society where Spanish-surname children are now more segregated than blacks, according to some measures, and where the Supreme Court has found such segregation unconstitutional, a program that tends to increase separation, raises very serious questions. In a number of cities, officials in bilingual programs have attacked desegregation orders and asked that Hispanic schools be exempted for educational reasons.

When the bilingual education title is revised I would strongly recommend that Congress require integrated bilingual student bodies wherever possible.[99]

Another reality that we are facing is the effect that desegregation plans are having on bilingual education. We believe that the issue is not so much a conflict in goals as it is the need for resources to expand the program in order to provide more multicultural settings for bilingual education.[100]

The 1978 law addressed the issue in two ways: by aiming the program at children with limited English language proficiency, it permitted flexibility of classroom placement. In addition, it specifically provided for up to forty percent English-speaking students in the classrooms.

> In order to prevent the segregation of children on the basis of national origin in programs assisted under this title, and in order to broaden the understanding of children about languages and cultural heritages other than their own, a program of bilintual instruction may include the participation of children whose language is English, but in no event shall the percentage of such children exceed 40 per centum. The objective of the program shall be to assist children of limited English proficiency to improve their English language skills and the participation of other children in the program must be for the principal purpose of contributing to the achievement of that objective.[101]

The Senate committee elaborated on the requirement:

> The issue of the extent to which English-speaking children should be permitted in Title VII projects was addressed by the Committee in the following manner. The bill allows the participation of English-speaking children but adds that they shall not exceed 40 percent. It was felt that the presence of English-speaking children would provide peer models for children with limited English proficiency. This is an important aspect of these children learning English. It was also felt that the presence of English speakers would reduce the segregation of children with limited English proficiency and provide positive experiences for English speakers by exposing them to other languages and cultures. The 40 percent maximum allows a wide range of flexibility for adaptation to local situations.[102]

To Maintain and Increase Mother Tongue Skills

The other goals of bilingual education, use of the native tongue and support for the cultural heritage of the minority language student, were retained in the 1978 law, but were specifically subordinated to the English language emphasis. Thus, bilingual education is defined as a program designed for children with limited English language skills in which there is "instruction . . . in English and, to the *extent necessary to allow a child to achieve competence in the English language, the native language* of the children of limited English proficiency. . . ." (emphasis supplied)[103]

The House Report attempted to deal with the transition v. maintenance argument by its reaffirmation of the native language role:

Since the inception of the Act, debate has raged unresolved over the extent to which native languages should be taught and at what stage students are ready to move out of the bilingual program.

Controversies over so-called maintenance or transitional approaches tend to confuse the issue, since these terms mean different things to different people and since there is general agreement that some instruction in the native language is necessary to help students strengthen language skills and develop in other academic subjects.[104]

The House also saw the broadened outreach as supportive of native language maintenance.

The Committee bill deals, to a certain degree, with this issue by broadening the definition of children who can participate in programs to include those with an adequate English-speaking ability but who have difficulty reading, writing or understanding English. Under this broadened definition, though, the local school district would still have the responsibility for making determinations of which individuals would participate in accordance with the other requirements of the Act.[105]

The 1976 General Accounting Office (GAO) report, which examined the bilingual educational program, had found as one of the factors adversely affecting academic achievement of limited English-speaking children, the fact that "the dominant language of the limited English-speaking children might not have been used enough for classroom instruction."[106] The 1978 legislation did not follow up on this comment.

To Support the Child's Cultural Heritage

Although Congress did not adopt the specific mention of *bicultural* along with *bilingual* as suggested by the U.S. Commission on Civil Rights[107] in 1975 and the National Council of La Raza[108] in 1977, it continued its support of the cultural heritage goal in the 1978 law.

The 1974 law had included in its statement of policy the following language which is still in the statute:

Sec. 702(a). Recognizing . . . (2) that many . . . children have a cultural heritage which differs from that of English-speaking persons; (3) that a primary means by which a child learns is through the use of such child's language and cultural heritage; . . . (5) that . . . children . . . benefit through the fullest utilization of multiple language and cultural resources. . . .

In 1978 even very strong transition program advocates supported the cultural continuance aspect of the program.

> MR. HEFTEL (D. Hawaii): The children with the assistance of volunteer instructors within the system develop self-appreciation programs for their own cultures. I have attended their programs and it is apparent this need exists. . . .
>
> MR. McGUIRE: I would agree that the ability to speak, to write English, is very important. I think the key to this is the sensitivity with which we build their English proficiency. The sensitivity issue and the bicultural issue comes [sic] in so that as children come in, it must not be done at the expense of their own culture.[109]

But again there was a modification of the bilingual education law in the 1978 amendments (shown in the italicized portion below) toward the integrating and balancing this cultural requirement with the cultural interests of English-speaking students. Bilingual instruction for children of limited English proficiency is to be given "with appreciation for the cultural heritage of such children, *and of other children in American Society. . . ."* (emphasis supplied).[110]

The house of Representatives 1978 Report explained the amendment as follows:

> Regarding the question of whether bilingual programs should have a cultural component, the Committee bill amends the present law to require that, if instruction is included on the cultural heritage of the children with limited English language skills, instruction must be also included on the cultural heritage of other children. In addition, the bill requires that research be conducted on the degree to which the inclusion of cultural heritage instruction in a bilingual education program serves to assist children in learning English.[111]

Program Design

The legislation envisions the funds will be used for instruction, teacher training, curriculum development, research, and evaluation.

Instruction

There appears to have been general agreement from the outset on the definition of bilingual education as the use of English and another language as instructional mediums in an educational program. The legislation calls for the "instruction . . .

in, and study of, English and, to the extent necessary, to allow a child to achieve competence in the English language, the native language . . . and such instruction [shall be] given with appreciation for the cultural heritage of such children, and of other children in American society. . . ."[112] Bilingual education is to range over the entire curriculum; "to the extent necessary, . . . in all courses or subjects of study which will allow a child to progress effectively through the educational system. . . ."[113]

The 1968 definition of limited English-speaking ability as "children who come from environments where the dominant language is other than English" made no distinction in levels of proficiency nor did it speak to the participation of minority language children in the integrated classroom. In a number of cases, school systems installed bilingual programs and concentrated on teaching English-dominant minority children, placing such children in remedial bilingual programs with minimal use of the non-English language.

Therefore, the present legislation is concerned wtih integrating the students of limited English proficiency with the rest of the school children both on educational and ethnic grounds. Thus, in "such courses or subjects of study as art, music, and physical education," the statute requires bilingual education programs to provide for participation "in regular classes."[114] The same rationale lies behind the legislative charge that children in bilingual education programs "be placed to the extent practicable, in classes with children of approximately the same age and level of educational attainment."[115] If children of "varying ages or levels of educational attainment are placed in the same class," instruction should be appropriate for their level of attainment.[116] Although teacher training and curriculum development may be centralized, the program shall serve children "in the school which they normally attend."[117]

There was considerable discussion of when and how to include English-speaking students in bilingual education programs. The original 1968 law made no provision for the participation of the English-speaking student in the bilingual program. The 1978 Senate bill allowed the participation of English-speaking children in the bilingual programs provided the number did not exceed forty percent. This was a slight reduction from the 50/50 ratio used in Colorado which Congress was advised had worked rather well[118] but still permitted flexibility.[119] The purpose of this provision was to reduce the possibility of segregation in the program and to provide peer models for children with limited English proficiency.

The House bill handled the question somewhat differently, adopting separate rules for programs which remove the children from regular classroom activities, so-called "pull-out" programs. For those programs where the children have the benefit of teaching specialists, only children with limited English proficiency would be eligible. All regular classroom instruction would permit a mix.[120] This approach, perhaps, reflected the GAO criticism: "[T]here often seemed to be too many English-speaking children in the project classrooms, thereby diluting program services for the limited English-speaking children."[121] The final law adopted the Senate language.[122]

The 1975 study conducted by OE's Office of Planning, Budget, and Evaluation identified four exemplary basic classroom bilingual projects that could serve as replicable models for districts contemplating similar programs. The descriptions of these programs were packaged and distributed to interested applicants as Project Information Packages.[123] They were also describing to the Congress by the administration, without, however, any suggestion that these would be only models utilized or even the preferred ones. The structure of the models varies; for example, one project uses English primarily, with one-third of the day in French, while another begins primarily in Spanish and introduces English as the student demonstrates readiness and understanding. In 1978 the Congress required the development of other models as well.

Training

From the outset the need was recognized for specialized training to create the teaching corps and ancillary personnel to serve the program. Thus, the 1968 Bilingual Education Act provided for "pre-service training, designed to prepare persons to participate in bilingual education."[124] The GAO and the American Institutes for Research in their evaluations, the administration in its presentation, and Congress after reviewing the program have all agreed on the need for additional qualified teachers.[125] The issue is one of both equality and quantity.

The 1974 amendments expanded the training component of the existing legislation requiring a fifteen percent set-aside of local bilingual education funding for inservice training.[126] The 1978 legislation removed the fifteen percent inservice training requirement[127] of the statute.

Regarding in-service training, the mandatory 15% set-aside for that purpose is very crucial for some local programs. For others, the need may have been fulfilled and therefore the funds may be used for other purposes. The Committee bill, therefore, removes the requirements in present law that each local project must expend at least 15% of its funds on in-service teacher training. Rather, the decision on the exact degree of such funding would be left with the local school district, with the expectation that in-service training is an important component of these programs. However, it must be noted that this set-aside funds in-service training programs that are non-degree in nature and therefore may not completely solve the need for highly qualified teachers.[128]

The commissioner may provide a wide range of training through grants, contracts, and fellowships (including stipends and allowances for dependents) to met specific needs and to promote general career development.[129] The training may be given to teachers, administrators, counselors, paraprofessionals, teacher aids, and parents.[130] Fellowship assistance must be repaid by the trainee either in cash or by an equivalent period of work in bilingual education training. The commission may waive repayment "in extraordinary circumstances."[131]

HEW requires grantees to give priority to persons who are bilingual and who demonstrate a high degree of interest in bilingual education.[132] A grantee which provides training leading to an undergraduate degree or a teaching certificate or training of personnel at an institute of higher education "shall require that all participants in its training program demonstrate proficiency in English and in the target language as a condition of successful completion of the program.[133]

Training may be conducted by: (1) local educational agencies, (2) state educational agencies, and (3) institutions of higher education (including junior colleges and community colleges). Private nonprofit organizations may also provide training if they apply after consultation with, or jointly with, local educational agencies or the state education agency.[134] (The requirement of consultation may be contrasted with the program grant requirements in which a joint application with the local education agency is required.) The commissioner must give priority to applicants with "demonstrated competence and experience in the field of bilingual education."[135]

Curriculum
Development

As the federal bilingual education program has expanded (there are now over 70 languages serving 302,000 children) the need for materials has expanded also. The program has not been able to meet this need especially in the less frequently used languages in the United States.

A recent study of the state of bilingual materials, published after the 1978 legislation and passed Congress, reaffirmed this shortage.[136] The study was optimistic in believing that "with growing numbers of bilingual programs and students, bilingual materials development in the U.S. will increase in the years ahead, particularly for the major languages."[137]

In 1975 the Office of Bilingual Education began to fund a network of institutions (materials development centers, dissemination and assessment centers, and training resource centers) pursuant to the statutory mandate that the commissioner and the directors of the National Institute of Education "shall, through competitive contracts with appropriate public agencies and private institutions and organizations, develop and disseminate instructional materials and equipment suitable for bilingual education programs."[138] At present there are thirty-three centers serving more than 500 local education agencies in thirty-nine states, the District of Columbia, Puerto Rico, and the territories of the United States. Each center has specific territorial and linguistic responsibilities.

This program has had considerable impact but the continuing shortages in some areas and weakness in others led to the 1978 amendment requiring the bilingual material to be equal in quality to those developed for regular English instruction.[139]

Despite the progress of the materials development centers, a need still exists for high quality materials, especially in some of the Native American, Asian and Pacific, and Indo-European languages. Some Native American projects experience particular problems with languages than do have a written orthography; local teachers and directors must spend considerable time developing materials in these instances, a task for which few have adequate training.

Existing materials are often unsatisfactory. The GAO report found that 60 percent of project directors and teachers surveyed felt their materials were inadequate. Much of the material sent to the disseminarion centers is found to be unsuitable. One dissemination center director estimated that only 10 to 15% of materials received is suitable for dissemination.[140]

The availability of materials already in existence must be considered, and "special attention shall be given to language groups for whom private organizatons are unlikely to develop such materials."[141]

Research

The failure to prove the effectiveness of bilingual education and the devastating evaluations by GAO and the Americn Institutes of Research disturbed the Congress, and it responded by increasing the amount available for research[142] fourfold to $20 million for 1979.[143]

The House Committee Report commented:

Based on the lack of national data regarding the other types of Title VII programs, the lack of national evaluations of other approaches to English instruction, the evidence of gains in individual projects, and the support for the bilingual approach from involved teachers and students and language group organizations, the Committee feels the need for program change as well as for further research, demonstration and evaluation to determine what constitutes a good program of bilingual education.

The Commissioner's Report on the Condition of Bilingual Education of 1977 found that "there is little to guide educators in designing and implementing effective bilingual projects." The National Association for Bilingual Education testified that only a small number of program models have been identified to date.

　　Consequently, the Committee bill increases the authorization of appropriations for research and development in bilingual education from $5 million a year to $20 million a year.[144]

The commissioner is charged to carry out a research program through competitive contracts with institutions of higher education, private and nonprofit organizatons, state educational agencies, and individuals.

The research activities to be funded are set forth in the statute are wide-ranging. Almost all arose in 1978 at Senate initiative:

1. Studies to determine and evaluate effective models for bilingual bicultural programs;
2. studies to determine
   a. language acquisition characteristics and
   b. the most effective method of teaching English within the context of a bilingual bicultural program;
3. a five-year longitudinal study to measure the effect of bilingual education on students who have non-English language proficiencies;
4. studies to identify the most effective and reliable method of identifying students entitled to bilingual education services;
5. the operation of a clearinghouse of information for bilingual education;
6. studies to determine the most effective method of teaching reading to children and adults who have language proficiencies other than English;
7. studies to determine the effectiveness of teacher training preservice and inservice programs funded under this title;
8. studies to determine the critical cultural characteristics of selected groups of individuals in order to teach about culture in the program.[145]

Evaluation

　　Like research, evaluation gained strong support from the Congress in the 1978 legislation primarily because of the GAO report.

The House Committee commented:

　　At the local level, a GAO report on bilingual educationed noted that evaluations for individual projects "have been inadequate for measuring programs' effect on student achievement and . . . have been inadequate for identifying projects worthy of replication." Poor self-evaluation designs proliferated even among the best projects, GAO continued.[146]

The need for local evaluation is also noted in the Senate Report.

The bill also requires that the Commissioner develop guidelines for local evaluations. It is hoped that these guidelines will provide scientifically valid information as well as descrbe the unique features of each project in order that local level projects can be validly compared.[147]

The statute also provides that any child enrolled more than two years in the program shall have an individual evaluation.[143] Although designed primarily to transfer responsibility of the program to the states, the provision also assures additional educational data.

The
Allocation
Process

Although the bilingual education program is a discretionary grant program, the legislation itself and the legislative history impose a structure on the allocation of funds. From the outset, in 1968, there were three general standards imposed:

1. The geographic distribution of children of limited English proficiency in the nation;
2. the capability of local educational agencies to carry out the programs; and
3. the relative number of persons from low-income families to be benefited by such programs.[149]

Geographic Distribution

The requirement to consider the location of children of limited English proficiency in the distribution of bilingual education funds parallels the approach of formula grant programs. The Office of Education has not published data or statistics setting forth the placement of numbers of students with limited English proficiency. The National Center for Education Statistics has tabulated and displayed states with children 4-13 years old with a household language other than English.[150]

There are two other geographical requirements which are to receive priority treatment by the commissioner:

1. Areas having the greatest need for programs;[151] and
2. applicants from local educational agencies which are located in various geographical regions of the nation and which propose to assist children of limited English proficiency who have historically been underserved by programs of bilingual education.[152]

The 1978 House Report elaborated on the first standard:

"Areas of greatest need" should be defined as including those which, within the immediately five preceding years, have had a significantly above-average influx of individuals of limited English language skills.[153]

The second "priority" is weakened considerably by the statutory condition "taking into consideration the relative numbers of such children in the schools for such local educational agencies and the relative need of such programs."[154] Its basic purpose was, given the limited amount of bilingual education funds, "to utilize scarce funds for demonstration programs and projects with a view toward stimulating interest and initiatives among State and local educational agencies throughout the Nation which ultimately would lead to successful non-Federal programs."[155]

Local Education Agency Capability

The regulations setting forth criteria for evaluating individual applicants require the application to discuss methods of administration, financial management procedures, coordination of funded and nonfunded activities under the program, and a plan for continuing the program after federal funding is completed.[156]

The 1978 amendments require the commissioner to determine that the assistance

will contribute toward building the capacity of the applicant to provide a program of bilingual education on a regular basis . . . of sufficient size, scope, and quality to promise significant improvement in the education of children of limited English proficiency and that the applicant will have the resources and commitment to continue the program when assistance under the Title is reduced or no longer available.[157]

Low Income

The low-income criterion originated in the 1968 Senate bill which had required the commissioner to allot funds based on the number of Spanish-speaking students in the states and the per capita income of the states "in such manner as he determines will best carry out the purpose of this title."[158]

The 1968 House bills focused more closely on the low-income question, perhaps reinforced by the experiences of Head Start and other poverty programs which had experimented with bilingual education. Thus, one House bill spoke of projects providing "reasonable assurances of making a substantive impact in meeting the special educational needs of persons who come from non-English-speaking low-income families."[159] Another required the commissioner to "develop criteria and procedures to assure that funds will go to areas of greatest needs," taking into consideration the number of children from non-English-speaking backgrounds and the per capita income from each state.[160]

The 1968 act was a compromise granting the commissioner some discretion while at the same time emphasizing the poverty criteria both in the geographical distribution of the program and in funding specific applications. The commissioner was charged with giving "highest priority to States and areas within States having the greatest need for programs . . . taking into consideration the number of children with limited English speaking ability between the ages of three and eighteen within each State,"[161] and approving those applications "designed to meet the special educational needs of children of limited English speaking abilities in schools having a high concentration of such children from families (a) with income below $3,000 per year, or (b) [receiving payments from State-approved AFDC programs]."[162]

The present law as a result of the 1974 amendments softens somewhat the low-income requirements. It mandates the commissioner *"to the extent feasible* [to] allocate funds appropriated in proportion to the geographical distribution of children of limited English proficiency throughout the Nation with due regard for the relative ability of particular local educational agencies to carry out such programs and the *relative numbers of persons from low-income families sought to be benefited by such programs* (emphasis supplied)."[163]

Low income is defined in the regulations issued by the Office of Education as an annual family income that does not exceed the poverty level determined under Setion 111(c)(2) of Title I of the Elementary and Secondary Education Act of 1965 as amended.[164]

The Application Process for Program Grants

To receive bilingual education program grants, one or more local educational agencies or an institution of higher education (including junior and community colleges), in conjunction with one or more local educational agencies, may apply.

Eligibility

State education agencies may apply for funds to provide technical assistance and coordination of bilingual programs within the state. These funds must supplement not supplant other funds available to the state.[165] The state agency may only receive up to five percent of the total that school districts in that state receive for the program.[166] This statutory limitation has caused administrative difficulties in some of the states with smaller bilingual education programs.[167]

Content of Grant Applications

Each grant aplication must set forth a description of the activities to be funded and provide evidence that the activities "will make substantial progress toward making programs of bilingual education available to children having need thereof in the area served by the applicant."[168]

By regulation, the commissioner has requested evidence assuring applicant supervision and information on the method of administration.[169] Similarly the applicant must set forth the description of fiscal control and the budget justification.

The applicant must indicate (a) the total number and percentage of children of limited English-speaking ability enrolled in the schools of the applicant and the number and percentage to be served by the proposed program; (b) when and how the applicant identified the children; (c) the number of low-income persons sought to be benefited and how they will benefit; (d) provisions for involving qualified personnel with experience in the educational problems of children of limited English-speaking ability and the use of cultural and educational resources in the area to be served; and (e) the evaluation design of the proposed program including, provisions for comparing performance of participating children on tests of reading skills in English and the other language with an estimate of performance in the absence of the program or with nonparticipating children;[170] the instruments of measurement; and provisions for reporting pretest and posttest scores.[171]

The 1978 amendments provide for increased parental participation. An application for a program of bilingual edcation shall be developed in consultation with an advisory council, a majority of which shall be parents and other representatives of children of limited English proficiency. The application must contain documentation of the advisory council's consultation and comments on the project.[172]

Finally, the application must assure that, after approval, the applicant will provide for continuing consultation and participation by a committee of parents, teachers, and other interested individuals. It would appear that the postapproval consultative group need not be the same as the advisory council. On the committee parents of children participating in the program must predominate, and a majority must be parents of children with limited English proficiency.[173] All parents of participating children must be informed of the institutional goals of the program and the progress of their children.[174]

Duration

In 1978, as in 1974, the duration of project funding was an issue discussed at some length by both the administration and Congress. The Carter administration proposed a five year funding limitation, a position which was supported by the House bill.

The Committee bill proposes a general rule that assistance under the Act be limited to no more than 5 years for any particular school or group of schools. However, a waiver of this rule is mandated whenever the school district shows a clear fiscal inability to carry on the program; shows adequate progress in the program; and either has a continuing presence of a substantial number of students with limited English-speaking skills in such school or schools, has experienced a recent substantial increase in the number of such students, or is under an obligation to provide bilingual education pursuant to a court order or a Title VI plan.[175]

The Senate opposed such a limitation; although it recognized that state and local commitment is important for the success of the program, the educational needs of the children, in their view, predominated.

Many local districts are hard pressed for funds at present, and bilingual education for minority students may be a low priority. Without federal funding many children will not receive the help they need. There is no educational base for such a limitation. In most areas with high concentrations of children with limited English proficiency, there are children continually entering the school system—some because of local births and some because of migration. The presence of children needing bilingual education will not disappear after five years. The Committee also noted that no other program in ESEA has such a limitation.[176]

The issue of duration reflected more than budgetary concerns. A firm time limit in Title VII program grants was consistent wtih a limited federal commitment to bilingual education as a reserach and development program and a transitional program;[177] open-ended grants suggested a broader federal involvement, a service program, and a maintenance effort.[178]

The 1978 law permits initial funding of one to three years and limits the ability of the commissioner to terminate the program. The commissioner's decision regarding the length of initial funding depends upon (a) the severity of the problem to be addressed, (b) the nature of the activities proposed, (c) the likely duration of the problems addressed by the application, and (d) other criteria the commissioner may establish to assure the effective use of the funds.[179] In addition the commissioner must determine that federal assistance will contribute toward building local capacity to provide a self-sustaining bilingual education program.[180]

Termination provisions are very formal. The commissioner, after reviewing program operations, may, upon finding that a school does not have a long-term need for continued assistance, issue an order to the local educational agency to prepare and submit within one year a revised application setting forth a schedule for termination of federal funding "in the fifth year following the issuance of such an order."[181] The commissioner's finding may not be issued without notice and opportunity for hearing. The reduction schedule shall be in accordance with criteria established by the commissioner designed to ensure gradual assumption of the cost by the applicant.[182]

The commissioner may not issue an "order to submit an application in preparation for termination of assistance . . . to any local educational agency" which shows adequate progress in meeting the goals of the program and a "fiscal inability" to carry on a program without the federal assistance. Further, to prevent termination there must also be either a continuing presence of a substantial number of students of limited English proficiency in bilingual education programs under Title VII; a recent, substantial increase in the number of students of limited English proficiency who have enrolled in such a program; or a state or federal court order or plan approved by the secretary under Title VI of the Civil Rights Act of 1964 affecting services for more children.[183] Once a termination order is issued, the commissioner is further charged to annually review the conditions to see if the order should be withdrawn or suspended.[184]

Program Administration

The law establishes an Office of Bilingual Education run by a director "to whom the Commissioner shall delegate all of his delegable functions relating to bilingual education." Under the 1978 amendments "the director shall also be assigned responsibility for coordinating the bilingual education aspects of other programs administered by the Commissioner."[185]

The statute requires the secretary to establish a National Advisory Council on Bilingual Education composed of fifteen members.[186] At least eight shall be persons experienced in "dealing with the educational problems of children and other persons who are of limited English proficiency." At least one of these eight shall represent persons serving on boards of education operating bilingual education. The group shall consist of at least two experienced teacher trainers, two persons with general experience in elementary and secondary education, two classroom teachers who have utilized bilingual methods and techniques, two parents of students whose language is other than English, one representative of a state educational agency, and one at-large member.

The council shall generally represent the geographical areas and population of persons with limited English proficiency. The secretary shall designate the chairperson and provide staff assistance and information necessary to the council's activities.

The council's function is to advise the commissioner in the preparation of general regulations and administrative and operational policy matters including approval criteria for applications. Each year by March 31, the council shall submit a report to the Congress and the president on the condition of bilingual education in the nation and on the administration and operations of Title VII.

FUTURE DIRECTIONS

Service Rather Than Demonstration

The bilingual education program as originally formulated, and as presently authorized, is a research and demonstration program. Congress acted on an intuitive judgment that teaching children in the language they understand was likely to be helpful. Testimony in 1967 had focused on need with a conscious awareness that solutions as yet were uncertain. The declaration of policy in the 1968 act articulated this perception by looking to local educational agencies "to develop and carry out new and imaginative elementary and secondary school programs."[187]

This language was reinforced in subsequent sections of the act which spoke of "the development of programs . . . including research projects, *pilot* projects . . . designed to *test the effectiveness* . . . " (emphasis supplied). Congress, in addition, envisioned "the development and dissemination of special instructional materials."[188] In subsequent years as the program has expanded, this initial experimental thrust has become diluted, and the program has moved toward a service emphasis.

Both the 1978 law and congressional reports emphasized once more the research and demonstration character of the program, stressing the need for additional study and evaluation of the approaches. The 1978 amendments specifically added in the statement of policy a subsection to note this direction: "Recognizing . . . (7) research and evaluation capabilities in the field of bilingual education need to be stregthened."

> The Committee bill . . . provides increased authorizations for training activities, research and evaluation and grants. . . . The committee is pleased to note that its faith in the efficacy of bilingual education is being affirmed in a growing number of States which have adopted sound bilingual programs to meet specific needs. It may be that a more direct Federal contribution to such State and local activities is appropriate for the future; but little progress toward such a service orientation can be made until Federal officials charged with carrying out the Title VII program do the job so clearly theirs under the law.[189]

The reaffirmation of the demonstration nature of the program resulted from two congressional concerns: (1) the absence of documentation and statistics which had been requested in 1974 and (2) the damaging reports of GAO[190] and the American Institutes for Research.[191] The AIR study concluded that "there is no compelling evidence in the current data of the Impact Study that Title VII bilingual education as presently implemented is the most appropriate approach for these students." This latter, most recent evaluation troubled the Congress and, although challenged by NIE and others, affected the 1978 legislation, reinforcing the committee's feeling that the appropriate approach and utility of bilingual education needed to be demonstrated.

> The first national evaluation of bilingual education supported by the Office of Education and conducted the American Institutes for Research raises some serious questions about the viability of the bilingual approach.
>
> A recent GAO report on bilingual education pointed out that evaluations for individual projects "have been inadequate for measuring programs' effect on student achievement and . . . have been inadequate for identifying projects worthy of replication."
>
> Consequently, the Committee bill increases the authorization of appropriations for research and development on bilingual education from $5 million a year to $20 million a year. The bill also requires each local project to provide for its own evaluation. It is hoped that these amendments will all lead to greater knowledge within the next several years about what is most effective in bilingual education.[192]

To assure that additional data is available and that there is an understanding in the Congress of the overall direction of the program, the 1978 amendments require the individual grant applications to include an evaluation component.[193] In addition, the Commissioner of Education is required to report annually to the Congress. The 1978 law reiterates the 1974 requirements with minor modifications. The commissioner, in consultation with the National Advisory Council, shall submit:

1. A national assessment of the educational needs of children and other persons with limited English proficiency
2. A report on the degree to which these needs are being met by federal, state, and local efforts
3. A plan, including cost estimates, for extending bilingual education to serve preschool and elementary children and other persons of limited English proficiency, including a phased plan for training of necessary teachers and other educational personnel
4. An evaluation of the bilingual program
5. A description of the staffing of the program by HEW
6. An assessment of the number of teachers and other personnel needed to carry out a program of biligual education for persons of limited English proficiency
7. An estimate of the number of teacher training fellowships for bilingual education which will be necessary for the two succeeding fiscal years[194]

Most importantly, the secretary is charged with additional actions and reports which elaborate upon these requirements. By September 30, 1980, the secretary is to develop (a) methods to identify children of limited English proficiency who are in need of bilingual education programs; (b) "evaluation and data gathering models, which take into account linguistic and cultural differences of the child, which consider the availability and the operations of State programs for such children, and shall include allowances for variables which are applicable" to bilingual education programs "such as pupil-teacher ratios, teacher qualifications, length of the program, hours of instruction, percentage of children in the classroom who are English dominant and the percentage who have limited English proficiency."[195]

As part of this developmental effort, the commissioner was to publish within six months of the date of passage of the Education Amendments of 1978 "(1) models for programs of bilingual education which may include suggested teacher-pupil ratios, teacher qualifications, and other factors affecting the quality of instruction offered, and which shall represent a variety of types of such programs, and (2) models for the evaluation of such programs as to the progress made by participants therein attaining English skills."[196] The House of Representatives reported the following explanation of this mandate:

> The Commissioner's Report on the Condition of Bilingual Education of 1977 found that "there is little to guide educators in designing and implementing effective bilingual projects." The National Association for Bilingual Education testified that only a small number of program models have been identified to date.[197]

Although the committee's reports reflected the skepticism and concern with the evaluations to date, the lack of data on student needs and teacher availability, and the absence of clear instruction models, the act looked toward developing a service program on a broad level throughout the United States, once models had been developed and proved. The steady increase in appropriations from $7.5 million in fiscal year 1969 to $158.6 million in fiscal year 1979,[198] indicates both a desire and possible capacity to effect such a conversion. Such a modification envisions changing, as well, the method of distributing funds from a discretionary grant program to formula distribution.

> (f) The Secretary shall prepare and submit to the President and to the Congress not later than December 31, 1981, a report setting forth recommendations on the methods of converting, not later than July 1, 1984, the bilingual education program from a discretionary grant program to a formula grant program to serve students of limited English proficiency and recommendations on whether or not such conversion would best serve the needs of such students. The study required by this subsection shall consider the findings of other studies required to be made under this section, and

shall include cost estimates for the phasing in of the formula grant program.[199]

The discussion to convert from a research and demonstration program to a service program is likely to center not only on measurable success but also on cost. The general charge to utilize funds to initiate bilingual programs has continued, but the 1978 House Report specifically noted the cost question in its lengthy discussion of demonstration v. service. It hoped that once a program was established, costs would decrease and local districts would continue the program.[200] One can conjecture that if the demonstrations prove favorable, if the costs of continuing a program are shown to be substantially less than initiating a program, and if local districts are unable to meet the entire financial burden, Congress will support a bilingual education service program.

A Co-ordinated Bilingual Education Program with Increased Significance

Bilingual education programs are funded not only under Title VII but also under a number of other programs in HEW.[201] The increased power granted to the director of the Title VII office over these other programs and the transfer of Section 708(c) of the Emergency School Aid Act to Title VII[202] foreshadow a centralized administration and, perhaps, an overall, cohesive, educational concern with minority language children.

The Emergency School Aid Act bilingual set-aside funds, curriculum development, teacher training, and interethnic understanding programs help provide equal educational opportunity for children with language difficulties. The funds may be utilized to assist school districts to meet *Lau* remedy court orders.

The House Committee commented on the provision: "The Committee was disturbed to find little coordination between this program and Title VII . . . this tranfer will achieve a greater coordination between the two programs."[203]

Further evidence of this centralized direction is seen in the new legislation establishing a Department of Education. This legislation establishes an Office of Bilingual Education and Minority Languages Affairs headed by a director who "shall coordinate the administration of bilingual education programs by the Department and shall consult with the Secretary concerning policy decisions affecting bilingual education and minority language affairs."[204] The Senate bill called for an Office of Bilingual Education and Minority Affairs. In adopting the House nomenclature, the final law singled out the problems of language and language minority individuals from persons designated for special treatment by race, color, sex, or income. The role of the director is not confined to bilingual education. He is given a broader consultative role in minority language affairs as well.

The director gains additional stature under the reorganization. He/she reports directly to the secretary[205] and is expected to be established at a GS-18, the top level of the Civil Service. The Senate bill specified a GS-18 rating for the director while the House stated no specific grade level. The grade was omitted in the final law with the comment in the committee report that "the conferees wish to indicate their intentions that this official should be so classified by the Office of Personnel Management."[206]

CONCLUSION

Over the last ten years since the Bilingual Education Act was first passed, Title VII programs have expanded considerably in numbers, and funding has continually increased. As this has occurred, Congress has sought greater formalization of the program, clarification of its goals and direction, and development of standards of success.

It appears likely that the future of the program depends upon establishing clear evaluative criteria and a record of success. The new law seeks local capacity building to assure continuity, but is less clear on the long-range federal commitment.

With the broader stature of the director of bilingual education in the new Department of Education, there is increased opportunity to bring together minority language education programs. One of the major challenges facing the director will be the coordination of the various minority language programs outside of Title VII.

SELECTED LEGISLATIVE HISTORY DOCUMENTS

1968

Bilingual Education Act:
P.L. 90-247, (Jan. 2, 1968), 81 Stat. 816, 20 U.S.C.A. 880 (b)

Rules and Regulations:
39 Fed. Reg. 17963 (May 22, 1974)

Congressional Reports:
U.S. Sen., Committee on Labor and Public Welfare, Elementary and Secondary Education Act Amendments of 1967, Report No. 90-726 (90th Cong., 1st Sess.)

House of Rep., Committee on Education and Labor, Elementary and Secondary Education Act Amendments of 1967, Report No. 90-1049 (90th Cong., 1st Sess.)

Congressional Hearings:
U.S. Sen., Bilingual Education, Hearings before the Special Subcommittee on Bilingual Education of the Committee on Labor and Public Welfare on S. 428 (2 vols.) (90th Cong., 1st Sess.)

House of Rep., Bilingual Education Programs, Hearings before the General Subcommittee on Education of the Committee on Education and Labor on H.R. 9840 and H.R. 10224 (90th Cong., 1st Sess.)

1974

Bilingual Education Act:

P.L. 93-380, (Aug. 21, 1974), 88 Stat. 503

Rules and Regulations:

45 C.F.R. 581, Part 123 Biligual Education

Congressional Reports:

U.S. Sen., Committee on Labor and Public Welfare, Education Amendments of 1974, Report No. 93-763 (93rd Cong., 2nd Sess.)

House of Rep., Committee on Education and Labor, Education Amendments of 1974, Report No. 93-1211 (93rd Cong., 2nd Sess.)

House of Rep., Committee on Education and Labor, Education Amendments of 1974, Report No. 93-805 (93rd Cong., 2nd Sess.)

Congressional Hearings:

U.S. Sen., Education Legislation, 1973, Hearings before the Subcommittee on Education of the Committee on Labor and Public Welfare on S. 1539 (93rd Cong., 1st Sess.), Part 7

House of Rep., Elementary and Secondary Education Amendments of 1973, Hearings before the General Subcommittee on Education of the Committee on Education and Labor on H.R. 16, H.R. 69, H.R. 5163, and H.R. 5823 (93rd Cong., 1st Sess.)

1978

Bilingual Education Act:

P.L. 95-561, (Nov. 1, 1978), 92 Stat. 2270

Rules and Regulations (Proposed):

44 Fed. Reg. 38415 (June 29, 1979)

Rules and Regulations (Final):

45 Fed. Reg. 23208 (April 4, 1980)

Congressional Reports:

U.S. Sen., Committee on Human Resources, Educational Amendments of 1978, Report No. 95-856 (95th Cong., 2nd Sess.)

House of Rep., Committee on Education and Labor, Education Amendments of 1978, Report No. 95-1137 (95th Cong., 2nd Sess.)

House of Rep., Committee on Education and Labor, Education Amendments of 1978, Report No. 95-1753 (95th Cong., 2nd Sess.) (Conference Report)

Congressional Hearings:

U.S. Sen., Education Amendments of 1978, Hearings before the Subcommittee on Education of the Committee on Human Resources on S. 1753 (95th Cong., 1st Sess.)

House of Rep., Bilingual Education, Hearings before the Subcommittee on Elementary, Secondary, and Vocational Education of the Committee on Education and Labor on H.R. 15 (95th Cong., 1st Sess.)

NOTES

1. To a degree, of course, there is some implicit recognition of English since the Constitution is written in that language.
2. See generally, E. McWhinney, *Federal Constitution-Making for a Multi-National World* (1966); R. Bowie and C. Friedrich, *Studies in Federalism* (1954). The bilingual experience of Canada is detailed in Royal Commission on Biculturalism and Bilingualism, *A Preliminary Report* 33 (1965).
3. R. Fitzgibbon, *The Constitutions of the Americas* 228, 323, 398, 448, 556, 605 (1948) cites the following constitutions in the Western Hemisphere that designate official languages: Cuba, article 6; Ecuador, article 7; Guatemala, article 4; Haiti, article 29; Nicaragua, article 7; and Panama, article 7.
4. *The Federalist Papers,* No. II (1788).
5. H. Manuel, *Spanish-Speaking Children of the Southwest* (1956).
6. T. Fehrenbach, *Lone Star: A History of Texas and the Texans* 167 (1968).
7. D. Ferris, *Judge Marvin and the Founding of the California Public School System* 92 (1962).
8. Calif. Stat. Ch. 556, Sec. 55 (1870).
9. L. Pit, *The Decline of the Californios* 226 (1966).
10. In 1884 the law required "Each of the voting precincts of a county shall be and constitute a school district in which shall be . . . taught reading, writing . . . in either English or Spanish or both, as the directors may determine." H. Kloss, *The American Bilingual Tradition* 134 (1977).
11. J. Forbes, "Mexican-Americans: A Handbook for Educators," *in Hearings before the House General Subcommittee on Education of the Committee on Education and Labor on H.P. 9840 and H. 10224, 90th Cong., 1st Sess., 508* (1967).
12. Kloss 134-135 (1977).
13. N. Gonzales, "The Spanish Americans of New Mexico: A Distinctive Heritage" in University of California, *Mexican-American Study Project* 36-38 (1967); W. Keleher, *The Fabulous Frontier* 90 (1945).
14. F. Cohen, *Handbook of Federal Indian Law* 234 (1942).
15. Ibid., 240.
16. One treaty did, however, include a reference to the language to be employed.

This notable exception appears in the Treaty of May 6, 1828, with the Cherokee Nation. Article 5 reads in part: "It is further agreed by the U.S. to pay $1,000 . . . towards the purchase of a Printing Press and Types to aid towards the Cherokees in the progress of education, and the benefit and enlighten them as people, *in their own language*" (emphasis supplied).

17. *The Education of American Indians, A Survey of the Literature,* prepared for the Senate Special Subcommittee on Indian Education of the Committee on Labor and Public Welfare, 91st Cong., 1st Sess., 11 (1969).

18. "The Indians being the prior occupants, possess the right of the soil. It cannot be taken from them unless by their consent, or by rights of conquest in case of a just war. To dispossess them on any other principle would be a great violation of the fundamental laws of nature." Statement of Henry Knox quoted in D. McNickle, *The Indian Tribes of the United States: Ethnic and Cultural Survival* 32 (1962). See also *Johnson* v. *MacIntosh* 21 U.S. (8 Wheat.) 543 (1823); *Cherokee Nation* v. *Georgia* 30 U.S. (5 Pet.) 1 (1831); and *Worchester* v. *Georgia* 31 U.S. (6 Pet.) 515 (1832).

19. Quoted in Senate Special Subcommittee on Indian Education of the Committee on Labor and Public Welfare, *Indian Education: A National Tragedy—A National Challenge,* 91st Cong., 1st Sess., 143 (1969) (hereinafter cited as *Indian Education).*

20. The Dawes Severalty Act, which ushered in the allotment period of Indian history, was passed in 1884. Its essential features were: (1) tribal lands were to be divided and the president was authorized to assign or allot 160 acres to each Indian family head; (2) each Indian would make his selection, but if he failed or refused, a government agent would make the selection; (3) title to the land was placed in trust for twenty-five years; (4) citizenship was conferred upon all allottees and upon other Indians who abandoned their tribes and adopted "the habits of civilized life"; (5) surplus tribal lands remaining after allotment might be sold to the United States. McNickle 48-49. The allotment law and subsequent statutes set up procedures which resulted in the transfer of some ninety million acres from Indian to white owners in the next forty-five years. *Indian Education,* pp. 150-151; *Blackfeet et al. Nation* v. *United States,* 81 Ct. Cls. 101, 115, 140 (1935).

21. A. Josephy, Jr., *The Indian Heritage of America* 339 (1947).

22. Superintendent of Indian Schools, *Sixth Annual Report* 10 (1887).

23. A. Faust, *The German Element in the United States* 204 (1969).

24. For example, Missouri in 1817; Illinois in 1825; Michigan in 1835; and Iowa in 1841. H. Kloss, *The Bilingual Tradition in the United States* 200 (1970).

25. Faust 151.

26. Ibid.

27. Ibid., 152.

28. L. Jorgensen, *The Founding of Public Education in Wisconsin* 146 (1956).

29. M. Jones, *American Immigration* 103 (1960).

30. The text has limited itself to immigration from Europe. Similar pressures arose against the Chinese and Japanese migrant in the western states and in Hawaii culminating in a series of laws aimed at restricting immigration, ownership of land, and, subsequently, in pressure to close the private Japanese foreign language schools. See *Farrington* v. *Tokushige* 273 U.S. 284 (1927). See generally M. Konvitz, *The Alien and Asiatic in American Law* (1946) and R. Daniels, *The Politics of Prejudice: The Anti-Japanese Movement in California and the Struggle for Japanese Exclusion* (1969).

31. D. Eaton, *The Government of Municipalities* 123-126 (1899).

32. The detailing of these political and economic requirements and their original purpose is set forth in A. Leibowitz, "English Literacy: Legal Sanction for Discrimination," 45 *Notre Dame Lawyer* 7 (1969).

33. A. Leibowitz, *Educational Policy and Political Acceptance: The Imposition of English as the Language of Instruction in American Schools* (1971).

34. *Meyers* v. *Nebraska* 262 U.S. 390 (1923).

35. *Lassiter* v. *Northhampton Election Board* 360 U.S. 45 (1959); but see *Cardona* v. *Power* 384 U.S. 672 (1966) and *Puerto Rican Organization for Political Action* v. *Kusper* 490 F. 2nd 575 (7th Cir. 1975).

36. Economic Opportunity Act of 1964. P.L. 88-452, 78 Stat. 508.

37. Elementary and Secondary Education Act of 1965. P.L. 89-10, 79 Stat. 27.

38. The 1930 Census identified "Mexicans" (persons of Spanish colonial descent) as a racial classification. In 1940, on the basis of a five percent sample, the Census counted persons speaking Spanish as the mother tongue. The 1950 and 1960 Censuses, on the basis of a twenty and twenty-five percent sample, respectively, identified the Spanish-surnamed populace in the five southwestern states. These states had accounted for more than eighty percent of all persons with Spanish as the mother tongue. The 1970 Census used four different means of identifying persons of Spanish ancestry: (1) birthplace, (2) Spanish surname, (3) mother tongue, and (4) Spanish origin based on self-identification.

39. The precise figures of 1960 for these three states are: Arizona—194,356 Spanish-surnamed, out of a total populace of 1,302,161; New Mexico—269,122 out of a total population of 951,023; and Colorado—157,173 out of a total population of 1,753,050.

40. Hearings before the Senate Special Subcommittee on Bilingual Education of the Committee on Labor and Public Welfare, 90th Cong., 1st Sess., 75 (1967) (hereinafter cited as 1967 Senate Hearings, Bilingual Education).

41. The Nixon administration expanded its jurisdiction and renamed it the Cabinet Committee on Opportunity for the Spanish-Speaking.

42. Upheld by the Supreme Court in *South Carolina* v. *Katzenbach* 383 U.S. 301 (1966). In extending the Voting Rights Act in 1970 and 1975, Congress suspended and then banned the English literacy test.

43. The provision was upheld by the Supreme Court in *Katzenbach* v. *Morgan* 384 U.S. 641 (1966) reversing 247 F. Supp. 196 (DDC 1965).

44. New York City Board of Education, *Puerto Rican Study 1953-1957* (1958).

45. Colorado Commission on Spanish Citizens, *The Status of Spanish-Surnamed Citizens in Colorado* (1967).

46. For example, H.R., Con. Res. 108 (83rd Cong., 1st Sess.).

47. Bilingualism in education, off-reservation boarding schools, and termination were not necessarily at odds although in practice they were seen that way. The most notable experiment in bilingual education in an off-reservation boarding school (which in practice was linked to relocation) was the special Navajo education program which began in 1946 at the Sherman Institute in Riverside, California, L. Coombs, *Doorway toward the Light* (1962).

48. Senate Special Subcommittee on Indian Education of the Committee on Labor and Public Welfare, *Indian Education: A National Tragedy—A National Challenge*, 91st Cong., 1st Sess., 19 (1969). The point in the text is well taken. However, it should be noted that the Cherokees were far from typical. They were the only North American tribe which had developed an indigenous written language.

49. H.R., Doc. 272 (90th Cong., 2nd Sess.), 5. President Johnson's message on Indian affairs, the most liberal statement of Indian policy ever made, although it stressed Indian education and its control by Indians, did not mention the subject of language. Message from the President of the United States transmitting Indian Policy. H.R. Doc. No. 91-363 (91st Cong., 2nd Sess.).

50. Statement of Dr. Joshua Fishman, Research Professor of Social Sciences, Yeshiva University, 1967 Senate Hearings, Bilingual Education, pp. 133-134.

51. See the testimony of various officials in 1967 Senate Hearings, Bilingual Education; and House of Representatives, Bilingual Education Programs, Hearings before the General Subcommittee on Education of the Committee on Education and Labor, 90th Cong., 1st Sess. (1967) (hereinafter cited as 1967 House Hearings, Bilingual Programs).

52. The literature is vast and rarely are distinctions made between bilingual and other language programs. Good reviews of the literature only slightly dated are P. Engle, *The Use of the Vernacular Languages in Education Revisited: A Literature Review prepared for the Ford Foundation, Office of Mexico, Central American and the Carribean* (1973); J. Rubin and B. Jernudd, *References for Students of Language Planning* (1974). See also the listing Office of Education, *Publications on Comparative Education* (March 1, 1975). For more substantive material see the papers from the Section on Language Planning submitted to the VIII World Congress of Sociology (Toronto, 1974); the International Conference on Language Planning (Skokloster, Sweden, 1973); and J. Fishman, ed., *Readings in the Sociology of Language* (1965).

53. House Report 95-1137, Education Amendments of 1978 (95th Cong., 2nd Sess.) 84 (hereinafter cited as 1978 House Report).

54. S. 428 (90th Cong. 1st Sess., 1967), §702.

55. Statement of Senator Yarborough, 1967 Senate Hearings, Bilingual Education, p. 37.

56. S. 428 (90th Cong. 1st Sess., 1967), §703 (b).

57. Statement of Schmuel Lapin, General Secretary, YIVO Institute of Jewish Research, 1967 Senate Hearings, Bilingual Education, p. 602.

58. Statement of Honorable Henry B. González (Democrat, Texas), 1967 Senate Hearings, Bilingual Education, p. 600.

59. 1967 House Hearings, Bilingual Programs.

60. 20 U.S.C. 880 (0) (1968), P.L. 90-247, Title VII, §702, 81 Stat. 816.

61. 1967 Senate Hearings, Bilingual Education, pp. 33-34.

62. Bilingual Education Act as amended §703 (a) (1).

63. Senate Report 95-856, Education Amendments of 1978 (95th Cong., 2nd Sess.) 69 (hereinafter cited as 1978 Senate Report).

64. House of Representatives, Bilingual Education, Hearings before the Subcommittee on Elementary, Secondary, and Vocational Education of the Committee on Education and Labor, 95th Cong., 1st Sess., Part 3, 306-308 (1977) (hereinafter cited as 1977 House Hearings, Bilingual Education).

65. Ibid., 332-333.

66. 1978 House Report, p. 87.

67. P.L. 95-561 (95th Cong., 2nd Sess.). Education Amendments of 1978, 92 Stat. 2143 (hereinafter "Bilingual Education Act as amended"), §703 (a) (1).

68. 1978 Senate Report, p. 70.

69. Ibid. The regulations judge groups of children to be "historically underserved" by "comparing the number and distribution, by language group, of children of limited English proficiency who are in need of bilingual education with the number and distribution, by language group, of children of limited English proficiency who are being served by programs of bilingual education." 45 CFR 123a.30.

70. Statement of Bruce Gaarder, Chief, Modern Language Section, U.S. Office of Education, 1967 House Hearings, Bilingual Programs, pp. 351-357.

71. Ibid., 399.

72. Bilingual Education Act of 1968, §706 (a). The section referred to in this footnote is as a result of a 1970 amendment, P.L. 91-230, April 13, 1970; 84 Stat. 151.

73. Ibid., see §706(b).

74. Bilingual Education Act as amended, §722(b); cf., Bilingual Education Act of 1968, §706(b).

75. 1978 Senate Report, p. 78.

76. Bilingual Education Act as amended, §721(f). See also 45 CFR 123a.21.

77. 1978 House Report, p. 86.

78. Bilingual Education Act of 1968, 81 Stat. 816, §702.

79. S. 428, (90th Cong., 1st Sess., 1967).

80. 1967 Senate Hearings, Bilingual Education, p. 410.

81. Statement of Senator Ralph Yarborough, ibid., p. 1.

82. C. Lavatelli, *Piaget's Theory Applied to an Early Childhood Education* 42 (1973).

83. Statement of Leonard Pacheco, Project Director, Project Head Start, Alhambra, California, 1967 Senate Hearings, Bilingual Education, p. 422.

84. Statement of Honorable Ernest D. Debs, Supervisor, Los Angeles County, ibid., p. 432.

85. Statement of Robert S. Randall, Associate Director, Research and Evaluation, Southwest Educational Development Laboratory, Austin, Texas, ibid., p. 608.

86. Statement of Professor Julian Nava, Member-Elect, Los Angeles City Board of Education, ibid., p. 436.

87. Statement of Luis Alvarez, Coordinator, Federated Puerto Rican Parents, ibid., p. 567.

88. Statement of Schmuel Lapin, General Secretary, YIVO Institute for Jewish Research, ibid., p. 602.

89. P.L. 90-247, Jan. 2, 1968, Stat. 816, §702.

90. Senate Report 90-726, Elementary and Secondary Education Act Amendments of 1967 (90th Cong., 1st Sess.) 49.

91. Ibid., 50.

92. 1967 House Hearings, Bilingual Programs, pp. 44-45.

93. Senate Report 93-763, Education Amendments of 1974 (93rd Cong., 2nd Sess.) 42 (hereinafter cited as 1974 Senate Report).

94. Quoted in T. Andersson, "Bilingual Education: The American Experience," paper presented at the Ontario Institute for Studies in Education Conference on Bilingual Education, Toronto, Canada, March 13, 1971, p. 14, ED 048 581.

95. 1974 Senate Report, p. 45.

96. Bilingual Education Act as amended, §702 (a) (7) (B).

97. Ibid. §731 (c) (3).

98. American Institutes for Research, *Evaluation of the Impact of ESEA Title VII, Spanish/English Bilingual Education Program: Overview of Study and Findings* 14, 10-11 (1978).

99. Statement of Gary Orfield, Department of Political Science, University of Illinois at Urbana, 1977 House Hearings, Bilingual Education, pp. 336-337.

100. Statement of Maria Swanson, President, National Association for Bilingual Education, ibid., p. 333.

101. Bilingual Education Act as amended, §703 (a) (4) (B).

102. 1978 Senate Report, p. 71.

103. Bilingual Education Act as amended, §703(a)(4)(A)(i).

104. 1978 House Report, p. 87.

105. Ibid.

106. Comptroller General of the United States, *Bilingual Education: An Unmet Need* 45 (1976).

107. U.S. Civil Rights Commission, *A Better Chance to Learn: Bilingual Bicultural Education* (1975).

108. 1977 House Hearings, Bilingual Education, pp. 306-321.

109. Ibid., 345-346.

110. Bilingual Education Act as amended, §703(a)(4)(A)(i).

111. 1978 House Report 95-1137, p. 87.

112. Bilingual Education Act as amended, §703(a)(4)(A).

113. Ibid.

114. Ibid., §703(a)(4)(C).

115. Ibid., §703(a)(4)(D).

116. Ibid.

117. Ibid., §703(a)(4)(B).

118. 1978 House Report, p. 86.

119. 1978 Senate Report, p. 71.

120. 1978 House Report, p. 303.

121. Comptroller General of the United States, *Bilingual Education: An Unmet Need* (1976).

122. Bilingual Education Act as amended, §703(a)(4)(B).

123. Office of Education, Project Savior; Project Venceremos, Project Nuevos Horizontes, Project Adelante.

124. Bilingual Education Act of 1968, §704(b).

125. Comptroller General of the United States, 14. American Institutes for Research, *Evaluation of the Impact of ESEA Title VII, Spanish/English Bilingual Education Program* (1978). The House of Representatives in its 1978 report estimated a national requirement of 129,000 teachers.

126. Bilingual Education Act of 1974, §721(b)(2)(B).

127. Bilingual Education Act as amended, §72(b)(2)(B).

128. 1978 House Report, p. 89.

129. Bilingual Education Act as amended, §723(a)(1)(2).

130. Some of the needs of bilingual teachers and their specialized training is set forth in H. Casso, *Bilingual/Bicultural Education and Teacher Training* (1976).

131. Bilingual Education Act as amended, §723(a)(6); cash repayment is envisioned over fifteen years at an interest rate of seven percent per annum, 45 CFR 123h.44.

132. 45 CFR 123h.30.

133. 45 CFR 123e.41.

134. Bilingual Education Act as amended, §723(b).

135. Ibid., §723(a)(4).

136. Development Associates, Inc., *A Study of the State of Bilingual Materials Development and the Transition of Materials to the Classroom* (3 vols.) 6, vol. 1 (1978).

137. Ibid., p. 25.

138. Bilingual Education Act as amended, §742(e).

139. Ibid.

140. 1978 House Report, p. 86.

141. Ibid.

142. 1978 House Report, p. 84. Although not official, perhaps equally influential was the critical review—N. Epstein, *Language Ethnicity and the Schools: Policy Alternatives for Bilingual Bicultural Education* (1977).

143. Bilingual Education Act as amended, §742.

144. 1978 House Report, p. 85.

145. Bilingual Education Act as amended, §742(b).

146. 1978 House Report, p. 85.

147. 1978 Senate Report, p. 69.

148. Bilingual Education Act as amended, §721(b)(3)(F).

149. Bilingual Education Act as amended, §721(b)(4); Bilingual Education Act of 1968, §705(b)(2). See also Bilingual Education Act as amended §721(b)(3)(A).

150. National Center for Education Statistics, *The Condition of Education: Statistical Report 37* Chart 1.15 (1978).

151. Bilingual Education Act as amended, §721(c). The final regulations deemphasized this criterion when comment on the draft regulations regarded it as unfairly discriminating against school districts which were small, rural, or did not have a heavy concentration of children of limited English proficiency. 45 Fed. Reg. 23231 (April 4, 1980).

152. Ibid., §721(b)(4).

153. 1978 House Report, p. 91.

154. Bilingual Education Act as amended, §721(b)(4).

155. 1978 Senate Report, p. 70.

156. 45 CFR, 123a.30.

157. Bilingual Education Act as amended, §721(b)(3)(E).

158. S. 428 (90th Cong., 1st Sess., 1967), §703(b).

159. H.R. 9840 (90th Cong., 1st Sess., 1967), §703(b).

160. H.R. 10224 (90th Cong., 1st Sess., 1967), §703(b).

161. Bilingual Education Act of 1968, §703(b).

162. Ibid., §704(a&c).

163. Bilingual Education Act as amended, §721(b)(4) (emphasis supplied).

164. 45 CFR 123.01(e); the allocation formula of Title I is discussed in 1978 House Report, pp. 8-17.

165. Bilingual Education Act as amended, §721(b)(5)(A).

166. Ibid., §721(b)(5)(B).

167. 1977 House Hearings, Bilingual Education, p. 87.

168. Bilingual Education Act as amended, §721(b)(1)(B).

169. 45 CFR 123a.30.

170. Ibid.

171. Ibid.

172. Bilingual Education Act as amended, §703(a)(4)(E).

173. Ibid., §703(a)(4)(E)(iii), 45 CFR 123a.44.

174. Ibid., §703(a)(4)(F).

175. 1978 House Report, p. 88.

176. 1978 Senate Report, p. 71.

177. The time limitation was embodied in the HEW regulation published in October 1973. 45 Fed. Reg. 123 (Oct. 1, 1973).

178. The issue is discussed with respect to the 1974 law in some detail in S. Schneider, *Revolution, Reaction, or Reform: The 1974 Bilingual Education Act* 104 (1976).

179. Bilingual Education Act as amended, §721(e)(1).

180. Ibid., §721(b)(3)(E).

181. Ibid., §721(b)(2)(B).

182. Ibid.

183. Ibid., §721(b)(2)(A)(iii).

184. Ibid., §721(b)(2)(C).

185. Ibid., §731.

186. The role of the Council is set forth ibid., §732.

187. Bilingual Education Act of 1968, §702.

188. Ibid., §704(a).

189. 1978 Senate Report, p. 68. The regulations focus at some length on demonstration projects including additional target populations (children of migratory workers, recent immigrants, high school students preparing to enter the job market, and exceptional children), exemplary approaches to instruction including use of computer assisted instruction, high probability of replication in other similar school districts, and approaches to obtain community/parental involvement. 45 CFR 123b.10, 45 CFR 123b.30.

190. Comtroller General of the United States, *Bilingual Education: An Unmet Need* (1976).

191. American Institutes for Research. *Evaluation of the Impact of ESEA Title VII, Spanish/English Bilingual Education Program* (1978).

192. 1978 House Report, pp. 84-85.

193. Bilingual Education Act as amended, §721(b)(3)(C)(iii).

194. Ibid., §731(c)(1)-(6).
195. Ibid., §731(e).
196. Ibid., §731(d).
197. 1978 House Report, p. 85.
198. "House-Senate Conference Committee Agrees on Bilingual Education Budget," *FORUM* II(8), September 1979, p. 2.
199. Bilingual Education Act as amended, §731(f).
200. 1978 House Report, pp. 87-88.
201. A good listing is found in HEW, *The Condition of Bilingual Education in the Nation: First Report by the U.S. Commissioner of Education to the President and the Congress* (1976).
202. Bilingual Education Act as amended, §751.
203. 1978 House Report, p. 90.
204. House Report 96-459 to accompany S. 210, Department of Education Organization Act (96th Cong., 1st Sess., 1979), p. 9.
205. Ibid., pp. 41-42.
206. Ibid., p. 42.